PERFECT

COCKTAILS

Max Ernst, Cocktail Drinker, *1945.*

PERFECT

COCKTAILS

TREASURE PRESS

First published in Great Britain in 1985 by
Treasure Press
59 Grosvenor Street
London W1

Originally published in France in 1983 by
Librairie Larousse under the title
Larousse des Cocktails

French text by Jacques Sallé
English translation by Naomi Good and Rachel Grenfell

ISBN 1 85051 079 2

Printed in Hong Kong

Preface

Louis Delluc said that a cocktail is not just the sum of its ingredients; it is the way in which they are put together. In fact, the art of creating cocktails lies not just in choosing ingredients but in combining them in the correct proportions. This sort of expertise can only be achieved by someone who has studied well-tried and proven cocktail recipes. It is important to have a thorough knowledge of the classic cocktails, because improvization is not recommended to a beginner unfamiliar with the strengths and weaknesses of alcoholic drinks and mixes. You can learn the rules which govern cocktail-making by trying out some of the many recipes which have been invented to date; most of them are listed in this book.

For, in fact, it is not immediately obvious which alcohols and wines go well together. Harmony has its own rules and demands. For example, David Embury describes whisky as 'a gloomy old bachelor fiercely determined to guard his independence and rarely showing any disposition to marry'. And who would risk mixing whisky with other drinks unless they had first tried *Rob Roy* or *Rusty Nail?* The same could be said of vodka, gin, brandy etc. The possibilities are infinite but the basic recipes provide the key. It is with this in mind that the author has designed this collection and devoted a chapter to each principal ingredient.

From Alphonse Allais' Captain Cap who has given us *Whisky Cocktail* and *Whisky Stone Fence*, to Jean Cocteau, great admirer of this alchemy; from Lemmy Caution, Peter Cheney's secret agent and great lover of cocktails and of women, to the Hollywood stars sipping long drinks in their luxurious living rooms; from Otto Dix's painting of Silvia von Harden with a cocktail at a café table to Max Ernst's very personal vision of the Cocktail Drinker . . . the cocktail seems to be one manifestation of the art of twentieth-century living. The fantasy of its presentation aims to please the eye and offer an entertainment to suit the hour and the mood. Even when made only from fruit juices, a cocktail is nonetheless a symbol of sophistication and harmony.

Contents

Preface   5

Cocktails   9

The origins of the cocktail   9

The bar   11

The art of mixing cocktails   14

The main types of cocktail   19

The recipes   22

Brandy-based Cocktails   23

Cocktails based on Calvados and other cider brandies   35

Rum-based Cocktails   38

Gin-based Cocktails   55

Vodka-based Cocktails   72

Cocktails based on Bourbon, Rye Whiskey and Canadian Whisky   79

Cocktails based on Scotch and Irish   88

Tequila-based Cocktails   95

Cocktails based on Apéritifs and Cocktail Apéritifs   100

Cocktails based on Digestives and Cocktail Digestives   112

Punches   123

Milk-based Cocktails   126

Cocktails based on Wine and Beer   128

Hot Drinks   136

Non-alcoholic Cocktails and Drinks   141

Glossary   150

Index   155

Acknowledgements

p.2 Kunstsammlung Nordrhein-Westfalen, Dusseldorf. Photo: Fondation Maeght.

p.9 Private Collection, Paris. Photo: Lauros-Giraudon.

p.10 Photo: Studio Boré.

p.11 Musee de l'Ile-de-France, Sceaux. Photo: Lauros-Giraudon.

p.12 Courtauld Collection, London. Photo: Courtauld Institute Galleries.

p.13 Museo Risorgimento, Turin. Photo: Fiore.

p.14 Photo: Studio Boré.

p.15 Photo: Studio Boré.

pp.16-17 Photo: Paul Williams.

p.18 Musée des Beaux Arts, Besançon. Photo: Giraudon.

pp.20-21 Photo: Paul Williams.

p.22 Atelier Cappiello. Photo: Poster Museum, Paris.

p.23 Photo: Remy Martin.

p.24 Forney Library, Paris. Photo: L.L.

p.25 Photo: Studio Boré.

p.26 Forney Library, Paris. Photo: L.L.

p.29 Photo: Martell.

p.31 Photo: Studio Boré.

p.33 Photo: Studio Boré.

p.34 Photo: Studio Boré.

p.35 Photo: Jacques Sallé.

p.36 Photo: Studio Boré.

p.37 Photo: Studio Boré.

p.38 Photo: Library of the Decorative Arts, Paris.

p.41 Photo: Studio Boré.

p.42 Harry N. Abrams Family Collection, New York. Photo: Fabbri.

p.43 Forney Library, Paris. Photo: L.L.

p.44 Photo: Studio Boré.

p.45 Photo: Studio Boré.

p.47 Photo: Studio Boré.

p.49 Photo: Studio Boré.

p.50 Photo: Studio Boré.

p.51 Photo: Poster Museum, Paris.

p.52 Photo: Studio Boré.

p.53 Photo: Studio Boré.

p.54 Photo: Studio Boré.

p.55 Photo: Fiore.

p.56 Forney Library, Paris. Photo: L.L.

p.58 Grand Marnier Archives.

p.59 Photo: Studio Boré.

p.60 National Museum of Modern Art, Paris. Photo: Lauros-Giraudon.

Photo: Larousse.

p.62 Photo: Studio Boré.

p.63 Forney Library, Paris. Photo: L.L.

p.65 Photo: Studio Boré.

p.66 Photo: Studio Boré.

p.67 Photo: Studio Boré.

p.70 Photo: Studio Boré.

p.71 Photo: Studio Boré.

p.73 Photo: Studio Boré.

p.74 Photo: Studio Boré.

p.75 Photo: Studio Boré.

p.77 Photo: Studio Boré.

p.79 Jack Daniels Archives.

p.83 Photo: Studio Boré.

p.84 Photo: Studio Boré.

p.89 Simon-Frères Archives.

p.91 Bénédictine Archives.

p.92 Photo: Fiore.

p.93 Photo: Studio Boré.

p.96 Photo: Fiore.

p.97 Photo: Studio Boré.

p.99 Photo: Studio Boré.

p.100 Photo: Library of the Decorative Arts, Paris.

p.103 Photo: L.L.

p.104 Forney Library, Paris. Photo: L.L.

p.105 Photo: Studio Boré.

p.106 Photo: Poster Museum, Paris.

p.108 Pernod Archives.

p.109 Photo: Studio Boré.

p.111 Pernod Archives.

p.115 Cointreau Archives.

p.116 Fernet-Branca Archives.

p.117 Photo: Studio Boré.

p.118 Photo: Studio Boré.

p.121 Forney Library, Paris. Photo: L.L.

p.123 Forney Library, Paris. Photo: L.L.

p.125 Photo: Studio Boré.

p.126 Photo: Studio Boré.

p.128 Forney Library, Paris. Photo: L.L.

p.129 Mumm Archives.

p.131 Photo: Studio Boré.

p.132 Photo: Studio Boré.

p.133 Photo: Studio Boré.

p.134 Photo: Studio Boré.

p.135 Photo: Studio Boré.

p.136 Forney Library, Paris. Photo: L.L.

p.138 Photo: Studio Boré.

p.139 Photo: Studio Boré.

p.140 Photo: Studio Boré.

p.141 Photo: Encyclopédie Contemporaine.

p.143 Photo: Studio Boré.

p.146 Photo: Studio Boré.

p.148 Photo: Studio Boré.

p.150 Forney Library, Paris. Photo: L.L.

p.151 Bibliothèque de l'Arsenal. Photo: Lauros-Giraudon.

p.152 Simon Frères Archives.

p.153 Cusenier Archives.

p.155 Photo: Fiore.

Cocktails

Cocktail is a strange, rather crude word for such an elegant drink: it derives from the eighteenth-century slang term for a docked tail, first applied to a horse of mixed breed and then to a nag on a race course. A combined allusion to the society in which drinks are popular and the notion of mixed breeding must have led to the word being applied to alcoholic recipes.

The first cocktails originated in England at the height of the Victorian era. When the English entertained at home they remained faithful to the grape: sherry as an apéritif, claret with the meal, vintage port after that, and to clear the palate, a little madeira. But in the men's clubs, drinking habits were very different: it was not uncommon to drink mixtures such as *Claret Cuo* based on Bordeaux, or *Sherry Cobblers* based on sherry. These mixtures were often served in famous cups won in the sporting field.

Many cocktails were being made by the end of the century, and some of their names are still in use: Cobblers, Coolers, Crustas, Cups, Daisies, Fixes, Flips, Juleps, Negus, Nogs, Possets, Punches, Rickeys, Sangarees, Slings, Smashes. All suggest the hilarious nature of those gentlemen's club evenings, and the colonial origins of some of the mixes.

Working people in the big cities drank neither wine nor port because they were so heavily taxed; instead they drank beer or gin. Gin palaces were built, richly decorated with panelling of exotic woods and cut glass mirrors—some of them still survive in the more splendid public houses. Gin was not then a very good alcohol. Distilled in primitive fashion, it was cloudy and had to be flavoured with juniper berries and coriander, and sometimes sugar was added to make it drinkable. What would be more natural than to try to mask the strong taste of gin with various additions? On returning home from duty in the empire, nineteenth-century army officers brought the habit of drinking gin spliced with quinine, to fight off fever: that was how gin and tonic was first introduced, together with a number of other combinations.

While there was some tradition for mixed drinks, cocktails as we know them now came into their own in the 1920s. People wished to forget the calamities of the First World War, and set about amusing themselves. This was the era of Montparnasse where all nationalities met: French, English and American poets, mad Italian artists of all sorts. American jazz rang out in London and Paris, and the idea of the 'lounge lizard'—a languid, tango-dancing heart-throb—added a thrill to the hours *cinq à sept*. Suddenly everything went electric: people drove motor cars, and flew about in aeroplanes. The style of life was fast and sophisticated.

Peter Stampfli, Party, 1964

This was the time when Prohibition was introduced to the USA: the consumption of alcohol was forbidden between 1919 and 1933 by the 18th Amendment. The fight against intemperance intensified among well-intentioned Americans. They believed drink was a decadent European habit brought into the USA by Catholic immigrants from Italy, Ireland and so on, and that it was imperative to restore America to health and democracy once more. Needless to say, the measure only criminalized the sources of alcohol.

Secret distilleries, smuggling and speak-easies or illicit drinking dens were organized to the great financial benefit of their owners, and considerable loss to federal tax. In the face of weak and often

A selection of cocktails (left to right): Snowball, Amer Picon Cooler, Black Russian, Rose, Salty Dog, Blue Lagoon, Fond de Culotte, Manhattan.

colluding authorities, gangsters played an active part in the drinks business. It was the golden age of Al Capone and the crime syndicates. Adulterated alcohol was sold at a very high price, but Americans still bought it. It was rarely consumed in its natural state, it was so poorly-made—but the ostensible reason was to hide the taste of alcohol in case of a police raid. The cocktail was in its heyday. The barmen of the speak-easies racked their imaginations to devise recipes in which the hooch was hidden—like *Pussyfoot*, and many others. American travel agents found a new and profitable trade in 'wet weekends' to Cuba, where people were allowed to drink freely. For several years, Havana became the capital of the cocktail world, where such exotic concoctions as *Daiquiri*, *Cuban Cocktail*, and *Cuba Libre* were evolved.

While Wall Street began to totter, Europe and America virtually lived for the cocktail hour. The *Bloody Mary* was invented in Paris in 1921 and the *Side Car* in 1924. The whole world was drinking *Martini*, *Gin Fizz*, *Americano*, *John* or *Tom Collins*, or *Manhattan*, while imaginative barmen thought up still more creative combinations. The cocktail party replaced the tea dance, and even the hour of the evening meal was put back, nationwide in America, for the evening hour of the drink. Such flagrant disregard for the law only made the American authorities look foolish. The offending Amendment was repealed in 1933.

The Bar

There is nowhere quite like New York for the splendour, number, and variety of its bars. From the downright seedy and serious-drinking to the utmost elegance in decor and company, New York is truly a cocktail sipper's paradise. Fortunately, the recent popularity of cocktails (not a little helped by those famous words from James Bond when ordering his Martini) has enormously improved the cocktail bar, as opposed to the pub in Britain, in the past few years. This must also be due to the women's influence: smelly, smoky pub rooms with little or no seating are not to their taste every time. Some of the liveliest clubs and bars recall the golden era of the cocktail bar with their subdued lights, polished wooden bars, eau de nil or peach Art Deco walls, and etched-glass panels. A lucky visitor may even encounter a barman happy to be tested on his knowledge of mixes, or even to take up a recipe from a keen customer. In New York, San Francisco or Los Angeles, this would be a certainty.

A good barman is a pleasing sight to behold at his work: he knows the epic and adventurous tradition of his trade! His bottles are always lined up in such a way that he reaches almost without glancing for the appropriate alcohol; sharp, smart knives are at the ready to twist and carve the lemons, oranges, cucumbers and other tangy bits for his mixtures. An expert cocktail-maker, he knows how to handle glasses and bottles—siphons by the upper part, glasses by the stem or base, bottles by the lower half. A real professional will not smoke but will have matches or a lighter at hand, and will know how to prepare and light a cigar. As everyone knows, a true-born barman listens quite attentively, but seldom talks. . .

A good cocktail need not be sought out only in a bar, however. M.F.K. Fisher, one of the wittiest and most justly famous of this century's writers on food and taste, had much to say about cocktail drinking in her wonderful book *How to Cook a Wolf*, first published during the Second World War, when supplies were short and memories of a good drink high on the list of missed pleasures. Perhaps the best piece of advice she gives, without shame, is to learn to love to drink *alone*, with perhaps one good friend. '*Alone* does necessarily connotate salaciously, lasciviously, or even amorously, since if you like a person well enough to drink alone with him, he will be the kind who will have worked all day and be glad as you to sit back and absorb a little quick relaxation from a glass and then eat, quaffing immortality with joy', she writes. Splendid advice, still worth following to this day (though the job is not really a necessity). More in that vein is the writer's added note that some of her best drinking companions were old ladies, one of whom, eighty-two on her last birthday, gave her a lesson in both self-control and sensual pleasure from her obvious enjoyment of a *weekly* glass of dry champagne.

It is very much the theme of this new guide to cocktails that moderation is part of the art of cocktail drinking—they are meant to whet the appetite for further delights, not dull the senses into oblivion. Edward Anthony expressed this idea succinctly when quoting Don Marquis from O Rare Don Marquis: ' I drink only to make my friends seem interesting.' Drink only for pleasure, never to drown sorrows, and the spirit does not weaken. As one of Miss Fisher's connections once put it, echoing the words of Omar Khayyam: 'A horn of gin, a good cigar, and *you*, Babe.'

Jean Beraud, The cyclists' chalet in the Bois de Boulogne, *c.1900.*

A Bar in the House

For serving cocktails at home it is not necessary to have a bar; this is more common in America but for some reason is considered a little *de trop* in England where most people prefer a drinks cupboard in the sitting room.

A bar in the sitting room is of course very convenient, but it is quite enough to have a cupboard which keeps the bottles out of sight and protects them from dust and light (the latter causes some liqueurs to oxidize).

Another possibility is a mobile bar which can be moved to wherever your guests are, or a drinks trolley with bottles on the lower shelf, glasses and equipment on top.

The choice of bottles
It is perfectly possible to make cocktails with only three or four bottles of alcohol. But it is useful to have a somewhat larger selection and here is a basic list from which to choose:

- whisky (blended Scotch, Irish whiskey)
- bourbon or rye whiskey
- gin (London dry)
- vodka
- rum (white and golden)
- tequila
- cognac
- armagnac
- Calvados
- Campari
- vermouth: sweet – Martini or Cinzano

- dry – Noilly Prat, Martini dry
- pastis – Pernod
- orange liqueur – Grand Marnier, Cointreau, triple-sec, curaçao
- peppermint liqueur – crème de menthe, green and colourless
- chocolate liqueur – crème de cacao, brown and colourless
- coffee liqueur – Tia Maria or Kahlúa
- blackcurrant liqueur – crème de cassis from Dijon
- apricot liqueur – crème d'abricot or apricot brandy
- strawberry and raspberry liqueurs
- banana liqueur – crème de banane
- mandarin liqueur (tangerine flavoured)
- noyaux liqueur (almond flavoured)
- herb-based liqueurs – Chartreuse,

Edouard Manet, A bar at the Folies-Bergère, 1882.

green and yellow, Benedictine, Verveine du Velay, Izarra, green and yellow etc
○ aniseed liqueurs – anisette
○ other liqueurs – Drambuie, Southern Comfort, Strega, Galliano

Occasionally a recipe calls for tonic, bitter lemon, cola, ginger ale, beer, wine, champagne and orange juice.

Freshly pressed orange juice is the best. Certain types of orange give more juice than others but you can get more juice out of any orange by plunging it in hot water before pressing it. Fresh juice will not last for more than a day and it should be kept in the refrigerator.

For a home bar a dozen bottles should suffice to make your favourite cocktails.

The cost of such a bar is often overestimated. With a wide range of basic ingredients it is tempting and easy to serve cocktails, which in fact are often cheaper than the dreary traditional apéritif. Similarly the alcohol content of a cocktail is always less than that of its strongest ingredient: the majority of cocktails are less than 18°. But that does not mean that cocktails are innocuous, or that they cannot make you drunk.

Mixtures
If during a meal you drink two or three different wines one after the other, you can feel rather uncomfortable. Oddly this effect is less noticeable if you drink good wines or spirits in moderation.

It is not easy to define good wines or spirits without reference to chemistry or oenology. A good wine will have been carefully made from the healthy grapes of noble vines grown in good soil, allowed some time to mature, and properly bottled and corked when ready. Sadly, a bad wine corrupts taste. The same goes for spirits and liqueurs, although production is more complicated. You can take it for granted that the proper distillation of sound ingredients is the key to all good spirits. The ageing and blending of brandies, for example, can only improve the qualities they already have.

Mixing poor ingredients will never give a good result, but it is not always essential to use the very best, especially among the brandies.

The old Cafe Carpano at Turin

Storing spirits and liqueurs
Although wine bottles should be stored on their sides to keep the wine in contact with the cork, bottles of spirits and liqueurs should always be kept upright. Spirits and liqueurs only age in the cask; once they are bottled the ageing process stops.

Like wines, spirits dislike the light and prefer the dark. Oxidization caused by light can cause irreversible deterioration in certain fruit liqueurs.

It is not necessary to keep spirits in a cellar—humidity has no effect on them. A good cupboard is perfectly suitable.

KEEPING INSECTS AWAY
When it is very hot you can get rid of insects with the help of an orange studded with cloves: it can be decorative and useful on a buffet table.

The Art of Mixing Cocktails

Wines and spirits are nearly always the result of mixtures. Wines are blended, so are great brandies, and a great majority of commercial drinks are mixtures of some kind.

In theory it is simple: the qualities of two or more different products are enhanced by mixing them. But in practice it is not so simple—in this process the defects are also aggravated, so it is impossible to make a good product by mixing two poor ones.

This is also the art in mixing cocktails—to marry together two good products to make a better one. It has often been called the cooking of drinks; and just as in cooking, there are specific utensils, strict rules or rituals, which need to be observed. What could be more amusing than to bring a touch of originality and sophistication to a few dull hours than by devoting yourself to the pleasures of a master drinks maker?

A shaker, some beautiful glasses, some bottles and a little fruit are enough to surprise both host and company, but be careful not to be carried away. Lurking under an attractive appearance is a possibly dangerous alcoholic drink.

There are some essential rules to be observed in mixing alcoholic drinks. Do not mix the products of grain and grape, that is, grain spirits such as whisky, gin and vodka with spirits based on the grape like cognac, armagnac etc (though there are occasional exceptions to this rule). Nor should one mix spirits of the same kind, for example, whisky and gin, whisky and vodka or cognac or armagnac. And there are other mixtures which are unnatural to taste like rum and Calvados, rum and gin or whisky and rum etc.

The Ritual

For every cocktail there are one or more basic ingredients which give substance to the mixture, and other items which are supposed to modify its taste and

Accessories for the well-equipped bar.

Bar accessories: Ice bucket and small dishes by Cartier; glass from the Danish Boutique, Paris; serving dish for cocktail snacks by Hermès.

colour. There are four ways of making a cocktail: directly into a glass, in a mixing glass, in a shaker, or in an electic mixer.

Directly into a glass is the simplest and quickest method: to get a good mix, stir with a spoon or a mixer stick.

To use a mixing glass, put some cubes of ice in the glass, pour the ingredients over and stir with a spoon. The purpose of the mixing glass is to cool the ingredients while they are being mixed. The ice should be dry to prevent too much dilution and the stirring energetic and brief—about 10 seconds.

For the shaker, put ice cubes or crushed ice in the shaker, pour over the ingredients, screw down the top and shake it energetically but not too violently for about 10 seconds; remove the cover and pour into a glass through a strainer to leave the ice behind. The shaker makes for a homogenous and cool mixture, and the action helps to aerate the liquid.

50 ESSENTIAL COCKTAILS TO KNOW

Apple Brandy Cocktail
Benedictine Cocktail *114*
Between the Sheets
Black Velvet
Blood and Sand *89*
Bloody Mary
Bourbon Highball
Brandy Cocktail
Brandy Eggnog
Brandy Punch
Buck's Fizz
Champagne Cocktail
Corpse Reviver
Cuba Libre
Cuban Cocktail
Daiquiri
Dubonnet Fizz

Frozen Daiquiri
Fruit Punch
Gibson
Gimlet
Gin and Tonic
Gin Fizz
Gin Sling
Grog
Grasshopper
Harvey Wallbanger
Horse's Neck
Hot Brandy Flip
Irish Coffee
Manhattan *82*
Margarita *97*
Martini *65*

Mint Julep
Negroni
Pimms
Pina Colada
Pink Gin
Planter's Punch
Rum Collins
Sangria
Screwdriver
Sherry Cocktail
Snowball
Spritzer
Tequila Sunrise
Tom Collins
Whisky Cobbler
Whisky Toddy
White Lady

To use the electric mixer, put crushed ice and the ingredients in the mixer and process for a few seconds. The result is a very cold cocktail which can be strained or poured directly into a glass.

Bar Equipment and Ingredients

Apart from bottles, the well-stocked bar needs certain minimal equipment, basic ingredients and essential fresh produce.

EQUIPMENT
- bottle opener (waiter's friend)
- kitchen knife with small board for chopping fruits, cutting straws etc
- small fork
- mixing spoon
- mixing glass
- cocktail shaker (in three parts) or Boston shaker (two parts)
- electric mixer
- Hawthorne strainer
- funnel
- ice tongs
- insulated ice container
- lemon squeezer
- heat resistant pitcher for hot drinks
- champagne bucket
- measuring glass
- ice crusher
- decanter for wine and/or port

ACCESSORIES
- glasses (cocktail, tumbler, balloon, flute, tulip etc)
- hand towels and a glass-drying cloth, preferably linen
- straw dispenser
- fancy straws
- cocktail sticks (wood or plastic)
- mixer sticks
- swizzle sticks
- decorations (parasols, plastic figures and animals etc)

BASIC INGREDIENTS
- Angostura bitters
- soda water siphon
- cocktail cherries
- green olives stuffed with almonds, pimento or anchovy
- cocktail onions

- sugar cubes
- sugar, white, caster, and soft brown
- salt
- celery salt
- pepper
- nutmeg and grater
- cinnamon sticks and powder
- cloves
- Worcestershire sauce
- Tabasco
- ground coffee and instant coffee
- chocolate powder
- vanilla pod and essence
- herbal tea bags – verbena, mint, lime camomile, orange

- tea
- sugar syrup
- grenadine syrup
- maraschino syrup
- orgeat syrup
- other syrups (maple, raspberry, strawberry etc)
- orange juice
- lemon juice
- lime juice
- grapefruit juice
- pineapple juice
- other fruit juices (bilberry, black-currant, passion fruit etc)
- cream of coconut

FRESH PRODUCE
- lemons
- limes
- oranges
- fruit – bananas, grapefruit, coconut, pineapple, cherries, strawberries, apricots
- cucumber
- fresh mint
- milk
- eggs
- cream

A selection of glasses (top row, left to right): large brandy snifter, cocktail glass, old fashioned glass, small brandy snifter, handled glass; (bottom row, left to right): balloon glass, champagne flute, liqueur glass, champagne saucer, tulip glass, fancy glass.

COCKTAIL SNACKS

To avoid drinking on an empty stomach, it is a good idea to offer small snacks which can be prepared in advance. Here are some examples:

- peanuts, pistachio, cashew nuts and almonds
- black and green olives
- sausage and chorizo
- cubes of Emmenthal or Cantal cheese on cocktail sticks
- radishes, sliced sticks of carrot, celery, and cucumber
- quail's eggs

Canapés made with
- lumpfish roes or caviare
- anchovy fillets or paste
- sardines and lemon juice
- devilled crab and onion
- smoked salmon or salmon mousse
- liver mousse or pate
- melon cubes and Parma ham
- cream cheese with chopped herbs
- avocado mousse and tomato

A GLASS AT THE RIGHT TEMPERATURE:

The glass must be cooled before serving an iced drink or warmed before serving a hot one.

To cool a glass, put some crushed ice in it and stir it round until the inside has cooled. Alternatively, glasses can be kept in the refrigerator as long as it is free of food smells. For a frosty-looking drink, place the glass in the freezer for a few minutes before pouring.

It is advisable to use heat-resistant glasses for serving hot drinks. To warm a glass pour in hot water, leave for a few seconds, then add some boiling water. Pour the water away and wipe the glass before pouring in the hot drink. If there is no time to heat the glass, take care to put a metal spoon in the glass before pouring in the hot drink—this should prevent the cold glass from cracking on contact with the hot liquid.

Serving Cocktails

The preparation of cocktails calls for a certain ritual, and so does the business of serving them. A cocktail should not be served like a glass of water. After pouring the contents of the shaker or mixer into the chilled or heated glass, the cocktail should be decorated with pieces of fresh fruit, a slice of lemon or orange, or a twist of lime or lemon peel.

Some classic cocktails should be served and decorated exactly in the way described in the recipes which follow, but on the whole there is no set rule about decoration: it will depend on the style of glass that is used, the type of drink, and its ingredients. When the drink is ready, add one or two straws cut to a length to suit the glass as a finishing touch.

Pierre Bonnard, Tom Thumb's Café, *1928.*

WARNING!
Like all fizzy drinks, champagne should never be put in a shaker or electric mixer. To preserve the bubbles, pour the champagne directly into the glass.

The Main Types of Cocktail

There is no official classification of cocktails: custom becomes law, and thanks to the inventiveness of its originator, a single cocktail recipe can generate a whole new family of related drinks.

Short and long drinks
Short drinks are served in glasses which vary in size from 90–120 ml (1–4 fl oz). Their alcoholic strength can vary from about 40°, the strength of the original spirit, to 10° or 12° when diluted by additions containing little or no alcohol; for example, crustas, fixes, daisies, frappés, smashes, sours, straights etc.

Long drinks are served in glasses varying in size from 120–33 ml (4–11 fl oz) and sometimes even larger. Composed of spirits or liqueurs mixed with soda, tonic, fruit juice, beer, wines etc, they are generally less alcoholic and more thirst-quenching than short drinks.

Classifications
BUCK
A long, thirst-quenching drink made with soda or some other fizzy liquid like tonic, ginger ale or Coca-Cola, or with sparkling wine or champagne. Gin has usually provided the alcohol in a buck, but it is now made with many other spirits.

COBBLER
A long drink based on wine, fortified wine or spirits, easy to make and thirst-quenching. The ingredients are poured into a glass over ice cubes, decorated with fruits in season or fresh mint leaves and served with straws. Wine cobblers are made with bordeaux, burgundy, Rhine wines, sherry, port etc, and spirit cobblers with rum, whisky, cognac, gin etc.

COLLINS
A long drink made in a collins glass with spirit, lemon juice, soda and ice. Decorate with a slice of lemon or a cherry. *Tom Collins* is supposed to be made with dry gin and *John Collins* with Hollands.

COOLER
A vague term for a long drink mixed in a large glass (250 or 330 m (8–11 fl oz). It should not be too sweet nor too alcoholic or it will not make a good thirst-quencher. It is usually made of spirit, sugar or a syrup and ginger ale or similar fizzy drink. The best-known coolers are based on rum, gin or Calvados, to which lemon juice and sugar are added. Coolers are also made with red or white wine.

CRUSTA
A short drink served in a small-stemmed glass (90–150 ml (3–5 fl oz) and resembling a sour. The crusta can be made with any spirit or liqueur but it is most often made with brandy.
Recipe: moisten the rim of a glass with lemon juice and dip it in powdered sugar to frost it. In a mixing glass put some ice cubes, 1 dash of Angostura bitters, 3 dashes of Maraschino, and 1 measure of spirit. Stir well and strain into the glass. Decorate with a cherry and the peel of a lemon or orange cut in a long spiral.
N.B. In some recipes Maraschino is replaced by the juice of half a lemon and 1 teaspoon of powdered sugar or syrup.

CUP
Usually a long drink with a wine base, served on ice and decorated with pieces of fruit, cucumber slices, mint leaves etc. In the past it used to be served in a large silver bowl resembling a sports trophy, hence its name. It can and sometimes must be prepared in advance and is often served at receptions. A cup is served in a stemmed glass holding 250 ml (8 fl oz) or in a glass with a handle. It is related to cold punches but is more sophisticated in decoration and often takes longer to prepare because it is left to macerate for several hours before being served.

Sangria and *Claret Cup* are among the best-known examples. *Pimms* is not properly speaking a cup because it is made with a spirit and not with wine.

DAIQUIRI
See Rum-based cocktails (page 38).

DAISY
A short drink based on spirit (bourbon being the most popular), accompanied by lemon juice to which 1 teaspoon of grenadine or raspberry syrup is added. The drink is served in a small tumbler holding 120 ml (4 fl oz). It is generally mixed in a cocktail shaker or an electric mixer, and poured into a small tumbler containing crushed ice. It is then topped up with soda and decorated with fresh mint, raspberries or orange.

EGGNOG
Hot or cold drink based on egg and milk to which brandy or rum is added. It can be served in a tumbler or a stemmed glass.

FIX
A short drink with a spirit base. It is made by filling a glass holding 120 ml(4 fl oz) with crushed ice, juice of a lemon quarter, 1 teaspoon of pineapple syrup and 1 measure of cognac (or rum, gin, anis, armagnac, whisky, Calvados). Stir well with a spoon, decorate with cubes of pineapple and a half slice of lemon, and serve with straws.

FIZZ
A drink prepared in a shaker and served in a small tumbler. Fizzes are sweeter than sours because they contain more sugar or syrup, thus reducing the acidity of the lemon.
Egg white is usually added to a fizz, but never to a gin fizz (if it is, it becomes a silver fizz) nor to a *Bucks Fizz* which is made of champagne and orange juice and is not a true fizz. A fizz can be based on any spirit but gin is the most popular. Lemon juice enhances the taste and adds a touch of bitter sharpness which sugar, egg white and soda tone down.

FLIP

Originally a hot drink made with beaten eggs, hot beer, rum, powdered ginger and grated nutmeg. Nowadays it can be hot or cold, made with egg yolk, spirit and dusted with grated nutmeg. The best known is cold *Port Flip*, but it can also be made with cognac, gin, rum, whisky, sherry, Calvados or even with beer as in the past (Ale Flip).

FLOATER

A long drink made by pouring chilled soda into an old fashioned glass or tumbler and then covering it with a measure of brandy or liqueur poured very gently over the back of a spoon held over the glass.

FRAPPÉ

A short drink, made by pouring a liqueur over finely crushed ice in a small tumbler or brandy snifter, and served with short straws.

To make a peppermint frappé pour 2 measures of green crème de menthe into a brandy glass one-third full of finely crushed ice.

FROZEN

An iced drink prepared in an electric mixer with finely-crushed ice. A frozen is served with straws and should be drunk slowly.

GROG

A hot drink containing spirit (rum, whisky, cognac, Calvados etc) and boiling water, sweetened with 1–2 teaspoons of sugar or honey, and decorated with a slice of lemon stuck with a couple of cloves. Cinnamon in powder or stick form can also be added.

Like all hot drinks, grog should be served in a heatproof handled glass.

HIGHBALL

A long drink prepared in a large drinking glass with any spirit, ice and a fizzy addition (tonic, ginger ale, Coca-Cola, bitter lemon etc). Easy to make and popular.

JULEP

The essential element is fresh mint. Crush some leaves in sugar and a little water to extract the flavour. Add finely-crushed ice, a spirit (cognac, gin, rum, whisky) or white wine or champagne. Stir until the glass becomes cold and frosted. Serve with straws.

MULLED WINE

Heat red or white wine, add a little sugar and spice. Do not let the mixture boil, but serve very hot. Add spirit to give strength to the wine, but remember that alcohol evaporates quickly when heated.

OLD FASHIONED

Put a sugar lump in an old fashioned glass, sprinkle it with 3 dashes of Angostura, add 1 measure of rye (or bourbon or other spirit) and crushed ice. Stir, add soda to taste, and garnish with a half slice of orange and a cherry.

Pousse-café
An after-dinner drink which consists of a series of liqueurs, syrups, spirits etc, poured successively into a straight-sided glass so that they lie on top of each other but do not mix, forming a kind of rainbow. The key to success is to put the heaviest, that is the sweetest, ingredient first and then add the rest in decreasingly sweet order. As each must be added very carefully, it helps to pour very slowly over the back of a spoon. If successfully poured, a Pousse-Café is pretty to look at and surprising to drink.

Punch
Long cold or hot drink of which the alcohol base can be varied, e.g. rum, cognac, whisky, wine, cider. It is served in a tumbler or handled glass holding about 250 ml (8 fl oz), garnished with fresh fruit. Punch can be prepared in advance and served in a punch bowl.

Rickey
A medium-sized drink belonging to the Collins group and served in an old fashioned glass. It consists of spirit, lemon juice and soda (but no sugar).

Recipe: put some ice cubes in the glass, pour over the juice of half a lemon and 2 measures of whisky (or gin, Calvados, cognac etc). Mix with a spoon, add soda and garnish with a slice of lemon.

Sangaree
A medium-sized drink like a Rickey but with a base of beer, wine, port or sherry, and a dusting of grated nutmeg. Usually served in old fashioned glass with straws.

Shrub
Variety of grog to which fruit liqueur or fruit syrup is added. In the old days shrub was made by macerating fruit in spirit; it was then heated and strained. Now liqueurs or syrups made from blackcurrant, raspberry, strawberry etc are used. A measure of fruit liqueur is added to 1 measure of cognac or rum and 2 teaspoons of sugar. It is then topped up with boiling water.

Sling
A long hot or cold drink made of spirit (gin, cognac, rum, whisky, Calvados etc), lemon juice and a little sugar syrup in a tumbler, topped up with iced or hot water.

The best known are *Gin Slings*, hot weather drinks harking back to the old colonial days.

Smash
A short version of *Mint Julep* but made only with spirit and garnished with fresh mint, a slice of orange, and lemon peel cut in a spiral. Serve with short straws in an old fashioned glass.

Sour
A short drink based on lemon juice and spirits. In order to preserve its astringency little or no sugar is added—just soda and a slice of lemon; it is sometimes topped with a cherry. *Whisky Sour* is the best known, but sours can be made with gin, rum, cognac etc and also with wine, champagne, cider etc.

Toddy
A semi-long drink served cold or hot.

Recipe: put a measure of spirit (rum, whisky, cognac) and 1 teaspoon of sugar in a tumbler or stemmed glass holding 120 ml (4 fl oz). Top up with iced or hot water. A few drops of Angostura bitters can also be added.

The Recipes

The recipes which follow have been selected from among more than two thousand for their popularity and their appeal to the palate. On the whole they have been classified according to their chief ingredient, but with the help of the index it should be easy to track down a named cocktail.

The symbols by each cocktail tell you how it is made (by mixing glass, shaker or blender) and what kind of glass to serve it in. In most recipes the amount of the major ingredients is given in measures. The measure equals 3 cl (1 fl oz), but any other value can be given to it as long as the proportions are maintained.

    1 measure = 3 cl (1 fl oz)
    1 teaspoon = 5 ml
    1 tablespoon = 15 ml
    1 dash = a few drops

Terms used in the recipes

Alcoholic strength: this is indicated according to French practice: for example, 20° equals 20% of pure alcohol by volume.
Chill: this can be achieved by keeping bottles in the refrigerator for several hours or by putting them in a champagne bucket with ice and iced water for 10 to 20 minutes. The result should be cold but not icy.
Frost: damp the rim of a glass with water or lemon juice or syrup (grenadine gives a pretty red colour) and then turn it in a saucer filled with caster sugar until the sugar crystals stick to the rim.
Ice: it is essential to have a good supply of clean, dry ice. Some people make ice specially for cocktails out of bottled demineralized water, but it is not necessary to go so far. Ice is most often used in cubes, but some recipes need crushed ice—an ice crushing machine will do the job or you can wrap cubes in a tea cloth and beat them with a mallet or hammer.
Shake: shake the cocktail shaker vigorously for about 10 seconds.

Shakers: there are two kinds—
○ the traditional metal shaker consisting of a body, a cover with a built-in strainer and a stopper;
○ the Boston shaker made in two halves, metal and glass, which screw together. If you use this kind, you will need a strainer as well.

It is absolutely essential that the shaker is watertight. If the shaker contains hot liquid, wrap in a cloth before shaking.
Strain: use the integral strainer in the cocktail shaker or use a Hawthorne strainer to ensure that no ice or pips are poured into the cocktail glass.

Cappiello, Colour lithograph, 1923

Fruit juice: should always be freshly expressed and used immediately if at all possible, though the more exotic varieties can be purchased in bottle or can.
Sugar syrup: can be made with ½ litre (1 pint) water and 500 g (1 lb) sugar. It is quite easy to make: dissolve the sugar in the water, bring to the boil, and skim if necessary. Cool a little and strain through muslin into a clean warmed bottle. Cover when cold.
To make a gum syrup, add 100 g (3½ oz) gum arabic to the sugar and water mixture.

Key to symbols in the text
(Types of glasses).
1 *shaker*;
2 *mixing glass*;
3 *electric mixer*;
4 *goblet*;
5 *champagne flute*;
6 *liqueur pousse-café*;
7 *tulip*;
8 *lager*;
9 *Collins*;
10 *tumbler*;
11 *old fashioned*;
12 *fancy*;
13 *cocktail*;
14 *handled*;
15 *whisky tumbler*;
16 *balloon*;
17 *brandy snifter*;
18 *champagne saucer*

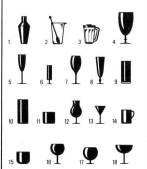

Brandy-based Cocktails

'The warm, champagny, old-particular brandy-punchy feeling' as Oliver Wendell Holmes describes it, captures the quality of brandy to perfection. In reality, the term brandy covers spirits distilled both from wine and from other ingredients, and are found in great variety. Brandy-based cocktails include those based on cognac, armagnac and other grape brandies.

Fruit brandies are not often used in mixtures because their strong aroma does not readily combine with other flavours. Calvados or applejack is distilled from cider and is so individual that it has a separate chapter devoted to it. Grape brandies are numerous but the most distinguished are cognac and armagnac.

Cognac is by far the best-known and most admired of the grape brandies because of its long-established quality and taste excellence. Only the brandy produced in the Charente region of France can be called cognac, just as armagnac applies to one region alone. English-speaking countries are the biggest importers of cognac, where it is usually known, simply and not quite correctly, as brandy.

Cognac has close connections with Britain, because many British names are associated with its history. Jean Martell, originally from the Channel Islands, Richard Hennessy from Ireland, Thomas Hine and James Delamain, English by birth or adoption, were all pioneers in the production of cognac in the Charente in the eighteenth century. They were soon followed by Frenchmen like Rémy Martin, Jean-Baptiste Camus and Emmanuel Courvoisier. But England and the countries once part of her empire have always remained faithful to 'brandy'.

Armagnac, a grape brandy produced in Gascony, has a reputation comparable to cognac, but is very different in character. It can be substituted for cognac in many of the recipes.

Other grape brandies are much less fine and of varying quality, but they can be used for mixing with a strongly-

A 1920 poster for Remy Martin cognac.

flavoured liqueur like peppermint, and less satisfactorily, with other spirits, such as gin or rum. There are many nationalities of cheaper brandies, from Spanish, Italian or German, to Portuguese, Greek and even American.

Happy Blends
Brandy goes well with all natural flavours, particularly fruit ones.
1 It mixes well with orange liqueurs such as Cointreau, Grand Marnier, triple-sec, curaçao, mandarin etc, the best example being the famous *Side Car*.
2 Combined with lemon, brandy brims over with vitality, freshness and pungency, as in a *Brandy Sour*, for example, but these characteristics are diminished by successive additions of sugar, grenadine syrup and soda.
3 The best of digestives, brandy combines with cream and chocolate in a

mellow cocktail, like the famous *Alexander* and others of the same type (see upper table below).

4 An unconventional and amusing combination is made with brandy and banana, for those who like an exotic touch (see lower left table).

Some Surprises
Cognac and ginger is surprising but much appreciated by some connoisseurs of cognac (see *Horse's Neck*).

Cognac and mint is an excellent digestive according to some and a marvellous pick-me-up according to others (see *Stinger*).

Cognac-Fernet is an elegant way of diluting Fernet-Branca and making it easier to drink.

Some Advice
Brandy is a spirit distilled from wine. It is not a good idea to mix it with grain spirits, such as whisky or bourbon, as

this will produce a fierce headache.

Every cognac and armagnac has been distilled and aged with care in order to preserve its aroma. Keep your Grande Champagne VSOP and Grand-Bas-Armagnac for yourself and your connoisseur friends to enjoy on its own. For cocktails use Cognac VS or 3 stars or an armagnac without pretensions. Even the youngest cognac and most modest armagnac, being fresher and younger, will work all the better in a mixture.

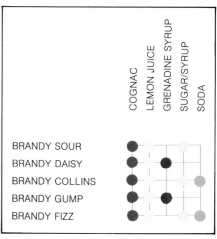

Poster by Bouchet for Cognac Jacquet, 1920.

	COGNAC	DOUBLE CREAM	CRÈME DE CACAO	CRÈME DE CAFÉ	DRY VERMOUTH	NUTMEG	ANGOSTURA BITTERS
ALEXANDER	●	●	●			●	
ALEXANDER'S SISTER	●	●		●			
CHOCOLATE SOLDIER	●			●	●		●

	COGNAC	CRÈME DE BANANE	DOUBLE CREAM	PINEAPPLE JUICE	ORANGE JUICE	ROYAL MINT CHOCOLATE	PASSION FRUIT SYRUP	FALERNUM	FROTHEE	ROYAL ORANGE CHOCOLATE
BANANA BLISS	●	●								
ARAGO	●	●								
SUMMER FUN	●	●		●	●					
ROSS ROYAL	●	●				●				
COGNAC PERINO	●	●			●		●	●		
DUNHILL "71"	●	●							●	●

	COGNAC	LEMON JUICE	GRENADINE SYRUP	SUGAR/SYRUP	SODA
BRANDY SOUR	●	●			
BRANDY DAISY	●	●	●		
BRANDY COLLINS	●	●			●
BRANDY GUMP	●	●	●		
BRANDY FIZZ	●	●		●	●

AFTERNOON COCKTAIL 🍸 🍸

Put some crushed ice into a mixing glass and pour in:

⅓ *maraschino*
⅓ *Fernet-Branca*
⅓ *cognac*

Mix well with a spoon and pour into a champagne saucer. Top up with soda and garnish with an orange slice. Serve with a straw.

ALEXANDER 🍸 🍸

Pour into a cocktail shaker containing some ice cubes:

1 *measure cognac*
1 *measure brown crème de cacao*
1 *measure double cream*

Shake well and strain into a cocktail glass. Sprinkle with grated nutmeg and chocolate.

ALEXANDER'S SISTER 🍸 🍸

Pour into a cocktail shaker over some ice cubes:

1 *measure cognac*
1 *measure Kahlúa*
1 *measure double cream*

Shake well and pour into a cocktail glass. Sprinkle with grated nutmeg.

ALEXIS HECK 🍸 🍸

Put some ice cubes in a mixing glass and add:

⅖ *Martell Medaillon Fine Cognac*
⅕ *Grand Marnier*
⅕ *golden rum*
⅕ *dry Cinzano*

Stir and strain into a champagne saucer.

Alexander in a Lalique crystal glass

AMERICAN BEAUTY 🍸 🍸

Put some ice cubes in a cocktail shaker and pour in:

1 *measure brandy*
1 *measure dry vermouth*
1 *measure orange juice*
1 *measure grenadine*
1 *dash crème de menthe*

Shake well and strain into a large cocktail glass. Tilt the glass and gently pour in a little ruby port so that it floats on top. Decorate with a sprig of fresh mint.

AMERICAN BEAUTY SPECIAL 🍸 🍸 🍸

Put some ice cubes in a shaker or mixing glass and pour in:

⅓ *cognac*
⅓ *Cointreau*
⅓ *golden rum*

Shake well and strain into a champagne saucer. Decorate with a twist of lemon peel and a small yellow flower.

AMERICAN ROSE 🍸 🍸

Pour into a shaker containing some ice cubes:

1 *measure cognac*
1 *dash Pernod*
1 *dash grenadine*
½ *ripe peach*

Shake well and strain into a balloon glass filled with crushed ice. Decorate with peach slices and a cherry on a cocktail stick. Top up with champagne just before serving.

ARAGO 🍸 🍸

Put some ice cubes in a shaker and pour in:

1 *measure crème de banane*
1 *measure double cream*
1 *measure cognac*

Shake well and strain into a cocktail glass. For a thick, frosty Arago, add a sliced banana to the ingredients with the ice and mix in an electric blender for 1 minute. Pour into a cocktail glass or tumbler.

ATLANTIC COGNAC

Put some ice cubes in a shaker and pour in:

⅔ cognac
⅓ crème de café

Shake and strain into a collins glass. Top up with as much fresh orange juice as you like. Stir well just before serving. Decorate with an orange slice and a maraschino cherry.

BANANA BLISS

Put some ice cubes in a mixing glass and pour in:

1 measure cognac
1 measure crème de banane

Stir with a spoon and strain into a cocktail glass. Decorate with banana slices on a cocktail stick.

B AND B (BENEDICTINE AND BRANDY)

In a liqueur glass put:

1 measure Benedictine

Gently pour in 1 measure cognac over the back of a spoon so that it floats on top.

BETWEEN THE SHEETS

Pour into a cocktail shaker containing some ice cubes:

1 measure cognac
1 measure white rum
1 measure Cointreau
1 dash lemon juice

Shake well. Pour into a champagne saucer. Decorate with a thin slice of lemon.

BILLY HAMILTON

Pour into a cocktail shaker containing some ice cubes:

⅓ brandy
⅓ curaçao
⅓ crème de cacao
1 egg white

Shake well and strain into a cocktail glass.

BOMBAY

Put some ice cubes in a mixing glass and pour in:

1 measure brandy
½ measure dry vermouth
½ measure sweet vermouth
1 dash pastis
2 dashes orange curaçao

Stir well and strain into an old fashioned glass over 2 ice cubes.

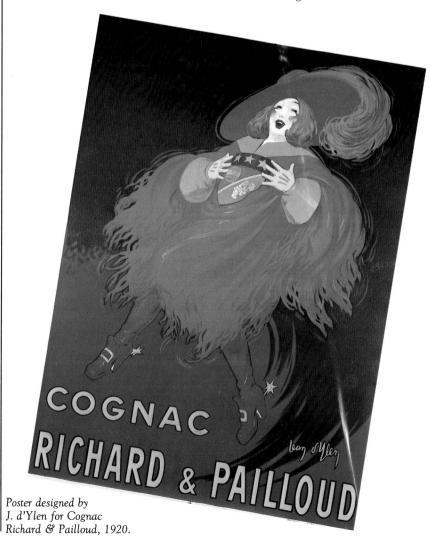

Poster designed by
J. d'Ylen for Cognac
Richard & Pailloud, 1920.

BOSOM CARESSER ♦ ᵧ

Put some ice cubes in a cocktail shaker and pour in:

2 measures brandy
1 measure curaçao
1 egg yolk
1 teaspoon grenadine

Shake vigorously and strain into a cocktail glass.

BRANDY BLAZER ♥

Dampen the rim of a heat-proof balloon glass and dip it into caster sugar to frost. Hold the glass over a low flame to caramelize the sugar. Pour in some hot coffee and add:

1½ measures cognac
½ measure Kahlúa
1 teaspoon sugar
1 piece orange peel
1 piece lemon peel

Stir well before serving.

BRANDY CHAMPERELLE ♥

Pour into a balloon glass:

1 measure brandy
1 measure curaçao
3 dashes Angostura bitters

Stir and serve.

BRANDY COCKTAIL 1 ⍭ ᵧ

Put some ice cubes in a mixing glass and pour in:

1½ measures brandy
½ measure Benedictine
1 dash Angostura bitters

Stir and strain into a cocktail glass. Decorate with a cherry.

BRANDY COCKTAIL 2 ⍭ ᵧ

Put some ice cubes in a mixing glass and pour in:

1 measure brandy
1 dash vermouth
1 dash curaçao
1 dash sugar syrup
2 dashes Angostura bitters

Stir well and strain into a cocktail glass. Decorate with a spiral of lemon peel and a cherry.

BRANDY COLLINS ▯

Fill a tumbler with ice cubes and pour in:

juice of ½ lemon
1 teaspoon sugar
1 measure brandy

Stir and top up with soda. Garnish with a slice of lemon.

BRANDY DAISY ♦ ▯

Put some ice cubes in a cocktail shaker and pour in:

2 measures brandy
1 tablespoon lemon juice
2 teaspoons grenadine

Shake and strain into a tumbler. Add a quarter peach, a quarter apricot and a quarter apple cut into pieces.

BRANDY FIZZ ♦ ▯

Pour into a cocktail shaker containing some ice cubes:

1 measure cognac
½ measure lemon juice
¼ measure sugar syrup or 1 teaspoon sugar

Shake well and strain into a collins glass full of ice cubes. Top up with

soda. Garnish with a slice of lemon and 2 cherries on a cocktail stick.

BRANDY FLIP ♦ ❢

Put some ice cubes in a cocktail shaker and pour in:

2 measures brandy
1 teaspoon sugar
1 egg

Shake well. Strain into a champagne flute and sprinkle with grated nutmeg.

BRANDY GUMP ♦ ᵧ

Pour into a cocktail shaker containing some ice cubes:

2 measures brandy
juice of ½ lemon
2 dashes grenadine

Shake and strain into a small cocktail glass.

BRANDY SOUR ♦ ❢

Put some ice cubes in a cocktail shaker and add:

1½ measures cognac
½ measure lemon juice
1 teaspoon sugar

Shake and strain into a tulip glass.

BRANDY TODDY ▪

In an old fashioned glass dissolve 1 scant teaspoon sugar in 2 teaspoons water. Add:

1 ice cube
2 measures brandy

Stir. Add a sliver of lemon peel.

BRANDY VERMOUTH COCKTAIL

Put some crushed ice in a cocktail shaker and pour in:

2 measures brandy
$\frac{1}{2}$ measure sweet vermouth
1 dash Angostura bitters

Shake well and strain into a small cocktail glass.

BREAKFAST NOG

Pour into a cocktail shaker containing some ice cubes:

1 measure cognac
1 measure Grand Marnier
1 egg
2 measures milk

Shake and strain into a tumbler. Sprinkle with grated nutmeg.

CACATOES

Pour into a cocktail shaker containing some ice cubes:

$\frac{4}{10}$ cognac
$\frac{1}{10}$ Marie Brizard crème de banane
$\frac{2}{10}$ Mandarine Impériale
$\frac{2}{10}$ orange juice
$\frac{1}{10}$ lemon juice
1 dash grenadine

Shake and strain into a cocktail glass. Decorate with a slice of orange, a cherry and a sprig of mint.

Yvon Bleses, Lyon.
ABF, France.

CALIMERO

Put some ice cubes in a cocktail shaker and pour in:

$\frac{3}{4}$ measure brandy
$\frac{1}{4}$ measure Grand Marnier
$\frac{1}{4}$ measure Tia Maria
$\frac{3}{4}$ measure orange juice
a few dashes lemon juice
1 teaspoon egg white

Shake very well and strain into a balloon glass. Garnish with a slice of orange.

CARNIVAL

Put some ice cubes in a cocktail shaker and pour in:

$\frac{1}{3}$ measure cognac
$\frac{1}{5}$ measure apricot brandy
$\frac{1}{3}$ measure Lillet
1 dash kirsch
1 dash orange juice

Shake and strain into a fancy glass. Decorate with a red and yellow flower if desired.

S.A. Rowe.
Torquay Carnival Cocktail Competition, 1948.
UKBG, Great Britain.

CARROL COCKTAIL

Put some crushed ice in a mixing glass and add:

1 measure cognac
$\frac{1}{2}$ measure sweet vermouth

Stir well and strain into a chilled cocktail glass. Garnish with either a cherry or cocktail onion.

CHAMPS-ELYSÉES

Put some ice cubes in a cocktail shaker and pour in:

$\frac{3}{5}$ brandy
$\frac{1}{5}$ yellow Chartreuse
$\frac{1}{5}$ lemon juice
1 dash Angostura bitters

Shake vigorously and strain into a small cocktail glass.

CHOCOLATE SOLDIER

Pour into a cocktail shaker containing some ice cubes:

1 measure brandy
1 measure dry vermouth
1 measure crème de cacao
2 dashes Angostura bitters

Shake and strain into a cocktail glass.

F.J. Cook.
European Cocktail Competition, Torquay, 1949.
UKBG, Great Britain.

CLASSIC COCKTAIL

Pour into a cocktail shaker containing some ice cubes:

2 measures cognac
2 teaspoons lemon juice
2 teaspoons maraschino
2 teaspoons curaçao

Shake well. Dampen the rim of a brandy snifter and frost with sugar. Pour in the cocktail and drop in an ice cube.

CLOSE ENCOUNTERS

Put into an electric blender:

2 tablespoons crushed ice
1 measure brandy
$\frac{1}{2}$ measure curaçao
4 measures orange juice
4 strawberries
1 dash Angostura bitters

Blend well and pour into a balloon glass. Decorate the rim of the glass with an orange slice and spear 2 strawberries on a cocktail stick.

Drawing by Emile Bourdelin of the vats at the Martell distillery at Cognac.

COFFEE NOG

For each person put 1 egg yolk and ½ measure double cream into a bowl and whisk until thick and mousse-like.
    Then pour into a saucepan:

200 ml/7 fl oz black coffee
1 measure cognac
½ measure crème de cacao
1 teaspoon cocoa powder
1 teaspoon sugar

Put the pan over low heat and, stirring constantly, bring the mixture to just under the boiling point. Pour into a heatproof handled glass and spoon the beaten cream on top. Grate some nutmeg over the top and serve.

COGNAC COCKTAIL

Put some ice cubes in a mixing glass and pour in:

2 measures cognac
2 measures lemon juice

1 dash Cointreau
1 dash Angostura bitters

Stir to mix and strain into a cocktail glass. Decorate with a twist of lemon peel.

COGNAC-MINT FRAPPÉ

Put some ice cubes in a mixing glass and pour in:

1 measure cognac
1 measure green crème de menthe

Stir well to mix. Strain into a tumbler filled with crushed ice. Crush some fresh mint between your fingertips and drop into the glass. Serve with straws.

COGNAC ORANGE

Fill a tumbler with crushed ice and add:

1 measure cognac
2 measures orange juice

Garnish with an orange slice. Serve with straws.

COGNAC PERINO

Put some crushed ice in a cocktail shaker and pour in:

1 measure Monnet Régal cognac
½ measure crème de banane
½ measure passion fruit syrup
¼ measure Falernum
¼ measure orange juice
2 dashes Frothée

Shake vigorously and strain into a cocktail glass.

Toby Cordero,
Perino's Restaurant, 1973.
USBG, USA.

CORPSE REVIVER 1

Pour into a mixing glass containing some ice cubes:

2 measures cognac
1 measure calvados
1 measure sweet vermouth

Stir to mix well and strain into a cocktail glass. Garnish with a twist of lemon peel.
N.B. Corpse Reviver 2, which is based on gin, can be found on page 61.

CORPSE REVIVER 3

Put some ice cubes in a cocktail shaker and add:

1 measure cognac
1 measure lemon juice
1 measure orange juice
2 dashes grenadine

Shake well and strain into a tulip glass. Top up with chilled champagne. Decorate with a slice of lemon or orange.

CUBAN ♦ 🍸

Put some ice cubes in a cocktail shaker and add:

1 measure brandy
½ measure apricot brandy
¼ measure lime juice

Shake and strain into a cocktail glass.

DUNHILL '71' ♦ 🍷

Put some ice cubes in a cocktail shaker and add:

¾ measure cognac
¾ measure Royal Orange Chocolate liqueur
¾ measure crème de banane

Shake. Strain into a balloon glass. Top with a thin layer of double cream.

BRIAN RUDDY,
1st prize National Cocktail Competition, London, 1971. UKBG, UK.

EAST INDIA 1 🍶 🍸

Pour into a mixing glass containing some ice cubes:

2 measures cognac
1 teaspoon pineapple juice
1 teaspoon curaçao
a few dashes Angostura bitters

Stir and strain into a cocktail glass. N.B. East India 2 is based on vermouth and sherry, see page 107.

ELLISSE ▮

Put some ice cubes in a tumbler and add:

2 dashes Angostura bitters
1½ measures brandy
1 dash Strega

Top up with ginger ale. Garnish with a spiral of lemon peel.

FAVOURITE ♦ 🍷

Put some ice cubes in a cocktail shaker and add:

½ measure brandy
½ measure gin
½ measure lemon juice
¼ measure grenadine

Shake well. Strain into a balloon glass. To garnish, place a slice of lemon across the rim of the glass.

FERNET 🍶 🍸

Pour into a mixing glass:

1 measure cognac
1 measure Fernet-Branca
1 dash Angostura bitters
2 dashes sugar syrup

Strain into a cocktail glass. Garnish with a twist of lemon peel.

GOLDEN GLEAM ♦ 🍷

Put some ice cubes in a cocktail shaker and add:

1 measure cognac
1 measure Grand Marnier
½ measure lemon juice
½ measure orange juice

Shake and strain into a tulip glass.

GOLDEN MEDALLION ♦ 🍸

Put some ice cubes in a cocktail shaker and add:

1 measure brandy
1 measure Galliano
1 measure orange juice
1 dash egg white

Shake. Strain into a cocktail glass. Grate a little orange peel over the top.

GREEN ROOM 🍶 ▮

Put some ice cubes in a mixing glass and add:

2 measures dry vermouth
1 measure cognac
2–3 dashes curaçao

Shake and strain into a small tumbler. cherry.

BOB LITTARDI,
Paris. ABF, France.

HARVARD COCKTAIL 🍶 🍸

Put some ice cubes in a mixing glass and add:

1 measure cognac
1 measure sweet vermouth
2 dashes Angostura bitters

Stir and strain into a cocktail glass.

HERCULYS ▮

Pour into a tumbler over some ice cubes:

$\frac{2}{10}$ cognac
$\frac{2}{10}$ Amaretto di Sarronna
$\frac{1}{10}$ grenadine
$\frac{5}{10}$ orange juice

Stir well to mix. Garnish with a slice of orange, lemon peel and a brandied

HORSE'S NECK ▮

Cut the peel of a lemon in a continuous spiral and put it in a tumbler. Fill with ice cubes and add:

1½ measures cognac
1 dash Angostura bitters

Top up with ginger ale and serve.

Horse's Neck in a Lalique crystal glass.

HOT BRANDY FLIP ⫿

For each person put 1 egg yolk and 1 teaspoon sugar into a mixing bowl and beat until thick and pale.
  In a small saucepan heat:

200 ml/7 fl oz strong black coffee
2 measures cognac
3 measures ruby port

Stirring constantly, bring the mixture to just under boiling point. Pour immediately over the egg yolk and sugar; stir until the mixture is smooth and thick. Pour into a heatproof handled glass; grate nutmeg on top.

KRISS ⫿⫿

Put some ice cubes in a mixing glass and add:

$\frac{5}{10}$ *cognac*
$\frac{2}{10}$ *dry vermouth*
$\frac{2}{10}$ *Amaretto di Sarrono*
$\frac{1}{10}$ *lemon juice*
a little sugar syrup

Stir. Strain into a collins glass. Top up with tonic water. Garnish with a slice of lemon and a cherry.

Umberto Caselli, Milan.
AIBES, Italy.

LAIT DE POULE ⫿ ⫿

Put some ice cubes in a cocktail shaker and add:

1 measure cognac
$\frac{1}{2}$ *measure crème de vanille*
2 measures milk
1 egg yolk

Shake energetically. Strain into a large cocktail glass. Sprinkle with grated nutmeg.

LAST ORDER ⫿

Heat over a low flame:

350 ml/12 fl oz brown ale
1 measure cognac
1 tablespoon raisins
2 slices stem ginger (preserved)

Just before the mixture comes to the boil pour it into a heatproof handled glass. Serve with a stick of cinnamon.

LIAISON ⫿ ⫿

In a cocktail shaker full of ice cubes put:

$\frac{5}{10}$ *cognac*
$\frac{3}{10}$ *Cointreau*
$\frac{2}{10}$ *cream of coconut*
1 dash Angostura bitters

Shake and pour into a fancy glass without straining.

Jean-Loup Timmerman,
1st prize Nantes meeting, France, June 1981.

MILLIONAIRE ⫿ ⫿

Put some ice cubes in a cocktail shaker and add:

2 measures cognac
$\frac{1}{4}$ *measure Cointreau*
1 dash crème de noyau
1 dash orgeat syrup
1 dash Angostura bitters

Shake well and strain into a cocktail glass.

MONTANA ⫿ ⫿

Put some ice cubes in a mixing glass and add:

1 measure cognac
1 measure dry vermouth
2 dashes port
2 dashes anisette
2 dashes Angostura bitters

Stir and strain into a cocktail glass.

MORNING GLORY 1 ⫿ ⫿

Put some ice cubes in a cocktail shaker and add:

1 measure cognac
$\frac{1}{2}$ *measure curaçao*
$\frac{1}{2}$ *measure lemon juice*
2 dashes Angostura bitters
2 dashes pastis
1 teaspoon sugar

Shake and strain into a tumbler. Add a long spiral of lemon peel and some ice cubes. Top up with soda.
N.B. Morning Glory 2 is based on rye whiskey, see page 84.

MOULIN ROUGE

Put some ice cubes in a collins glass and add:

1 measure cognac
4 measures pineapple juice

Stir to mix. Top up with chilled champagne or any other sparkling white wine. Garnish with a piece of pineapple and a cherry.

NEW FASHIONED

In an old fashioned glass put:

1 sugar cube
1 dash Angostura bitters
1 splash of the soda syphon
Then add:
$1\frac{1}{4}$ measures brandy

Put in 3 ice cubes and garnish with a slice of orange and a slice of lemon.

	COGNAC	COINTREAU/GRAND MARNIER	LEMON JUICE	ANGOSTURA BITTERS	ORANGE JUICE	GRENADINE SYRUP	MARASCHINO	RUM	DRY VERMOUTH	PASTIS	CREAM OF COCONUT	CRÈME DE NOYAUX	ORGEAT SYRUP	CHAMPAGNE	EGG	MILK	SUGAR/SYRUP	SODA
SIDE CAR	●	●	●															
COGNAC ORANGE	●				●													
BRANDY CHAMPERELLE	●	●		●														
COGNAC COCKTAIL	●	●	●	●														
CLOSE ENCOUNTERS	●	●		●	●													
GOLDEN GLEAM	●	●	●		●													
OLYMPIC	●	●			●													
PENGUIN (FANCY)	●	●	●		●	●												
PICK ME UP	●	●			●	●								●				
AMERICAN ROSE	●					●				●				●				
ROLLS ROYCE	●	●			●										●			
BOSOM CARESSER	●	●				●									●			
BREAKFAST NOG	●	●													●	●		
CLASSIC COCKTAIL	●	●	●				●										●	
GREEN ROOM	●	●							●									
ALEXIS HECK	●	●						●	●									
T.N.T.	●	●		●						●								
MORNING GLORY N° 1	●	●	●	●						●							●	●
LIAISON	●	●		●							●							
MILLIONNAIRE	●	●		●								●	●					

OLYMPIC

Put some ice cubes in a cocktail shaker and add:

1 measure cognac
1 measure Grand Marnier
1 measure orange juice

Shake and strain into an old fashioned glass.

PENGUIN

Into a mixing glass pour:

1 measure brandy
$\frac{1}{2}$ measure Cointreau
1 measure lemon juice
1 measure orange juice
1 dash grenadine

Stir well to mix. Pour into a large balloon glass filled with ice cubes. Garnish with a quarter slice each of orange and lemon placed on the rim of the glass, a cherry, and a paper parasol. Serve with 2 long straws.

PICK ME UP

Put some ice cubes in a cocktail shaker and add:

$\frac{3}{4}$ measure brandy
$\frac{1}{4}$ measure Grand Marnier
juice of $\frac{1}{2}$ orange
1 dash grenadine

Shake well and strain into a balloon glass. Top up with champagne. Garnish with a quarter slice of orange and a quarter slice of lemon placed on the rim of the glass, and a cherry. Serve with 2 straws.

PIPPI LONG DRINK

Put some ice cubes in a cocktail shaker and add:

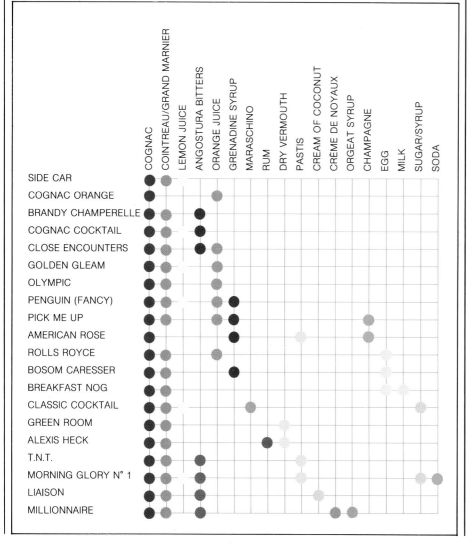

1 measure Bisquit cognac
1 measure apricot brandy
juice of 1 clementine
1 egg white

Shake well and strain into a tumbler.
Top up with Fanta lemonade.

First prize National Cocktail and Long Drink
Competition. DBL, Denmark.

PLAYMATE 🍸 ▪

Put some ice cubes in a cocktail
shaker and add:

½ *measure cognac*
½ *measure apricot brandy*
½ *measure Grand Marnier*
½ *measure orange syrup*
1 egg white
1 dash Angostura bitters

Shake and strain into an old fashioned
glass. Garnish with orange peel.

PRINCE CHARLES 🍸 🍷

Pour into cocktail shaker containing
some ice cubes:

1 measure brandy
1 measure Drambuie
1 measure lemon juice

Shake and strain into a balloon glass.
Decorate with a lemon slice across the
rim.

RED HACKLE 🍸 🍸

Place some ice cubes in a cocktail
shaker and pour in:
½ *brandy*
¼ *Dubonnet*
¼ *grenadine*

Shake and strain into a cocktail glass.

T. BLAKE,
Irish Cocktail Competition, 1961.

Side Car in a
Baccarat crystal glass.

ROLLS ROYCE 🍸 🍸

Place some ice cubes in a cocktail
shaker and add:

1 measure brandy
1 measure Cointreau
1 measure orange juice
1 egg white

Shake well. Strain into a cocktail glass.

UKBG, Great Britain.

SIDE CAR 🍸 🍸

Put some ice cubes in a cocktail
shaker and add:

1¼ *measures cognac*
½ *measure Cointreau*
½ *measure lemon juice*

Shake well and strain into a cocktail
glass.

STINGER ♠ ☘

Put some ice cubes in a cocktail shaker and add:

1½ measures cognac
½ measure white crème de menthe
1 dash lemon juice

Shake well and strain into a cocktail glass.

SUMMER FUN ♠ ▮

Pour into a cocktail shaker containing ice cubes:

1 measure cognac
¾ measure crème de banane
3 measures pineapple juice
3 measures orange juice

Shake well and pour into a tumbler. Decorate with a strawberry placed on the rim of the glass and a small paper parasol. Serve with straws.

SWEET EDEN ♠ ☘

Pour into a cocktail shaker containing some ice cubes:

4/10 cognac
3/10 Tia Maria
1/10 Bols blue curaçao
2/10 orange juice

Shake and strain into a cocktail glass. Garnish with a cherry and a half slice of orange.

FERNAND DINUOLO,
Paris. ABF, France.

THREE MILLER ♠ ☘

Put some ice cubes in a cocktail shaker and add:

1 measure brandy
½ measure white rum
1 teaspoon grenadine
1 dash lemon juice

Shake and strain into a cocktail glass.

T.N.T. ◹ ☘

Put some ice cubes in a mixing glass and add:

1 measure cognac
½ measure Cointreau
1 dash Angostura bitters
1 dash pastis

Stir well to mix. Strain into a cocktail glass.

Stinger in a glass from the Danish Boutique, Paris.

TOPS SMILE ◹ ☘

Put some ice cubes in a mixing glass and add:

¾ Courvoisier VSOP cognac
⅛ Cherry Heering
⅛ Drambuie
1 dash Marie Brizard anisette
2 dashes orange juice
2 dashes lemon juice

Stir and strain into a cocktail glass.

GUS TOPS,
UBB, Belgium.

VANDERBILT ◹ ☘

Pour into a mixing glass:

1 measure cognac
1 measure cherry brandy
2 dashes sugar syrup
2 dashes Angostura bitters

Stir to mix and strain into a cocktail glass. Garnish with a cherry and a twist of lemon peel.

WHIP ♠ ☘

Pour into a shaker:

½ measure brandy
½ measure dry vermouth
½ measure curaçao
½ measure pastis

Shake and strain into a cocktail glass.

YANKEE DOODLE ♠ ☘

Pour into a cocktail shaker containing some ice cubes:

⅓ brandy
⅓ crème de banane
⅓ Royal Mint Chocolate liqueur

Shake well and strain into a cocktail glass.

Calvados-based Cocktails

Spirits distilled from cider have a strong smell of apple, in varying degrees of intensity, which makes them very difficult to blend in cocktails. All these brandies are distilled from fermented apple juice. The local American variety, which is known as applejack or apple brandy, is a very powerful alcohol, often quite rough and lacking in subtlety. In Switzerland, they make Pomme, a clear and limpid liquid, very much like fruit brandy.

Many other countries produce cider-based brandies, and sometimes sweeten them. But the best-known and probably the finest in this group of spirits is Calvados. Like cognac, Calvados is aged and improved over a period of many years in wooden casks, which gives the drink a supple roundness and a beautiful golden-brown colouring. A good Calvados can be recognized by its nose: it should give out a subtle scent of new apples. With age it loses its freshness and vigour, but gains in its aroma and subtlety of flavour. Like all mature things, it wins in distinction what it loses in youth.

Happy Blends
Calvados and other cider brandies have a very pronounced character and do not blend well with most other spirits; their strong apple scent dominates the cocktails in which they are used. But they can tolerate some admixtures at least for the short period of time that it takes to drink them.

Calvados and lemon is a delight for anyone who likes lemon drinks; acid-flavoured mixtures are in the best tradition of cocktails (see *Apple Brandy Cocktail, Calvados Sour, Calvados Cooler, Calvados Rickey, Jack Rose* etc).

Calvados and orange juice is a smooth and subtle contrast of orange and apple flavours (see *Calvados Cocktail, Jack Rabbit*).

Calvados and cider is an unusual drink. Calvados is combined with the drink from which it derives, giving a distinctive character to some novel cocktails.

Some Surprises
Calvados and vermouth is a noteworthy treat. Such a surprising combination seems unnatural, but you will be astonished at the unexpected and original result (see *Apple Blossom, Princess Pride Cocktail*). Calvados and pineapple juice is a refreshing drink (see *Hawaiian Brandy Cocktail*).

Some Advice
Calvados enthusiasts will be curious to know how it behaves when skilfully blended: the recipes that follow are among the best. But they will certainly be disappointed if they are tempted to create more fanciful concoctions. Quite the best way to enjoy a good Calvados is in traditional fashion, in a brandy snifter at the end of a meal. An old Calvados has exceptional and subtle aromas, more clean flavoured and fruity than those of cognac, and it is one of the best spirits made in France. For cocktails, use the youngest Calvados available.

Calvados ageing in vats.

A.J. 🍶 🍸

Put some ice cubes in a cocktail shaker and add:

1 measure Calvados
1 measure grapefruit juice
1 dash grenadine

Shake vigorously and strain into a cocktail glass.

AMBROSIA 🍶 🥂

Put some ice cubes in a cocktail shaker and add:

½ Calvados
½ cognac
1–2 dashes raspberry syrup

Shake vigorously and strain into a champagne flute. Top up with champagne. Stir very gently to mix and garnish with two or three raspberries on a stick.

ANGEL FACE 🍶 🍸

Put some ice cubes in a cocktail shaker and add:

½ Calvados
¼ apricot brandy
½ gin

Shake vigorously and strain into a cocktail glass. Decorate the glass with an apricot slice if desired.

APPLE BLOSSOM 🍶 🍸

Put some ice cubes in a cocktail shaker and add:

1 measure Calvados
1 measure sweet vermouth

Shake well. Strain into a cocktail glass.

APPLE BRANDY COCKTAIL ♟️🍸

Place some ice cubes in a cocktail shaker and pour in:

1 measure Calvados
1 teaspoon grenadine
1 teaspoon lemon juice

Shake and strain into a cocktail glass.

APPLE BRANDY HIGHBALL ▯

Fill a tumbler with ice cubes and add:

1 measure Calvados

Top up with soda or ginger ale. Stir and decorate with a twist of lemon peel.

APPLE COCKTAIL ♟️🍸

Pour into a cocktail shaker containing some ice cubes:

1 measure Calvados
1 measure dry cider
½ measure gin
½ measure cognac

Shake and strain into a cocktail glass.

APPLEJACK COCKTAIL ♟️🍸

Pour into a cocktail shaker containing some ice cubes:

1 measure Calvados
½ measure grenadine
½ measure lemon juice

Shake and strain into a cocktail glass.

CALVADOS COCKTAIL ♟️▯

Pour into a cocktail shaker containing some ice cubes:

Calvados Cocktail in a glass from Cristal d'Arques.

1 measure Calvados
½ measure Cointreau
½ measure Angostura bitters
1 measure orange juice

Shake well. Put some crushed ice in a tumbler and strain the cocktail on to it. Decorate with an orange slice and serve with straws.

CALVADOS COOLER ▯

Put some crushed ice in a tumbler and add.

1 measure Calvados
juice of ¼ lemon
1 teaspoon sugar

Stir to mix and top up with soda.

CALVADOS RICKEY ▪

Put some ice cubes in an old fashioned glass and add:

1 measure Calvados
juice of ¼ lemon

Stir and top up with soda. Garnish with a slice of lemon.

CALVADOS SOUR ♟️🍸

Place some ice cubes in a cocktail shaker and add:

1 measure Calvados
½ teaspoon sugar
1 teaspoon lemon juice

Shake and strain into a large goblet. Garnish with half an orange slice and a cherry.

CAPE COD JACK ▪

Put some ice cubes in an old fashioned glass and add:

1 measure Calvados
1 measure bilberry juice
1–2 teaspoons sugar

Stir to mix. Serve with a stirrer.

CASTLE DIP ♟️🍸

Put some ice cubes in a cocktail shaker and add:

1 measure Calvados
1 measure white crème de menthe
3 dashes Pernod

Shake and strain into a cocktail glass.

HARVARD COOLER ♟️▯

Put some ice cubes in a cocktail shaker and add:

1 measure Calvados
juice of ½ lemon
1 scant teaspoon sugar

Shake well. Put some ice cubes in a tumbler and strain the mixture over them. Top up with soda. Stir gently before serving.

HAWAIIAN BRANDY COCKTAIL

Put some crushed ice in a cocktail shaker and add:

1 measure Calvados
½ measure pineapple juice
1 dash maraschino
1 dash lemon juice
½ teaspoon sugar

Shake well and strain into a cocktail glass.

HONEYMOON

Put some ice cubes in a cocktail shaker and add:

½ measure Calvados
½ measure Benedictine
juice of ½ lemon
3 dashes Cointreau

Shake and strain into a cocktail glass.

JACK RABBIT

Put some ice cubes in cocktail shaker and add:

1 measure Calvados
½ measure maple syrup
½ measure lemon juice
½ measure orange juice

Shake well and strain into a cocktail glass.

JACK ROSE

Put some ice cubes in a cocktail

shaker and add:

1 measure Calvados
1 teaspoon sugar
juice of ½ lemon or lime
3 dashes grenadine

Shake well. Strain into a cocktail glass.

MOONLIGHT COOLER

Put some ice cubes in a cocktail shaker and add:

1 measure Calvados
juice of 1 lemon
½ teaspoon sugar

Shake and strain into a tumbler. Add two ice cubes and top up with soda. Garnish with fresh fruit slices.

Moonlight Cooler in a Lalique crystal glass.

PO-POMME

Place some ice cubes in a mixing glass and add:

⅓ Calvados
⅔ cherry brandy
few dashes Angostura bitters

Stir well to mix and strain into a tumbler. Top up with dry cider (or sweet cider if you like). Add 2 ice cubes, some apple cut into cubes and 3 brandied cherries.

PRINCESS PRIDE COCKTAIL

Put some ice cubes in a cocktail shaker and add:

1 measure Calvados
½ measure sweet vermouth
½ measure Dubonnet

Shake vigorously and strain into a cocktail glass.

THREE-THREE-THREE (333)

Into a cocktail shaker containing some ice cubes pour:

½ measure Calvados
½ measure Cointreau
½ measure grapefruit juice

Shake and strain into a tulip glass. Garnish with a thin slice of lemon and a cherry.

WHIST

Into a cocktail shaker containing some ice cubes pour:

½ measure Calvados
½ measure rum
½ measure sweet vermouth

Shake and strain into a cocktail glass.

Rum-based Cocktails

A number of evocative images are brought to mind at the mention of the word rum—from swarthy pirates toasting captured treasure with flasks of dark Jamaican rum to tanned holidaymakers sipping exotic fruity cocktails on sun-drenched beaches.

There is an astonishing variety of rums. Produced mainly in the Caribbean, rum is distilled from the fermented juice of the sugar cane or more commonly from molasses (the residue left after the production of sugar from cane); a more strongly flavoured rum is produced by adding the residue of one distillation to the next. Rum is distilled in a number of ways and each country produces a spirit with its own distinctive characteristics. Roughly speaking, there are light-bodied white rums; golden rums which are lightly coloured by being aged in cask and sometimes darkened by the addition of caramel; and well-aged dark rums which often have a pungent flavour.

Rum has been imported into England since the eighteenth century and almost all the rum drunk here still comes from Commonwealth countries in the Caribbean.

Rum was also very popular in the American colonies, and the United States is now the largest consumer of rum in the world. It prefers its rum light and white, perhaps because of the bad memories left by the bathtub spirits of the Prohibition era.

In France the importation of rum was originally forbidden, and although the influence of the Empress Josephine brought West Indian products back into fashion, it was not until 1854 that most of the discriminatory duties were finally removed. Today the importation of rum is restricted to those varieties produced in French overseas departments and territories.

The subtlety and bouquet of a rum give a cocktail its personality. White rum is most frequently used in cocktails and comes from the distillation of molasses. Less aromatic than the darker rums, it works perfectly with fruit juices and certain liqueurs. Golden rum has a good colour and a stronger aroma and goes well in a number of cocktails and, when used for making hot drinks, gives most comforting results.

Happy Blends

Rum and lemon or lime is a winning combination, above all in the famous *Daiquiri*, originally from Cuba. The recipe varies according to fancy but always contains two basic ingredients: lemon juice and rum, as recommended at the beginning of the century by its inventor, Constante Ribalagua of the Florida Restaurant in Havana.

Bacardi, a variant of *Daiquiri*, is made only with Bacardi rum, originally from Cuba but now exported from Puerto Rico too. A related invention is *Cuba Libre* which took its name from the independence of the island in 1902.

Rum and lemon or lime are the base of all the traditional cocktails from sours, or *Collins* right up to the sophisticated and potent *Zombie* (see the table on this page).

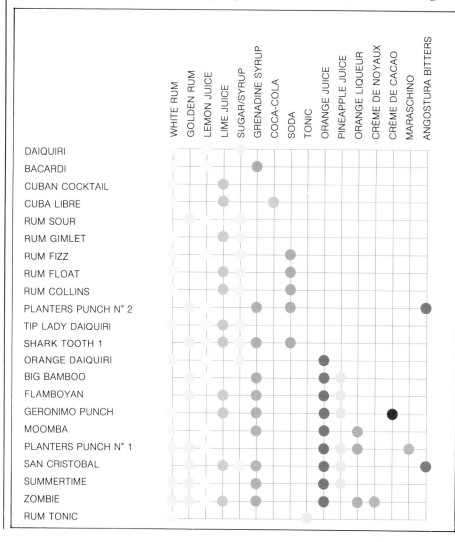

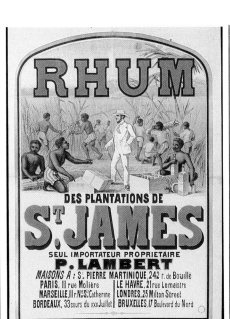

Calvados Cocktail in a glass from Cristal d'Arques.

Rum also goes very well with coconut and pineapple juice, as in the well-known *Piña Colada* and other cocktails of the same family: *Blue Hawaiian*, coloured with blue curaçao; *Casablanca*, coloured pink with grenadine syrup; and *Banana Royal*, which is a must if you like consuming thick cocktails with a spoon (see lower left table on page 40).

Orange juice is also an excellent partner for rum in a number of punches and in some long drinks (see lower right table on page 40).

Some Advice
According to professionals, rum is the best spirit base for cocktails. Fresher and more open than cognac and other brandies, rum—light, golden or dark—mixes extremely well with all kinds of fruit juice. It is often described as the most natural spirit, since sugar is the raw material of alcohol and the juice of the sugar cane, from which rum is made, is very rich in natural sugar.

ACAPULCO

Put some ice cubes in a cocktail shaker and add:

1 measure golden rum
½ measure Cointreau
2 teaspoons lemon juice
1 teaspoon sugar

Shake and strain into a cocktail glass.

ACAPULCO GOLD

Put some ice cubes in a cocktail shaker and add:

½ measure golden rum
½ measure tequila
1 measure pineapple juice
½ measure grapefruit juice
½ measure cream of coconut

Shake and strain into a small tumbler full of ice cubes.

ADIOS AMIGOS

Pour into a cocktail shaker containing ice cubes:

1 measure white rum
½ measure dry vermouth
½ measure cognac
½ measure gin
½ measure lime juice

Shake well. Serve in a large cocktail glass.

ALEXANDER BABY

Pour into a cocktail shaker containing some ice cubes:

1 measure dark rum
1 measure crème de cacao
1 measure double cream

Shake and strain into a cocktail glass. Sprinkle grated nutmeg on top.

AMERICAN FLYER

Pour into a cocktail shaker containing some ice cubes:

1 measure white rum
1 measure lime juice
½ teaspoon sugar

Shake and strain into a champagne flute. Top up with chilled champagne.

ANTILLES

Pour into a cocktail shaker containing ice cubes:

1 measure white rum
½ measure white Dubonnet

Shake and strain into a cocktail glass. Garnish with a twist of orange peel.

APRICOT DAIQUIRI

Put some crushed ice in an electric blender and add:

1 measure white rum
1 measure lemon juice
½ measure apricot liqueur or brandy
3 ripe apricots, stones removed

Blend for 1 minute or until the mixture is smooth. Pour into a champagne saucer. Garnish with a slice of apricot, a cherry and a sprig of fresh mint.

APRICOT NOG

Put some crushed ice in an electric blender and add:

1 measure white rum
½ measure apricot brandy
½ measure apricot juice
¼ measure double cream

Blend for a few seconds only. Pour into a collins glass.

AROUND THE WORLD 🗑🍸

Put 2 glasses crushed ice in an electric blender and add:

3 measures orange juice
3 measures lemon juice
3 measures white rum
1 measure orgeat syrup
½ measure cognac

Blend for a few seconds. Pour into two tumblers. Serve with straws.
SERVES 2

ASTRONAUT 🍸🍸

Put some ice cubes in a cocktail shaker and add:

½ measure white rum
½ measure vodka
½ measure lemon juice
1 dash passion fruit juice

Shake and strain into a tumbler filled with ice cubes. Garnish with a slice of lemon.

AURORE 🍸🍸

Put some ice cubes in a cocktail shaker and add:

⁶⁄₁₀ Duquesne white rum
²⁄₁₀ Mandarine Imperiale
²⁄₁₀ Saint-Raphael raspberry
  liqueur

Shake and strain into a cocktail glass. Garnish with a spiral of lemon and orange peel and a brandied cherry.

PIERRE SCHAEFFER, TROUVILLE, ABF, France.

BACARDI 🍸🍸

Put some ice cubes in a cocktail shaker and add:

1½ measures Bacardi white rum
½ measure lemon juice
1 dash grenadine

Shake well and strain into a cocktail glass.

BAHAMAS 🍸🍸

Put some ice cubes in a cocktail shaker and add:

1 measure white rum
1 measure Southern Comfort
1 measure lemon juice
1 dash crème de banane

Shake vigorously and strain into a cocktail glass. Decorate the glass with a thin slice of lemon if desired.

BAHIA 🗑🍸

Put some crushed ice in an electric blender and add:

1 measure golden rum
1 measure pineapple juice
½ measure cream of coconut

Blend at the highest speed for 15 to 20 seconds or until the mixture is light and foamy. Pour into a lager glass. Garnish with a sprig of fresh mint and a slice of pineapple.

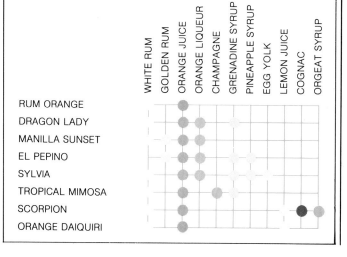

	WHITE RUM	GOLDEN RUM	PINEAPPLE JUICE	CREAM OF COCONUT	DOUBLE CREAM	BANANA	BLUE CURAÇAO	GRENADINE SYRUP	ANGOSTURA BITTERS
PIÑA COLADA	●		●	●					
BAHIA		●	●	●					
BANANA ROYAL		●	●	●		●			
BLUE HAWAIIAN	●		●	●	●		●		
CASABLANCA	●		●	●				●	●

	WHITE RUM	GOLDEN RUM	ORANGE JUICE	ORANGE LIQUEUR	CHAMPAGNE	GRENADINE SYRUP	PINEAPPLE SYRUP	EGG YOLK	LEMON JUICE	COGNAC	ORGEAT SYRUP
RUM ORANGE	●		●								
DRAGON LADY		●	●	●							
MANILLA SUNSET		●	●	●							
EL PEPINO		●	●	●							
SYLVIA		●	●		●						
TROPICAL MIMOSA		●	●		●		●				
SCORPION		●	●							●	●
ORANGE DAIQUIRI		●	●								

Bacardi in a Habitat glass.

BANANA COW 🍶🥛

Fill the goblet of an electric blender a quarter full of crushed ice and add:

4 measures coconut milk
1½ measures golden rum
1 ripe banana
1 teaspoon sugar

Blend for a minute or two or until the mixture is smooth. Pour into a tumbler and serve with straws.

BANANA DAIQUIRI 🍶🍸

Put three heaped tablespoons of crushed ice into the goblet of an electric blender and add:

1 measure golden rum
½ measure crème de banane
½ measure lemon juice
½ banana
2 teaspoons sugar

Blend for 15 to 30 seconds until the mixture is smooth and creamy. Pour without straining into a champagne saucer. Garnish with a slice of banana, a sprig of mint and a cherry. Serve with a straw.

BANANA ROYAL 🍶🥛

Put some crushed ice into an electric blender and add:

1½ measures coconut milk
3 measures pineapple juice
1½ measures golden rum
½ measure double cream
1 ripe banana

Blend for 15 to 30 seconds until smooth and creamy. Pour into a whisky tumbler and garnish with grated coconut.

BARRACUDA 🍾🥛

Fill a cocktail shaker one-third full of crushed ice and add:

1 measure golden rum
½ measure Galliano
1 measure pineapple juice
2 dashes sugar syrup
2 dashes lime juice

Shake and strain into a whisky tumbler. Top up with champagne. Garnish with a slice of lime and a cherry.

BIG BAMBOO 🍾🥛

Put some ice cubes in a cocktail shaker and add:

1 measure golden rum
1 measure orange juice
1 measure pineapple juice
⅓ measure lemon juice
⅚ measure grenadine

Shake well and strain into a tumbler over crushed ice. Garnish with an orange slice placed on the rim of the glass and a sprig of mint.

BLACK WIDOW 🍾🍸

Put some ice cubes in a cocktail shaker and add:

1 measure dark rum
½ measure Southern Comfort
juice of ½ lime
1 dash sugar syrup

Shake well and strain into a cocktail glass.

BLUE HAWAIIAN 🍶🍸

Put some crushed ice in an electric blender and add:

1 measure white rum
½ measure blue curaçao
2 measures pineapple juice
1 measure cream of coconut

Blend for 20 to 30 seconds. Pour into a champagne saucer. Decorate with a piece of pineapple.

BLUE SEA 🍾🥛

Put some ice cubes in a cocktail shaker and add:

4/10 Bacardi
3/10 blue curaçao
2/10 Cointreau
1/10 lemon juice
1 dash Pernod
1 egg white

Shake well. Strain into a tumbler. Top up with lemonade. Decorate with a slice of lemon and a sprig of mint.

Antonio de Jesus Estoril.
CBP, Portugal.

C 9 J PUNCH

Put some ice cubes in a cocktail shaker and add:

$\frac{5}{10}$ *Saint-James Impérial white*
rum
$\frac{2}{10}$ *Cointreau*
$\frac{2}{10}$ *peach juice*
$\frac{1}{10}$ *sugar syrup*
2 dashes grenadine

Shake vigorously and strain into a champagne saucer. To decorate, place a slice of peach across the rim of the glass. Add a maraschino cherry if desired.

YVON BOITEL, 3RD PRIZE,
Epinal meeting, France, October 1980.

CASABLANCA

Put some crushed ice in an electric blender and add:

1 measure white rum
1½ measures pineapple juice
½ measure cream of coconut
2 dashes grenadine
1 dash Angostura bitters

Blend at high speed for a few seconds or until the mixture is light and foamy. Pour into a large goblet and serve with straws.

CAVALIERI

Fill a cocktail shaker with ice cubes and add:

$\frac{1}{4}$ *measure white rum*
$\frac{1}{4}$ *measure Grand Marnier*
$\frac{1}{2}$ *measure dry Cinzano*
1½ measures strawberry juice

Shake vigorously and strain into a tumbler. Top up with ginger ale. Decorate with a strawberry and a half slice of orange.

CHINESE ITCH

Put some crushed ice into an electric blender and add:

1 measure golden rum
$\frac{3}{4}$ *measure passion fruit juice*
juice of 1 lime
1 dash orgeat syrup

Blend for 10 to 15 seconds. Pour into a champagne saucer. Decorate with a slice of lime.

COCO LOCO

Put some crushed ice in an electric blender and add:

4 measures coconut water
1 measure coconut milk
1 measure apricot brandy
1 measure white Puerto Rico rum

Blend at high speed. Serve in a coconut shell, sprinkled with cinnamon.

COCONUT TUMBLE

Put some crushed ice in a mixing glass and add:

1¼ measures Myers rum
$\frac{3}{4}$ *measure Cointreau*
1 measure cream of coconut
1 dash grenadine

Mix very well. Pour gently in a half coconut shell and serve with 2 straws. Decorate with a paper parasol and a maraschino cherry if desired.

CUBA LIBRE

Fill a collins glass three-quarters full of ice cubes. Squeeze the juice of half a lime into the glass and drop in the lime shell. Add 1 measure white rum. Top up with Coca-Cola. Stir well to mix. Serve immediately with 2 straws.
N.B. For Cuba Libre Supreme replace the rum with Southern Comfort.

Andy Warhol, Green Coca-Cola Bottles, *silk-screen on canvas*

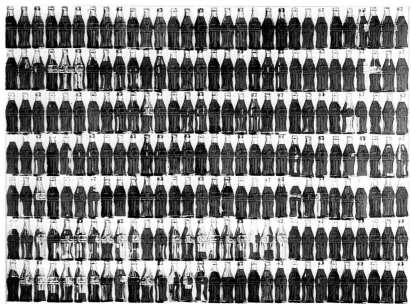

CUBAN COCKTAIL

Put some ice cubes in a cocktail shaker and add:

1 measure white rum
½ measure lime juice

Shake and strain into a cocktail glass. N.B. You may also add 3 dashes maraschino or curaçao, 1 dash Angostura bitters, 3 dashes grenadine, in various combinations.

CUP CRILLON

Put some ice cubes in a cocktail shaker and add:

1 measure white rum
¼ measure Grand Marnier
¼ measure crème de cassis
1 dash lemon juice

Shake well and strain into a tumbler. Top up with ginger ale. Decorate with a spiral of lemon peel and a cherry.

DAIQUIRI

Put some ice cubes in a cocktail shaker and add:

1 measure white rum
juice of ½ lemon
1 teaspoon sugar syrup

Shake and strain into a cocktail glass.

DON PABLO

Put some ice cubes in a mixing glass and add:

1½ measures golden rum
4 measures tomato juice
½ measure lime juice
1 dash Tabasco

Poster designed
by J. d'Ylen, 1920

RHUM PEPITA
LE MEILLEUR

celery salt or black pepper, to taste

Stir to mix. Strain into a collins glass containing ice cubes. Garnish with a tomato slice and a sprig of celery leaves.

DOUBLE 007

Put some ice cubes in a cocktail shaker and add:

$\frac{4}{10}$ Bacardi rum
$\frac{2}{10}$ sweet Martini
$\frac{2}{10}$ orange juice
$\frac{2}{10}$ lemon juice
1 dash sugar syrup

Shake and strain into a cocktail glass. Garnish with a cherry, an orange slice and a mint leaf.

LEPRINCE, PARIS.
ABF, France.

DRAGON LADY

Into a mixing glass containing some ice cubes pour:

1½ measures white rum
2 measures orange juice
¼ measure grenadine
1 dash curaçao

Stir well to mix. Strain into a tumbler and add two ice cubes. Garnish with a slice of orange and a cherry.

EL CONQUISTADOR

Put some crushed ice in an electric blender and add:

1 measure 75° proof rum
1½ measure white rum
½ measure triple sec
½ measure coconut milk
½ measure Mai Tai Mix*
½ measure lemon juice
2 dashes Angostura bitters

Blend well and pour into 2 cocktail glasses. Decorate with a slice of orange and a cherry. Serve with straws.
*See page 144.

Serves 2

EL JARDINERO

Pour into a cocktail shaker half full of ice cubes:

½ measure lime juice
1½ measures white rum
1 measure Sambuca

Shake well and strain into a marrow (see directions below). Decorate with a paper parasol; serve with straws.

EL PEPINO

Cut a marrow in half and gently scoop out the flesh of one half without piercing the skin to make the drink container. Put some ice cubes in a mixing glass and add:

1 measure golden rum
½ measure triple sec
1½ measures orange juice
1½ measures pineapple juice
1 dash grenadine

Stir very well and strain carefully into the marrow container. Decorate the marrow with a variety of tropical flowers and a paper parasol. Serve immediately with 2 straws.

EL PRESIDENTE

Put some ice cubes in a mixing glass and add:

1 measure white rum
½ measure dry vermouth
1 teaspoon grenadine
1 dash curaçao

Mix very well until the mixture becomes icy cold and strain into a chilled cocktail glass. Decorate the glass with a thin orange slice and fancy straws or mixer sticks if desired.

El Jardinero, a rum-based cocktail.

EL ZORZAL ❦ ▪

Half fill a cocktail shaker with ice cubes and add:

1 measure white rum
1 measure anisette
2 measures orange juice
1 dash grenadine

Shake vigorously and strain into an old fashioned glass containing ice cubes. Decorate the glass with a slice of orange, a piece of pineapple and a maraschino cherry.

ESTORIL 81 ❦ ▪

Put some ice cubes in a cocktail shaker and add:

$\frac{6}{10}$ Bacardi rum
$\frac{1}{10}$ Amaretto
$\frac{2}{10}$ lemon juice
$\frac{1}{10}$ orgeat syrup

Shake vigorously and strain into a tumbler. Top up with soda. Garnish with a thin slice of lemon and fancy straws or mixer sticks if desired.

Louis Grandi, Monte Carlo. ABF, France.

FIESTA ❦ ▼

Put some crushed ice in a mixing glass and add:

$1\frac{1}{4}$ measures white rum
$\frac{1}{4}$ measure Cointreau
$\frac{1}{2}$ measure lemon juice
1 teaspoon sugar
1 teaspoon grenadine

Mix very well. Strain the drink into a tulip glass. Top up with Seven Up or soda. Decorate the glass with a spiral of lemon peel, a paper parasol and a small paper doll. Add a small colourful flower if desired.

FIESTA COCKTAIL ❦ ▼

Put some cubes of ice in a cocktail shaker and add:

1 measure white rum
$\frac{1}{2}$ measure Calvados
$\frac{1}{2}$ measure dry vermouth

Shake vigorously and strain into a cocktail glass.

FLAMBOYAN ❦ ▪

Pour into a cocktail shaker containing some ice cubes:

2 measures pineapple juice
1 measure orange juice
$\frac{1}{4}$ measure lime juice
$1\frac{1}{2}$ measures crème de cacao
$1\frac{1}{2}$ measures golden rum
1 dash grenadine

Shake vigorously well and strain into a tumbler. Decorate the glass with a piece of pineapple and a slice of lime and serve with a fancy straw.

FROZEN DAIQUIRI ⊿ ▼

Put some crushed ice into an electric blender and add:

1 measure white rum
$\frac{1}{2}$ measure lemon juice
1 dash maraschino
$\frac{1}{2}$ measure sugar syrup

Blend at the highest speed for 1 to 2 minutes or until the mixture resembles frothy snow. Pour into a chilled champagne saucer or large wine glass and garnish with a cocktail cherry and a mint sprig if desired.

FROZEN MINT DAIQUIRI ⊿ ▼

Put some crushed ice in an electric blender and add:

Frozen Mint Daiquiri in Baccarat crystal.

1 measure white rum
$\frac{1}{2}$ measure white crème de menthe
$\frac{1}{2}$ measure lime juice

Blend at the highest speed for 10 to 20 seconds. Pour into a champagne saucer or large wine glass and garnish with a mint sprig.

FROZEN PINEAPPLE DAIQUIRI ⊿ ▼

Put a little crushed ice in an electric blender and add:

2–3 pineapple slices
$\frac{1}{2}$ measure lime juice
1 measure white rum
$\frac{1}{4}$ measure triple sec
1 teaspoon sugar

Blend at the highest speed until smooth. Pour into a champagne saucer and decorate with a piece of pineapple.

GERONIMO PUNCH ♦▮

Pour into a cocktail shaker containing some ice cubes:

1½ measures white rum
1 measure pineapple juice
1 measure orange juice
½ measure lime juice
2 dashes grenadine
1 dash Angostura bitters

Shake and strain into a collins glass full of ice cubes. Garnish with a slice of pineapple and a half slice of orange.

GOLDEN FLING ♦▮

Pour into a cocktail shaker containing some ice cubes:

1 measure mature golden rum
1 measure Galliano
1 measure pineapple juice

Shake well and strain into a tumbler. Top up with bitter lemon. Garnish with a strawberry, a piece of pineapple and a paper parasol.

GOLDEN GATE ▯ ⍟

Pour into a mixing glass containing some ice cubes:

1 measure white rum
⅕ measure dry sherry

Stir and strain into a cocktail glass. Garnish with lemon peel.

GOLDIE ♦▮

Pour into a cocktail shaker containing some ice cubes:

3/10 Bacardi rum
2/10 Cherry Heering
2/10 Cointreau
3/10 orange juice

Shake and strain into a tumbler. Top up with orangeade. Garnish with orange peel.

GENE TAKACS, COPENHAGEN.
DBL, Denmark.

GOLD TIME ♦⍟

Half fill a cocktail shaker with ice cubes and add:

1 measure golden rum
1 measure pineapple juice
1 egg yolk
1 dash lemon juice

Shake and strain into a fancy glass. Decorate with a lemon slice and a cherry. Serve with straws.

HAVANA BEACH COCKTAIL ♦⍟

Pour into a cocktail shaker containing some ice cubes:

1 measure white rum
1 measure pineapple juice
1 teaspoon sugar

Shake and strain into a cocktail glass.

HAWAIIAN COFFEE ▯⍟

Put some crushed ice into an electric blender and add:

1 cup black coffee, chilled
1 measure white rum
2 measures pineapple juice

Blend for 10 to 15 seconds. Pour without straining into fancy glasses.
SERVES 2

HEPMAÏSTOS ♦⍟

Pour into a cocktail shaker containing some ice cubes:

1 measure Bacardi rum
⅔ measure Dolfi strawberry liqueur
1 dash lemon juice

Shake. Strain into a cocktail glass and garnish with strawberries.

ERIC COUBARD, PARIS.
ABF, France.

HONEY SUCKLE ♦⍟

Pour into a cocktail shaker containing some ice cubes:

1 measure golden rum
juice of 1 lime
1 teaspoon clear honey

Shake well and strain into a cocktail glass.

INDIAN SUMMER ▯▮

Put some crushed ice into an electric blender and add:

3 measures coconut water
1 measure cream of coconut
1 measure white rum
1 measure gin
1 measure double cream

Blend at high speed for two minutes. Pour into a tumbler. Garnish with a piece of coconut and serve with straws.

KINGSTON ♦⍟

Put some ice cubes in a cocktail shaker and add:

4/10 Bacardi rum
3/10 Cointreau
1/10 crème de banane
1/10 pineapple juice
1 dash blue curaçao

Shake and strain into a cocktail glass. Garnish with a slice of lime.

CHRISTIAN JOLLY, PARIS.
ABF, France.

LA FLORIDA DAIQUIRI 🗑 🍸

Put some crushed ice in an electric blender and add:

1 measure white rum
1 teaspoon maraschino
juice of 1 lime
1 teaspoon sugar

Blend for a few seconds until the mixture is frothy. Pour without straining into a champagne saucer.

CONSTANTE RIBALAGUA,
Restaurant La Florida, Havana, Cuba.

MAHUI FIZZ 🗑 🍸

Fill the goblet of an electric blender one third full of crushed ice and add:

1 egg
4 measures pineapple juice
1 teaspoon sugar
1½ measures white rum

Blend at the highest speed until the mixture is smooth and mousse-like. Pour into a champagne saucer and decorate with a piece of pineapple and a cherry. Serve with fancy straws.

MAI TAI 🍹

Squeeze the juice of 1 lime on to some crushed ice in an old fashioned glass and add:

½ measure golden Martinique rum
½ measure Jamaican rum
¼ measure curaçao
⅛ measure sugar syrup
⅛ measure orgeat syrup

Stir to mix and garnish with a slice of lime, a mint sprig and a piece of fruit on a cocktail stick.

VICTOR J. BERGERON,
(Trader Vic), USA.

Mai Tai.

MANILLA SUNSET 🍹 🍺

Put some crushed ice in a mixing glass and add:

¾ measure white rum
¾ measure golden Jamaican rum
½ measure mandarine liqueur
½ measure orange juice

Stir well and strain into a tumbler. Garnish with a half slice of orange, a mint sprig and a small paper parasol.

MARIA BONITA 🍹 🍸

Fill a mixing glass with crushed ice and add:

3 measures pineapple juice
1½ measures white rum
½ measure Cointreau

Stir very well until the mixture is icy cold and strain into a tulip glass. Garnish with a small piece of pineapple, a maraschino cherry and a paper parasol if desired.

MAYA 🗑 🍺

Put some crushed ice in an electric blender and add:

1½ measures white rum
½ measure golden rum
¼ measure Cointreau
2 measures pineapple juice
1 teaspoon sugar

Blend for a few seconds until the mixture is light and frothy. Strain into a whisky tumbler and garnish with a piece of pineapple, a mint sprig and a cocktail cherry.

MOJITO

Crush some mint leaves with a teaspoon of sugar in a collins glass. Add:

2 measures golden rum
1 dash Angostura bitters
2–3 tablespoons crushed ice

Mix well with a spoon. Garnish the glass with an orange slice and a cocktail cherry.

MOOMBA

Put some ice cubes in a cocktail shaker and add:

$\frac{1}{2}$ measure white rum
$\frac{1}{2}$ measure Grand Marnier
$\frac{1}{2}$ measure orange juice
$\frac{1}{4}$ measure lemon juice
1 dash grenadine

Shake vigorously and strain into a cocktail glass. Garnish with a twist of orange peel.

MUCARO

Fill a cocktail shaker one-third full of ice cubes and add:

1 measure Tía Maria
1 measure golden rum
2 measures double cream

Shake well and strain into a cocktail glass. Sprinkle with cinnamon and serve with a cinnamon stick.

NOT TOO BAD

Put some ice cubes in a mixing glass and add:

$\frac{5}{10}$ Bacardi rum
$\frac{3}{10}$ crème de banane
$\frac{1}{10}$ Mandarine Imperiale
$\frac{1}{10}$ blue curaçao

Stir to mix and strain into a cocktail glass. Garnish with a slice of banana and a cherry.

KOLENICK, PARIS.
ABF, France.

ORANGE DAIQUIRI

Put some crushed ice into an electric blender and add:

$1\frac{1}{2}$ measures white rum
$\frac{1}{2}$ measure lemon juice
$\frac{1}{2}$ measure sugar syrup
$1\frac{1}{2}$ measures orange juice

Blend for 10 to 15 seconds until frothy. Pour into a champagne saucer and decorate with an orange slice.

PAPAYA ROYAL

Put some crushed ice in an electric blender and add:

175 g/6 oz peeled papaya (pawpaw), seeds removed
3 measures milk
1 teaspoon sugar
1 measure white Puerto Rican rum

Blend at high speed. Serve in a fancy glass or in a hollowed out papaya.

PEACH DAIQUIRI

Put three tablespoons of crushed ice in an electric blender and add:

1 measure white rum
$\frac{1}{2}$ measure lemon juice
$\frac{1}{2}$ measure peach liqueur
1 ripe peach, peeled and stoned
2 dashes maraschino

Blend for 1 minute or until smooth. Pour into a champagne saucer without straining. Garnish with a slice of peach, a cherry and a mint sprig.

PETIT FUTÉ

Pour into a cocktail shaker containing some ice cubes:

$\frac{5}{10}$ Saint-James Impérial white rum
$\frac{2}{10}$ dry Martini
$\frac{1}{10}$ sweet white Martini
$\frac{2}{10}$ passion fruit liqueur

Shake and strain into a cocktail glass. Garnish with a spiral of lemon peel and a candied fig.

ARIZO PLACUCCI, 2ND PRIZE,
Epinal meeting. France, October 1980.

PIÑA COLADA

Put some crushed ice in an electric blender and add:

1 measure white rum
2 measures pineapple juice
$\frac{1}{2}$ measure cream of coconut (Coco Lopez)
$\frac{1}{4}$ measure double cream

Blend for a few seconds and strain into a collins glass. Garnish with a piece of pineapple and serve with a straw.

PINEAPPLE FIZZ

Put some ice cubes in a collins glass and add:

1 measure golden rum
$1\frac{1}{2}$ measures pineapple juice
2 dashes sugar syrup

Stir to mix and top up with soda. Garnish with a piece of pineapple and a cherry.

PLANTER'S PUNCH 1

Put some ice cubes in a tumbler and add:

1 measure white rum
juice of ½ orange
juice of ½ lemon
1 dash maraschino
1 dash curaçao
2 dashes pineapple juice

Stir to mix. Garnish with a half slice of pineapple and two cherries. Top with a dash of golden rum.

PLANTER'S PUNCH 2

Put some ice cubes in a tumbler and add:

1 measure golden rum
1 measure lemon juice
1 dash Angostura bitters
4 dashes grenadine

Piña Colada served with a cream jug from the Danish Boutique, Paris.

Stir to mix. Top up with soda and garnish with a slice of orange and a cherry.
N.B. You can also make this recipe by adding 1 measure orange juice and reducing the lemon juice to a dash.

PUSSY FOOT 1

Put some crushed ice in an electric blender and add:

1½ measures white rum
1 measure double cream
1 measure pineapple juice
1 measure lime juice
1 measure cherry juice

Blend for 15 to 20 seconds and pour into a collins glass. Garnish with an orange slice and a cherry.

QUARTER DECK

Pour into a cocktail shaker containing some ice cubes:

1 measure golden rum
½ measure sweet sherry
1 teaspoon lime juice

Shake vigorously and strain into a cocktail glass.

RICOLIANO

Put some ice cubes in a goblet and add:

1¼ measures white rum
¼ measure Galliano
½ measure lime juice
1 teaspoon sugar

Stir to mix and top up with soda water. Garnish with half an orange slice and a cherry. Serve with two decorative straws.

ROYAL COCO PUNCH

Put some crushed ice into a cocktail shaker or electric blender and add:

3/10 Saint-James Royal golden rum
2/10 Cointreau
2/10 crème de cacao
3/10 cold black coffee
1 teaspoon cream of coconut (Coco Lopez)

Shake or blend well and pour into a champagne flute. Sprinkle with grated chocolate. Garnish with two brandied cherries and a quarter slice lime.

M. Sestillange. 1st prize,
Nantes meeting, June 1981. ABF, France.

Scorpion in a Lalique crystal glass.

RUM COLLINS

Pour into a collins glass:

1 measure white rum
1 teaspoon sugar syrup

Stir to mix. Squeeze in the juice of half a lime and drop in the squeezed out shell. Add some ice cubes and top up with soda.
N.B. Leave out the syrup for a *Rum Rickey.*

RUM FIZZ

Put some ice cubes in a cocktail shaker and add:

1 measure white rum
juice of 1 lemon
1 teaspoon sugar

Shake well and strain into a tumbler. Top up with soda.

RUM FLOAT

Fill a tumbler three-quarters full with ice cubes and pour in:

juice of ½ lime
1 teaspoon sugar

Top up with soda and stir gently. Carefully pour in 1 measure white rum over the back of a spoon so that it floats on top. Decorate the glass with a thin slice of lime.

RUM GIMLET

Put one ice cube in a cocktail glass and pour in:

1 measure white rum
½ measure lime juice
1 dash sugar syrup

Stir to mix. Garnish with a slice of lime.

RUM ORANGE

Put some ice cubes in a tumbler and add:

1 measure white rum

Top up with fresh orange juice and decorate with an orange slice.

RUM SOUR

Pour into a cocktail shaker containing some ice cubes:

1 measure golden rum
½ measure lime juice
1 dash sugar syrup

Shake well and strain into a balloon glass. Decorate with a slice of lime.

RUM TONIC

Half fill a tumbler with ice cubes and pour in:

1 measure white rum

Top up with tonic and garnish with two slices of lemon. Stir before serving.

SAN CRISTOBAL

Put some ice cubes in a cocktail shaker and add:

1 measure golden rum
1 measure orange juice
1 measure pineapple juice
½ measure lime juice
1 measure grenadine
1 teaspoon sugar
1 dash Angostura bitters

Shake vigorously. Strain into a collins glass containing ice cubes. Garnish with a half slice of pineapple and a slice of orange.

SCORPION 🍶 🍸

Put some crushed ice in a cocktail shaker and add:

1¼ measures white rum
¼ measure cognac
1 measure orange juice
1 measure lemon juice
1 dash orgeat syrup

Shake well and pour into a champagne saucer. Garnish with a gardenia.

SHARK'S TOOTH 1 ▯

Put some ice cubes in a tumbler and squeeze in the juice of half a lime. Add:

1 measure golden rum
1 dash grenadine
1 dash sugar syrup

Stir well to mix. Top up with soda. Stir lightly and garnish with a slice of lime and a sprig of mint.

SHARK'S TOOTH 2 🍶 🍸

Put some ice cubes in a cocktail shaker and add:

1 measure golden rum
1 teaspoon lemon juice
1 teaspoon dry vermouth
1 teaspoon passion fruit juice
1 teaspoon sloe gin
1 dash Angostura bitters

Shake and strain into a cocktail glass.

SIR WALTER 🍶 🍸

Put some ice cubes in a cocktail shaker and add:

½ measure white rum
½ measure brandy

1 teaspoon curaçao
1 teaspoon lemon juice
1 teaspoon grenadine

Shake and strain into a cocktail glass.

SLIM AND TRIM 🍶

Cut the top off a grapefruit leaving three-quarters of the fruit. Scoop out the pulp and squeeze it to extract the juice.
    Put some ice cubes in cocktail shaker and add:

4 measures grapefruit juice
1½ measures white rum
a little saccharine

Shake well and strain into the grapefruit shell. Serve with straws.

SOL Y SOMBRA 🍶

Cut the top off a small pineapple and scrape out the pulp. Squeeze the pulp to extract the juice.
    Put some crushed ice in a cocktail shaker and add:

1 measure golden rum
½ measure white rum
1½ measures apricot brandy
2 measures pineapple juice
juice of ½ lemon
2 dashes Angostura bitters

Shake well and pour into the pineapple shell. Cut out a section of the pineapple top to make space for 2 straws and replace it on top of the pineapple. Decorate with a paper parasol and serve standing in a bowl of crushed ice.
Serves 2

STRAWBERRY DAIQUIRI 🍶 🍸

Put some crushed ice in an electric blender and add:

1 measure white rum
½ measure lemon juice
¾ measure strawberry liqueur or syrup
5 or 6 strawberries

Blend at high speed for 1 minute or until smooth. Pour without straining into a champagne saucer. Garnish with a strawberry and a lemon or lime slice.

SUMMERTIME ▯

Pour into a collins glass:

1¼ measures white rum
¼ measure golden rum
1 measure pineapple juice
1 measure orange juice
½ measure lemon juice
1 dash grenadine

Add some crushed ice and stir to mix. Garnish with fresh fruit and a mint sprig. Serve with fancy straws and a stirrer.

Poster for Negrita Old Nick Rum, first made in 1884.

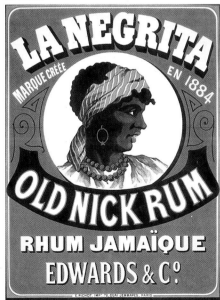

SUNSET ❖❖

Put some ice cubes in a cocktail shaker and add:

1 measure sugar syrup
3 measures fruit punch*
½ measure lime juice
1½ measures golden rum
½ measure apricot brandy

Shake and strain into a fancy glass.
*See page 124

SURFING ❖ Y

Put some ice cubes in a cocktail shaker and add:

½ measure Saint-James Royal golden rum
½ measure apricot liqueur
1 egg yolk
1 dash sugar syrup

Shake and strain into a cocktail glass. Sprinkle with grated nutmeg.

Yves Morinière, 3rd prize,
Nantes meeting 1981. ABF, France.

SYLVIA ❖❖

Pour into a cocktail shaker containing some ice cubes:

2/10 Bacardi rum
2/10 Grand Marnier
2/10 pineapple juice
4/10 orange juice
3 dashes grenadine
1 egg yolk

Shake and strain into a tumbler. Garnish with a slice of pineapple and cherries.

Martii Hämäläinen, Helsinki.
FBSK, Finland.

TALISMAN ❖❖

Fill a cocktail shaker one-third full of ice cubes and add:

1 measure white rum
1 measure golden rum
1 measure vodka
1 measure Grand Marnier
¼ measure lime juice
4 measures mango juice

Shake well. Fill a fancy glass such as the one shown in the photograph below a third full of crushed ice and pour in the mixture. Stir well to mix. Garnish with a slice of orange, a quarter slice of lime, a cherry and a mint sprig. Serve with two straws.

Talisman

TIP LADY DAIQUIRI ❖ Y

Pour into an electric blender:

1 measure white rum
¾ measure lemon juice
½ measure lime juice
1 teaspoon sugar
3 tablespoons crushed ice

Blend at the highest speed for 10 to 15 seconds or until the mixure is light and foamy. Pour into a champagne saucer without straining. Garnish with a peach slice, a maraschino cherry and a plastic mermaid if desired.

TRAPICHE COCKTAIL ❖ Y

Put some ice cubes in a mixing glass and add:

2 measures dark rum
3 measures Trapiche syrup*
1 dash lime juice

Stir vigorously to mix. Strain into a chilled balloon glass and garnish with a piece of sugar cane, if available, otherwise decorate with a thin slice of lime and a maraschino cherry. Serve with fancy straws.
*See page 148.

TROPICAL KISS ❖

Cut the top off a small pineapple and scrape out the pulp. Squeeze the pulp to extract the juice.
 Put some ice cubes in a cocktail shaker and add:

1 measure white rum
1 measure maraschino
3 measures pineapple juice
2 dashes grenadine

Shake well and strain into the pineapple shell. Garnish with a cherry and a fresh mint sprig. Serve with fancy straws.

TROPICAL MIMOSA ▮

Pour into a champagne flute:

3 measures orange juice
1 dash grenadine
1 measure white rum

Stir to mix and top up with champagne or sparkling white wine. Garnish with a spiral of orange peel.

TROPIC OF CAPRICORN ▮ ▮

Put some crushed ice in a cocktail shaker and add:

1½ measures Bacardi white rum
¾ measure crème de cacao
4 measures orange juice
1 egg white

Shake well and pour into a tumbler. Add a dash of blue curaçao. Garnish with two cherries, a slice of orange and a paper parasol. Serve with two fancy straws.

WARATAM ▮ ▮

Put some ice cubes in a mixing glass and pour in:

1½ measures white rum
¾ measure dry vermouth
4 dashes grenadine

Stir well and strain into a tulip glass. Garnish with a slice of lemon fixed on the rim of the glass.

WATERLOO ▮

Put some ice cubes in a goblet and add:

1 measure white rum
3 measures orange juice

Zombie.

Stir to mix. Pour over gently ½ measure mandarine liqueur. Serve without stirring.

WHITE WITCH ▮ ▮

Put some ice cubes in a cocktail shaker and add:

1 measure white rum
½ measure white crème de cacao
½ measure Cointreau
juice of ½ lime

Shake and strain into a tumbler containing some ice cubes. Top up with soda. Stir to mix. Garnish with a mint sprig and a slice of lime.

ZOMBIE ▮

Half fill a tumbler with crushed ice and add:

½ measure white rum
⅔ measure golden rum
⅔ measure lemon juice
1 measure orange juice
1 dash lime juice
1 teaspoon crème de noyau
1 teaspoon Grand Marnier
1 dash grenadine

Stir to mix. Garnish with a mint sprig, a slice of orange and a slice of lemon placed on the rim of the glass and a cherry on a cocktail stick. Serve with two straws.

Gin-based Cocktails

Gin originated in northern Europe, particularly Holland, where it was made from the end of the sixteenth century. But Geneva or Hollands, as it was known, found its true home in England. It drowned the sorrows of the urban working class in England in the eighteenth and nineteenth centuries, and was the ruin of many families, so vividly depicted in Hogarth's engravings. It was not until the beginning of the twentieth century that gin became almost acceptable in society, and gave rise to such mildly shocking jokes as 'I never drink anything stronger than gin before breakfast' from W.C. Fields.

Gin is distilled from grain or other raw materials and distinctively flavoured with juniper berries and coriander. Each make of gin combines the fruity and spicy elements in a secret recipe, but the overriding characteristic of gin is a delicious perfumed, fruity flavouring. It is the essential ingredient in many cocktails, none more famous than the classic *Dry Martini*.

In the opinion of connoisseurs the best is London dry gin, a spirit made from soft grain, dry and clean tasting. But England also produces a more scented variety, Plymouth gin, in the town of that name.

Holland still has a reputable gin called Genever or Hollands, richer and very scented, but less suitable for cocktails. The French make an alcohol flavoured with juniper which is traditionally drunk iced, to accompany beer.

Happy Blends
1 Gin and vermouth. Mixed with vermouth, gin becomes civilized: it mellows and combines well with the bitter flavours of aromatic wines (see table on right, page 57).

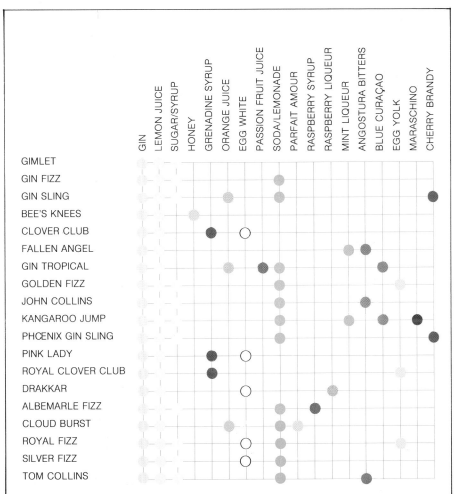

Poster for the world's best known vermouth.

2 Gin and orange. Orange juice and orange liqueur go so well with gin that even an orange-flavoured Martini, the *Bronx*, has been invented (see table on left, page 57).
3 Gin and lemon. Like all basic spirits gin cannot escape the traditional combination with lemon juice. The best known cocktail with this mix is *Gin Fizz*, (see table left).

56

ABBEY 🍸

Pour into a cocktail shaker containing several ice cubes:

1 measure gin
1 measure orange juice
1 dash Angostura bitters

Shake and strain into a cocktail glass. Garnish with a cherry.

ABBEY COCKTAIL 🍸

Pour into a cocktail shaker containing several ice cubes:

1 measure gin
½ measure sweet vermouth
½ measure orange juice
1 dash Angostura bitters

Shake and strain into a cocktail glass. Garnish with a cherry.

ACACIA 🍸

Pour into a cocktail shaker containing several ice cubes:

1 measure gin
½ measure Benedictine

Shake and strain into a cocktail glass.

AFTER ONE 🍸

Put some ice cubes into a cocktail shaker and add:

¼ Gordon's gin
¼ Galliano
¼ red Martini
¼ Campari

Shake well and strain into a cocktail glass. Garnish with a cherry and orange peel.

REINHOLD HUSAR, LOS ANGELES, 1973. *OBU, Austria.*

Poster by Grun
for Angostura Bitters.

AL 🍸

Put some ice cubes in a cocktail shaker and add:

1 measure gin
½ measure Grand Marnier
1 dash lemon juice
1 dash grenadine

Shake and strain into a cocktail glass. Garnish with a twist of lemon peel.

ALASKA 🍸

Pour into a mixing glass containing some ice cubes:

1 measure gin
⅓ measure yellow Chartreuse
1–2 dashes Angostura bitters

Stir well and strain into a cocktail glass. Garnish with a cherry impaled on a cocktail stick.

ALBEMARLE FIZZ

Put some ice cubes in a mixing glass and add:

1 measure gin
juice of ½ lemon
2 dashes raspberry syrup
½ teaspoon sugar

Stir to mix and strain into a tumbler. Top up with soda and add several ice cubes. Garnish with two cherries impaled on a cocktail stick and serve with two decorative straws.

ALCUDIA

Put some ice cubes in a cocktail shaker and add:

1 measure Beefeater gin
½ measure Galliano
½ measure Bols crème de banane
½ measure grapefruit juice

Shake and strain into a cocktail glass. Garnish with a twist of grapefruit peel.

DBL, Denmark, 1972.

ALFONSO

Put some ice cubes in a cocktail shaker and add:

1 measure gin
½ measure dry vermouth
½ measure Grand Marnier
2 dashes sweet vermouth

Shake well and strain into a large cocktail or a tulip glass. Add two or three ice cubes. Garnish with a half slice of orange astride the rim of the glass.

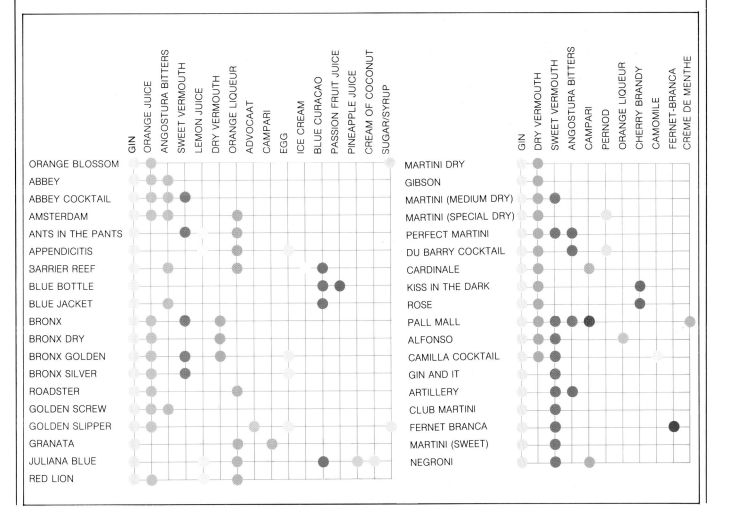

Poster designed for *Curaçao Marnier, 1889.*

AMERICAN FIZZ 👤▌

Put some ice cubes in a cocktail shaker and add:

1 measure gin
1 measure cognac
1 measure lemon juice
1 teaspoon sugar
1 dash grenadine

Shake and strain into a collins glass. Add some ice cubes and top up with soda. Garnish with a lemon slice placed on the rim of the glass.

AMSTERDAM 👤🍸

Put some ice cubes in a cocktail shaker and add:

1 measure Hollands gin
½ measure Cointreau
½ measure orange juice
2–3 dashes Angostura bitters

Shake and strain into a cocktail glass.

ANTS IN THE PANTS 👤🍸

Pour into a cocktail shaker containing some ice cubes:

1 measure gin
½ measure Grand Marnier
½ measure sweet vermouth
1 dash lemon juice

Shake and strain into a cocktail glass. Garnish with a twist of lemon peel.

APPENDICITIS 👤🍸

Pour into a cocktail shaker containing some ice cubes:

1 measure gin
¼ measure curaçao
¼ measure lemon juice
1 egg

Shake and strain into a cocktail glass.

ALLEN 👤🍸

Pour into a mixing glass containing some ice cubes:

1 measure gin
½ measure maraschino
1 dash lemon juice

Stir well to mix and strain into a cocktail glass.

AMBER DREAM 👤🍸

Put some ice cubes in a cocktail shaker and add:

1 measure gin
½ measure sweet vermouth
2 dashes yellow Chartreuse
1 dash Angostura bitters

Shake and strain into a cocktail glass. N.B. You may add more Chartreuse if you like.

ARTILLERY

Pour into a cocktail shaker containing several ice cubes:

1 measure gin
½ measure sweet vermouth
2 dashes Angostura bitters

Shake and strain into a large cocktail glass. Add two ice cubes and decorate with lemon peel.

BARRIER REEF

Pour into an electric blender:

1 measure gin
¾ measure Cointreau
1 dash Angostura bitters
1 scoop ice cream, vanilla or any other flavour

Blend for several seconds. Pour into a champagne saucer without straining. Sprinkle the top with a little blue curaçao.

BARTENDER

Put some ice cubes in a mixing glass and add:

½ measure gin
½ measure sherry
½ measure dry vermouth
½ measure Dubonnet
1 dash Grand Marnier

Stir to mix and strain into a cocktail glass.

BEE'S KNEES

Put some crushed ice into a cocktail shaker and add:

1 measure gin
1 measure lemon juice
1 teaspoon clear honey

Shake and strain into a cocktail glass.

BERMUDA ROSE COCKTAIL

Pour into a cocktail shaker containing several ice cubes:

1 measure gin
½ measure apricot brandy
2 dashes grenadine

Shake and strain into a cocktail glass.

BERMUDIAN COCKTAIL

Pour into a cocktail shaker containing several ice cubes:

1 measure gin
⅓ measure apricot brandy
⅓ measure grenadine
1 teaspoon lemon juice
1 teaspoon sugar

Shake well and strain into a cocktail glass.

Bronx served in a Habitat glass.

BLUE BOTTLE

Put some ice cubes in a mixing glass and add:

1 measure gin
½ measure blue curaçao
½ measure passion fruit juice

Stir to mix and strain into a cocktail glass.

BLUE JACKET

Put some ice cubes in a mixing glass and add:

1 measure gin
½ measure blue curaçao
1 dash Angostura bitters

Stir well and strain into a cocktail glass.

BRONX

Put some ice cubes in a cocktail shaker and add:

1 measure gin
½ measure orange juice
1 dash dry vermouth
1 dash sweet vermouth

Shake vigorously and strain into a cocktail glass. Decorate with a slice of orange, if desired.

BRONX DRY

Put some ice cubes in a cocktail shaker and add:

1 measure gin
1 measure orange juice
1 dash dry vermouth

Shake vigorously. and strain into a cocktail glass. Decorate with a slice of orange, if desired.

BRONX GOLDEN 🍾 🍸

Put some ice cubes in a cocktail shaker and add:

1 measure gin
½ measure orange juice
1 dash dry vermouth
1 dash sweet vermouth
1 egg yolk

Shake and strain into a cocktail glass.

BRONX SILVER 🍾 🍸

Pour into a cocktail shaker containing several ice cubes:

1 measure gin
½ measure sweet vermouth
2 dashes orange juice
½ egg white

Shake and strain into a cocktail glass. Sprinkle with a little grated nutmeg. N.B. For a drier cocktail use a dry vermouth instead of the sweet.

BYRRH SPECIAL 🍾 🍸

Put some ice cubes in a mixing glass and add:

1 measure gin
1 measure Byrrh

Stir to mix and strain into a cocktail glass.

CAFÉ DE PARIS 🍾 🍸

Pour into a cocktail shaker containing some ice cubes:

1 measure gin
1 teaspoon double cream
1 teaspoon Pernod
1 egg white

Shake vigorously. Strain into a cocktail glass and drop in an ice cube.

Otto Dix: Portrait of Silvia von Harden, *oil on wood, 1926.*

CAMILLA COCKTAIL 🍾 🍸

First infuse 2 sachets of camomile tea in 150 ml/¼ pint of boiling water. Allow to cool and discard the sachets.
    Fill a cocktail shaker one-third full of ice cubes and add:

the camomile infusion
4 measures gin
1 dash dry vermouth
1 dash sweet vermouth

Shake well and strain into four large cocktail glasses. Garnish each with a green olive.
SERVES 4

CARAMBA 🍾 🍷

Pour into a cocktail shaker containing several ice cubes:

4/10 Gordon's gin
1/10 Cherry Heering
1/10 raspberry liqueur
2/10 pineapple juice
2/10 grapefruit juice

Shake and strain into a balloon glass. Garnish with a twist of grapefruit peel and a brandied cherry.

MARTY SOSKIN, PARIS.
ABF, France.

CARDINAL

Put some ice cubes in a mixing glass and add:

$1\frac{1}{2}$ measures gin
$\frac{1}{4}$ measure dry vermouth
1 dash Campari

Stir well to mix and strain into a cocktail glass. Decorate with a piece of lemon peel.

CARIN

Put some ice cubes in a mixing glass and add:

1 measure gin
$\frac{1}{2}$ measure Dubonnet
$\frac{1}{2}$ measure mandarine liqueur

Stir to mix and strain into a cocktail glass. Garnish with a twist of lemon peel.

George Kuypers,
International Cocktail Competition, 1958.
UBB, Belgium.

CARUSO

Put some ice cubes in a mixing glass and add:

$\frac{1}{2}$ measure gin
$\frac{1}{2}$ measure dry vermouth
$\frac{1}{2}$ measure green crème de menthe

Stir well and strain into a cocktail glass.

CASINO

Pour into a cocktail shaker containing several ice cubes:

1 measure gin
$\frac{1}{2}$ measure maraschino
$\frac{1}{2}$ measure lemon juice
1 dash Angostura bitters

Shake and strain into a cocktail glass. Decorate with a cocktail cherry.

CLARIDGE COCKTAIL

Put some ice cubes in a mixing glass and add:

$\frac{1}{2}$ measure gin
$\frac{1}{2}$ measure dry vermouth
$\frac{1}{4}$ measure apricot brandy
$\frac{1}{4}$ measure Cointreau

Stir well and strain into a cocktail glass.

CLOUD BURST

Put some ice cubes in a cocktail shaker and pour in:

1 measure gin
$\frac{3}{4}$ measure crème de noyau
juice of $\frac{1}{2}$ lemon
juice of $\frac{1}{2}$ lime
1 dash egg white

Shake well and strain into a tumbler. Top up with soda. Add some ice cubes and lastly pour in $\frac{1}{4}$ measure Parfait Amour. Garnish with a slice of lemon and a paper parasol. Serve with straws.

CLOVER CLUB

Put some ice cubes in a cocktail shaker and pour in:

$1\frac{1}{2}$ measures gin
$\frac{1}{2}$ measure grenadine
juice of $\frac{1}{2}$ lemon
1 egg white

Shake well and strain into a cocktail glass or balloon glass.

CLUB MARTINI

Put some ice cubes in a mixing glass and add:

1 measure gin
$\frac{1}{2}$ measure sweet Martini or any other red vermouth

Stir and strain into a cocktail glass. Garnish with an olive.

CONCA D'ORA

Put some ice cubes in a mixing glass and pour in:

1 measure Gordon's gin
$\frac{1}{5}$ measure Cherry Heering
$\frac{1}{5}$ measure triple sec
$\frac{1}{5}$ measure maraschino

Stir well to mix. Strain into a cocktail glass or balloon glass.

Giuseppe Neri,
International Cocktail Competition,
Amsterdam, 1955.
AIBES, Italy.

CORPSE REVIVER 2

Put some ice cubes in a cocktail shaker and add:

1 measure gin
1 measure Cointreau
1 measure quinquina
1 measure lemon juice

Shake well and strain into a cocktail glass.

CROSS BOW

Put some ice cubes in a cocktail shaker and add:

$\frac{1}{2}$ measure gin
$\frac{1}{2}$ measure crème de cacao
$\frac{1}{2}$ measure Cointreau

Shake and strain into a cocktail glass.

J.L.Evans,
All Canadian Cocktail Competition, 1962.
BAC, Canada.

DEEP VALLEY ▮

Put 3 or 4 ice cubes in a collins glass and add:

1 measure gin
1 measure blue curaçao
1½ measures pineapple juice
2 dashes lemon juice

Top up with soda and stir to mix. Garnish with a spiral of lemon peel and a cherry.

DEMPSEY COCKTAIL ▯ ♈

Put some ice cubes in a mixing glass and add:

1 measure gin
1 measure calvados
2 dashes Pernod
2 dashes grenadine

Stir and strain into a cocktail glass. Add an ice cube.

D.O.M. COCKTAIL ♦ ♈

Pour into a cocktail shaker containing several ice cubes:

1 measure gin
¼ measure Benedictine
¼ measure orange juice

Shake and strain into a cocktail glass.

DRAKKAR ♦ ♈

Pour into a cocktail shaker containing several ice cubes:

1 measure Tanqueray gin
½ measure raspberry liqueur
2 dashes lemon juice
1 dash egg white

Shake and strain into a cocktail glass. Garnish with a raspberry.

BERNARD CORNO, PARIS.
ABF, France.

Poster by M. Du Dovich for Martini & Rossi's white vermouth.

DU BARRY COCKTAIL ▯ ♈

Put some ice cubes in a mixing glass and add:

1 measure gin
½ measure dry vermouth
½ teaspoon Pernod
1–2 dashes Angostura bitters

Stir well and strain into a cocktail glass. Garnish with a half slice of orange.

DUBONNET COCKTAIL ▯ ♈

Put some ice cubes in a mixing glass and add:

1 measure gin
1 measure Dubonnet

Stir well and strain into a cocktail glass. Garnish with a sliver of lemon peel.
N.B. There are a number of variations: you may add a dash of Angostura bitters or dry vermouth, or 2 dashes of maraschino.

FALLEN ANGEL

Pour into a cocktail shaker containing some ice cubes:

1 measure gin
1 measure lemon juice
½ teaspoon white crème de menthe
1 dash Angostura bitters

Shake and strain into a cocktail glass.

FERNET-BRANCA COCKTAIL

Put some ice cubes in a mixing glass and add:

1 measure gin
½ measure sweet vermouth
½ measure Fernet-Branca

Stir well and strain into a cocktail glass. Garnish with a cherry.

GATO

Put some crushed ice in an electric blender and add:

1 measure gin
6 strawberries
1 teaspoon sugar

Blend and strain into a champagne saucer. Garnish with a strawberry.

GIBSON

Put some ice cubes into a mixing glass and add:

1½ measures gin
1 dash dry vermouth

Stir well and strain into a cocktail glass. Garnish with a cocktail onion.

GIMLET

Put some ice cubes in a mixing glass and add:

1½ measures gin
½ measure lime juice
1 teaspoon sugar syrup

Stir well and strain into a cocktail glass. Garnish with a half slice of lime. If you like add a splash of soda before serving.

GIN AND BITTERS

Put a dash of Angostura bitters in a cocktail glass. Turn the glass until the inside is coated with the bitters. Pour away any excess. Pour in some gin and serve with a jug of water and some cocktail onions on cocktail sticks.
N.B. Although it is traditional to serve gin and bitters straight it is sometimes served on the rocks.

GIN AND IT

Put some ice cubes in a mixing glass and add:

1½ measures gin
½ measure sweet vermouth

Stir and strain into a cocktail glass. Garnish with a cherry.

GIN AND TONIC

Pour into a collins glass:

1½ measures gin
ice cubes

Top up with tonic and add a slice of lemon. Stir and serve.

GIN FIZZ

Put some ice cubes in a cocktail shaker and add:

1 measure gin
½ measure lemon juice
½ measure sugar syrup

Shake well and strain into a collins glass. Top up with soda and garnish with a lemon slice and two cherries on a cocktail stick.

GIN SLING

Pour into a cocktail shaker containing several ice cubes:

1½ measures gin
1 teaspoon sugar
1½ measures lemon juice
1 teaspoon orange juice

Shake well. Strain into a tumbler containing some ice cubes. Top up with soda. Pour in ¼ measure cherry brandy. Garnish with a piece of pineapple placed on the rim of the glass, a strawberry and a paper parasol. Serve with straws.

Gin Fizz in a Lalique crystal glass.

GIN TROPICAL 🍸▮

Put some ice cubes in a cocktail shaker and add:

1½ measures gin
1 measure lemon juice
1 measure passion fruit juice
½ measure orange juice

Shake well. Strain into a tumbler full of ice cubes. Top up with soda and stir gently. Add a dash of blue curaçao but do not stir. Garnish as usual with a parasol, cherry, strawberry, orange slice, etc. Serve with straws.

GOLDEN DAWN 🍸▾

Pour into a cocktail shaker containing some ice cubes:

½ measure gin
½ measure calvados
½ measure apricot brandy
½ measure orange juice

Shake and strain into a cocktail glass. Add a dash of grenadine and serve.

GOLDEN FIZZ 🍸▮

Put some ice cubes in a cocktail shaker and add:

1 measure gin
½ measure lemon juice
¼ measure sugar syrup
1 egg yolk

Shake and strain into a collins glass filled with ice cubes. Top up with soda and garnish with a slice of lemon fixed on the rim of the glass and two cherries on a cocktail stick.

GOLDEN SCREW ▪

Put some ice cubes in an old fashioned glass and put in:

1 measure gin
2–3 measures orange juice
1 dash Angostura bitters

Stir and garnish with an orange slice.

GOLDEN SLIPPER 🍸▾

Put some ice cubes in a cocktail shaker and add:

1 measure gin
1 measure advocaat
1 measure orange juice
1 teaspoon sugar
1 dash egg white

Shake and strain into a cocktail glass.

Lucien Quesnell, 1st prize,
Canadian Cocktail Competition, 1969.
Ontario, Canada.

GRANATA COCKTAIL 🍸▾

Pour into a cocktail shaker containing several ice cubes:

1 measure gin
¼ measure Cointreau
¼ measure Campari

Shake well and strain into a cocktail glass. Garnish with a spiral of lemon peel and a cherry.

GREEN LADY 🍸▾

Pour into a cocktail shaker containing some ice cubes:

5/10 Boodle's gin
2/10 green Chartreuse
2/10 yellow Chartreuse
1/10 lemon or lime juice

Shake and strain into a cocktail glass.

Georges Pesce, Le Fouquet's, Paris.
ABF, France.

HAWAIIAN 🍸▾🍷

Put some ice cubes in a cocktail shaker and add:

1 measure gin
1 measure pineapple juice
1 egg white
2 dashes Angostura bitters

Shake well and strain into a cocktail glass or a goblet.
N.B. For a change you can replace the pineapple juice and egg white with ½ measure orange juice and ½ measure curaçao. This cocktail can also be made with white rum.

HONOLULU 🍸▾

Put some ice cubes in a mixing glass and add:

½ measure gin
½ measure Benedictine
½ measure maraschino

Stir to mix. Strain into a cocktail glass.

JOHN COLLINS ▮

Into a collins glass filled with ice cubes pour:

1 measure Hollands gin
½ measure lemon juice
½ measure sugar syrup

Stir well and top up with soda. Stir again and garnish with a lemon slice fixed on the rim of the glass. Serve with a swizzle stick and straws.

JULIANA BLUE 🍸▮

Put some crushed ice in an electric blender and pour in:

Cappiello poster, for a brand of Curaçao made by Galland of Vienna, 1911.

1 measure gin
½ measure Cointreau
½ measure blue curaçao
2 measures pineapple juice
½ measure lime juice
1 measure cream of coconut

Blend at high speed for several seconds until the mixture has a consistency of soft snow. Put two ice cubes in a glass and strain the mixture on to them. Garnish the cocktail with tropical flowers for an extravagant and exotic look, or with a half slice of pineapple and two cherries. Serve with straws.

KANGAROO JUMP

Put some ice cubes in a cocktail shaker and add:

1 measure gin
1 measure lemon juice
1 dash gomme syrup
¼ measure maraschino

Shake well and strain into a tumbler. Top up with lemonade or soda. Add some ice cubes then add two dashes of green crème de menthe and one dash of blue curaçao. Garnish with a spiral of lemon peel and a cherry. Serve with a swizzle stick and straws.

KISS IN THE DARK

Pour into a cocktail shaker containing some ice cubes:

1 measure gin
1 measure cherry brandy
1 teaspoon dry vermouth

Shake and strain into a cocktail glass.

LONDON COCKTAIL

Put some ice cubes in a mixing glass and add:

1½ measures gin
2 dashes Angostura bitters
½ teaspoon sugar syrup
½ teaspoon maraschino

Stir well and strain into a cocktail glass. Garnish with a sliver of lemon peel.

MARTINI 1 (ORIGINAL RECIPE)

Into a mixing glass full of ice cubes pour:

1 measures gin
1 measure dry vermouth

Stir vigorously and strain at once into a cocktail glass. Squeeze on some lemon zest and drop the peel into the glass. You may garnish with an olive (not stuffed).

MARTINI 2 (DRY MARTINI)

Into a mixing glass full of ice cubes pour:

1½ measures gin
½ measure dry vermouth

Stir briskly and strain at once into a cocktail glass. Squeeze on some lemon zest and drop in the peel. If you like garnish with an olive (not stuffed).

MARTINI 3 (EXTRA DRY MARTINI) 🍸

Into a mixing glass filled with ice cubes pour in 1 measure dry vermouth. When the vermouth reaches the bottom of the glass pour it away but retain the ice cubes. Now pour in 1½ measures of gin and stir briskly for no more than 30 seconds. Strain into a cocktail glass. Squeeze on some lemon zest and throw away the peel.
N.B. You may also add a dash of Angostura bitters with the gin for a very dry and subtle drink.

MARTINI 4 (MEDIUM DRY MARTINI) 🍸

Put some ice cubes in a mixing glass and add:

1 measure gin
¼ measure dry vermouth
¼ measure sweet vermouth

Stir and strain into a cocktail glass. Garnish with a stuffed olive.

MARTINI 5 (SPECIAL DRY MARTINI) 🍸

Put some ice cubes in a mixing glass and add:

1 measure gin
¼ measure dry vermouth
½ teaspoon Pernod

Stir and strain into a cocktail glass. Garnish with a cocktail onion.

MARTINI 6 (SWEET MARTINI) 🍸

Put some ice cubes in a mixing glass and add:

1 measure gin
½ measure sweet vermouth

Dry Martini in a glass from the Danish Boutique, Paris.

Stir well and strain into a cocktail glass. Garnish with a maraschino cherry.
N.B. You can add a dash of Angostura bitters if you like to 'pep up' this sweet martini recipe.

MILLION DOLLAR 🍸

Pour into a cocktail shaker containing some ice cubes:

1 measure gin
½ measure sweet vermouth
1 egg white
2 teaspoons pineapple juice
1 teaspoon grenadine

Shake vigorously and strain into a cocktail glass.

MILVEA 🍸

Put some ice cubes in a cocktail shaker and add:

1 measure gin
½ measure crème de banane
½ measure St Raphael
1 dash double cream

Shake and strain into a cocktail glass. Garnish with a cherry.

A.GORDON, DUBLIN.
Irish Cocktail Competition, 1951.

MOON RIVER ⬙ ⛾

Put some ice cubes in a mixing glass and pour in:

$\frac{1}{2}$ *measure Gordon's gin*
$\frac{1}{2}$ *measure Marie Brizard apricot brandy*
$\frac{1}{2}$ *measure Cointreau*
$\frac{1}{4}$ *measure Galliano*
$\frac{1}{4}$ *measure lemon juice*

Stir and strain into a large cocktail glass. Garnish with a cherry.

DBL, DENMARK. 1ST PRIZE,
*National Cocktail and Long Drink
Competition, 1973.*

NEGRONI ▣

Put two or three ice cubes in an old fashioned glass and pour in:

1 measure gin
1 measure Campari
1 measure sweet vermouth

Stir to mix and garnish with a half slice of orange. Serve with a swizzle stick.

OPAL ⬗ ⛾

Pour into a cocktail shaker containing several ice cubes:

$\frac{6}{10}$ *Gordon's gin*
$\frac{1}{10}$ *lemon juice*
$\frac{2}{10}$ *Marie Brizard crème de banane*
$\frac{1}{10}$ *orgeat syrup*
1 dash Bols blue curaçao

Dampen the rim of a cocktail glass and frost with green sugar. Shake the cocktail well and pour into the glass. Garnish with a slice of lime cut in the shape of a heart.

MICHEL SARRI, CANNES.
ABF, France.

Negroni.

ORANGE BLOSSOM ⬗ ⛾

Pour into a cocktail shaker containing several ice cubes:

$1\frac{1}{2}$ *measures gin*
1 measure orange juice
1 teaspoon sugar

Shake well and strain into a cocktail glass. Garnish with a cherry.
N.B. You can vary the proportions of gin to orange juice according to taste.

PALL MALL ⬙ ⛾

Pour into a mixing glass containing some ice cubes:

$\frac{1}{3}$ *gin*
$\frac{1}{3}$ *sweet vermouth*
$\frac{1}{3}$ *dry vermouth*
1 teaspoon white crème de menthe
2 dashes Angostura bitters

Mix well and strain into a cocktail glass.

PENDENNIS COCKTAIL ♦ 🍸

Put some ice cubes in a cocktail shaker and add:

1 measure gin
½ measure apricot brandy
juice of ½ lime
1–2 dashes Peychaud bitters

Shake and strain into a cocktail glass.

PERFECT MARTINI 🍷 🍸

Put some ice cubes in a mixing glass and add:

1 measure gin
⅚ measure dry vermouth
⅚ measure sweet vermouth
1 dash Angostura bitters

Mix well and strain into a cocktail glass.

PHOENIX GIN SLING ▯

Pour into a tumbler:

1½ measures gin
¼ measure Cherry Heering
¼ measure lemon juice
¼ measure sugar syrup

Put in two to three tablespoons crushed ice and top up with soda. Stir to mix and garnish with a lemon slice and a cherry.

PINK GIN 🍷 🍸

Put some ice cubes in a mixing glass and add:

1½ measures gin
1–2 dashes Angostura bitters

Stir well to mix and strain into a cocktail glass.

PINK LADY ♦ 🍸

Put some ice cubes in a cocktail shaker and pour in:

1½ measures London dry gin
½ measure lemon juice
1 dash grenadine
1 teaspoon egg white

Shake well and strain into a cocktail glass.
N.B. As a variation, omit the teaspoon of egg white and replace it with a measure of double cream for a richer cocktail.

PLAYA DELIGHT ♦ 🍸

Put some ice cubes in a cocktail shaker and pour in:

1 measure gin
1 measure white rum
½ measure lime juice
3 measures orange juice
½ measure Galliano

Shake and strain into a cocktail glass. Garnish with a slice of lime fixed on the rim of the glass.
N.B. To make a long drink, omit the Galliano and strain the cocktail into a tumbler. Add two or three ice cubes and top up with soda. Garnish with a slice of lime fixed on the rim of the glass. Serve with two straws.

PRINCESS MARY ♦ 🍸

Put some ice cubes in a cocktail shaker and add:

½ measure gin
½ measure white crème de cacao
½ measure double cream

Shake and strain into a cocktail glass. Sprinkle with grated nutmeg or bitter chocolate.

PRINCETON 🍷 🍸

Pour into a mixing glass containing some ice cubes:

1 measure gin
½ measure port
1 dash Angostura bitters

Stir well and strain into a cocktail glass. Squeeze some lemon peel over the glass to extract the zest then drop in the peel.
N.B. Use white port for a lighter, more sophisticated cocktail, and ruby port for a fuller flavour.

RED LION ♦ 🍷

Put some ice cubes in a cocktail shaker and pour in:

½ measure gin
½ measure Grand Marnier
¼ measure orange juice
¼ measure lemon juice

Dampen the rim of a balloon glass and dip it into a thin layer of fine sugar to frost the rim. Shake the cocktail well and pour it into the glass. Drop in 2 or 3 ice cubes and serve garnished with a half slice of orange.

REGATE 🍷 🍸

Pour into a mixing glass containing some ice cubes:

4/10 Gordon's gin
3/10 Mandarine Imperiale
2/10 dry Martini
1/10 crème de banane

Stir well and pour into a cocktail glass. Garnish with a lemon slice, a cherry and a mint leaf.

Jean-Loup Timmerman, La Baule. ABF, France.

ROADSTER ♂ ♀

Pour into a cocktail shaker containing some ice cubes:

1 measure gin
1 measure Grand Marnier
1 measure orange juice

Shake and strain into a cocktail glass. Garnish with a twist of lemon peel.

ROMAN SLING ♂ ♀

Put some crushed ice into a cocktail shaker and add:

1½ measures London dry gin
¼ measure cognac
¼ measure Grand Marnier
½ measure orange juice
½ measure lemon juice

Shake and strain into a balloon glass. Garnish with a slice of orange and a cherry on a cocktail stick.

ROSE ♀ ♀

Put some ice cubes in a mixing glass and pour in:

1 measure London dry gin
½ measure dry vermouth
½ measure cherry brandy

Stir to mix and strain into a cocktail glass. Garnish with a cherry.

ROYAL CLOVER CLUB ♂ ♀

Put some ice cubes in a cocktail shaker and add:

1½ measures gin
¾ measure lemon juice
¾ measure grenadine
1 egg yolk

Shake well and strain into a cocktail glass.

ROYAL FIZZ ♂ ▌

Pour into a cocktail shaker containing several ice cubes:

1 measure London dry gin
½ measure lemon juice
1 teaspoon sugar
1 egg

Shake well and strain into a collins glass over two or three ice cubes. Top up with soda water and stir to mix. Garnish with two cherries and a lemon slice impaled on a cocktail stick. Serve with two decorative straws.
N.B. For variation, replace the soda with ginger ale.

ROYAL ROMANCE ♂ ♀

Put some ice cubes in a cocktail shaker and pour in:

1 measure gin
½ measure Grand Marnier
½ measure passion fruit juice
1 dash grenadine

Shake and strain into a cocktail glass.

JOHN PEROSINO, 1ST PRIZE,
British Empire Cocktail Competition, London, 1934.

ROYAL SMILE ♂ ♀

Put some ice cubes in a cocktail shaker and add:

1 measure gin
½ measure calvados
3 dashes grenadine
3 dashes lemon juice

Shake and strain into a cocktail glass. Decorate with a cherry.
N.B. For variation, replace the calvados with apricot brandy or cherry brandy.

SALOME ♀ ♀

Put some ice cubes in a mixing glass and pour in:

½ measure gin
½ measure Dubonnet
½ measure dry vermouth

Mix well and strain into a cocktail glass.

SILVER FIZZ ♂ ▌

Put some ice cubes in a cocktail shaker and pour in:

1 measure London dry gin
½ measure lemon juice
½ measure sugar syrup
1 egg white

Shake vigorously and strain into a collins glass full of ice cubes. Top up with soda and garnish with a lemon slice and two cherries on a cocktail stick.

SILVER JUBILEE ♂ ♀

Put some ice cubes in a cocktail shaker and pour in:

1 measure gin
½ measure crème de banane
½ measure double cream

Shake and strain into a cocktail glass.

SILVER STREAK ♀

Put 3 or 4 ice cubes in a balloon glass and pour in slowly:

1 measure gin
½ measure kummel

Serve without stirring.
N.B. You can replace the kummel with anisette.

SINGAPORE SLING ▮

Squeeze the juice of half a lime into a tumbler half full of ice cubes. Drop the lime shell into the glass and add:

1 measure gin
½ measure cherry brandy
1 teaspoon grenadine

Stir well. Top up with soda and garnish with a slice of lime. Serve with straws.

(Below): Silver Fizz. (Opposite): White Lady.

TOM COLLINS ▮

Pour into a collins glass:

1 measure gin
juice of 1 lemon
1 teaspoon sugar syrup

Stir well. Add ice cubes and top up with soda. Stir again and decorate with a lemon slice placed on the rim of the glass. Serve with a swizzle stick and two straws.

WAX ❦ ⏣

Put some ice cubes in a cocktail shaker and add:

1 measure gin
1 measure pastis
1 egg white
¼ measure sugar syrup

Shake well and strain into a large cocktail glass.

WESTERN ROSE ❦ ⏣

Put some ice cubes in a cocktail shaker and add:

1 measure gin
½ measure apricot brandy
½ measure dry vermouth
1 dash lemon juice

Shake and strain into a cocktail glass.

WHITE HEATHER ❦ ⏣

Put some ice cubes in a cocktail shaker and pour in:

1 measure gin
⅓ measure Cointreau
⅓ measure dry vermouth
⅓ measure pineapple juice
1 dash pastis

Shake and strain into a cocktail glass.

WHITE LADY ❦ ⏣

Put some ice cubes in a cocktail shaker and pour in:

1½ measures gin
½ measure Cointreau
½ measure lime juice

Shake and strain into a cocktail glass. Garnish with a cherry on a cocktail stick.
N.B. A dash of egg white is sometimes added to this cocktail.

WHITE LILY

Put several ice cubes in a mixing glass and pour in:

½ measure gin
½ measure white rum
½ measure Cointreau
1 dash pastis

Stir and strain into a cocktail glass.

WHITE ROSE

Put some ice cubes in a cocktail shaker and add:

1 measure gin
⅓ measure maraschino
1 dash orange juice
1 dash lemon juice
1 egg white

Shake well and strain into a cocktail glass.

YELLOW DAISY

Pour into a mixing glass containing several ice cubes:

½ measure gin
½ measure dry vermouth
¼ measure Grand Marnier

Stir well and strain into a cocktail glass.

ZA-ZA (ZARA)

Put some ice cubes in a mixing glass and pour in:

1½ measures gin
½ measure Dubonnet
1 dash Angostura bitters

Stir well and strain into a cocktail glass. Add a sliver of lemon peel. N.B. If you prefer change the proportions to 1 measure gin and 1 measure Dubonnet.

Vodka-based Cocktails

The traditional way to drink vodka in the Slav countries is to chill it well and to toss a small glassful to the back of the throat, between mouthfuls of caviare. It also combines well with smoked fish because it is unobtrusive and odourless. That also explains why it is used in so many cocktails, to give that hidden 'kick'.

Vodka is made from a variety of raw materials—grain, potato, molasses—from which is extracted a 96 per cent pure alcohol. It is often filtered through charcoal to remove all taste, good or bad, and then redistilled with aromatic herbs which give each vodka its special character. Sometimes aromatic extracts are added to the alcohol base. Either way, the best vodkas are produced from a rectified grain spirit redistilled with aromatic substances.

Polish vodkas are considered the best and are often strongly flavoured. Russian, Finnish and Swedish vodkas are less scented and more neutral in taste. Vodka mixes easily with a great number of spirits, diluting their flavour without reducing their strengths. It combines discreetly with fruit juices to which it adds alcoholic strength, without affecting the flavour, as in the famous *Screwdriver*. An eastern European habit is to slip lemon or orange peel into a bottle of vodka, for a simple home flavouring.

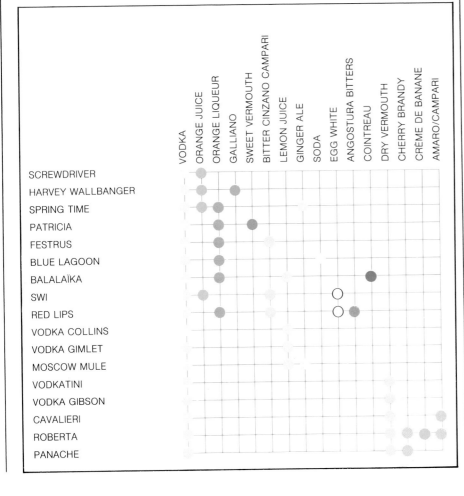

Chart columns: VODKA, ORANGE JUICE, ORANGE LIQUEUR, GALLIANO, SWEET VERMOUTH, BITTER CINZANO CAMPARI, LEMON JUICE, GINGER ALE, SODA, EGG WHITE, ANGOSTURA BITTERS, COINTREAU, DRY VERMOUTH, CHERRY BRANDY, CRÈME DE BANANE, AMARO/CAMPARI

Chart rows: SCREWDRIVER, HARVEY WALLBANGER, SPRING TIME, PATRICIA, FESTRUS, BLUE LAGOON, BALALAÏKA, SWI, RED LIPS, VODKA COLLINS, VODKA GIMLET, MOSCOW MULE, VODKATINI, VODKA GIBSON, CAVALIERI, ROBERTA, PANACHE

AMPAINEN

Fill a large tumbler with ice cubes and pour in:

1 measure vodka
1 measure crème de banane

Stir and top up with ginger ale. Garnish with a slice of orange.

ANGELO

Put some ice cubes in a cocktail shaker and add:

1 measure Smirnoff vodka
⅓ measure Galliano
⅓ measure Southern Comfort

Top up with pineapple and orange juice and shake. Strain into a cocktail glass. Add a dash of Frothee before serving.

Aart Leenheer.
NBC, Holland, 1977.

ANGEL'S SMILE

Put some ice cubes in a cocktail shaker and pour in:

½ measure vodka
½ measure Cointreau
½ measure kirsch
½ teaspoon grenadine

Shake well and strain into a cocktail glass. Garnish with a cherry.

APRÈS SKI

Put some ice cubes in a cocktail shaker and pour in:

½ measure vodka
½ measure green crème de menthe
½ measure Pernod

Shake and strain into a fancy glass. Add some ice cubes and top up with soda. Garnish with a lemon slice and a mint sprig. Serve with straws.

BALALAIKA ♦ ▼

Pour into a cocktail shaker containing several ice cubes:

1 measure vodka
1 measure Cointreau
1 measure lemon juice

Shake and strain into a cocktail glass.

BARBARA COCKTAIL ♦ ▼

Pour into a cocktail shaker containing several ice cubes:

1 measure vodka
½ measure crème de cacao
½ measure double cream

Shake and strain into a cocktail glass.

BELLADONNA ♦ ▼

Put some ice cubes in a cocktail shaker and add:

1 measure vodka
1 measure Pères Chartreux eau de noix
1 measure double cream

Shake and strain into a cocktail glass.

Jean Biolatto.
ABF, France.

BERNICE ♦ ▼

Put some ice cubes in a cocktail shaker and pour in:

1 measure vodka
½ measure Galliano
½ measure lime juice
3 dashes bitters

Shake and strain into a cocktail glass.

C.S. Berner,
U.S. (West Coast) Competition, 1950.
UKBG, Great Britain.

BLACK RUSSIAN ▪

Put 3 or 4 ice cubes in an old fashioned glass and add:

1 measure Russian vodka
1 measure Kahlúa

Stir well to mix.
N.B. If you replace the Kahlúa with Tía Maria the cocktail is called Black Cloud.

Black Russian in a Baccarat glass.

Bloody Mary in a glass of Saint-Louis crystal.

BLOODY MARY

Put some ice cubes in a mixing glass and pour in:

1 measure vodka
4 measures tomato juice
1 pinch of celery salt
1–2 drops Tabasco sauce
2–3 drops Worcestershire sauce

Mix well and strain into an old fashioned glass full of ice cubes. Garnish with a lemon slice.
N.B. You may add two or three dashes of lemon juice.

BLUE LAGOON

Put some ice cubes in a tumbler and add:

1 measure vodka
1 measure blue curaçao

Stir to mix. Top up with soda and serve with straws.

BULLSHOT

Pour into a tumbler:

1½ measures vodka
1½ measures cold beef consommé
2 dashes Worcestershire sauce
1 dash Tabasco sauce
1 pinch of salt

Stir well. Garnish with a lemon slice.
N.B. Add 1½ measures of tomato juice to make a Bloody Bullshot.

CAPE CODDER

Put some ice cubes in an old fashioned glass and pour in:

1 measure vodka

Top up with bilberry juice. Stir well before serving.
N.B. You can also add some lime juice and soda to taste.

CHI-CHI

Put some ice cubes in a cocktail shaker and pour in:

1½ measures vodka
2 measures pineapple juice
1 measure coconut cream
1 dash grenadine
juice of ½ lemon

Shake well and strain into a lager glass.

CAVALIERI

Put some ice cubes in a mixing glass and add:

1 measure vodka
½ measure dry vermouth
¼ measure Amaro Cora

Stir well and strain into a cocktail glass. Garnish with a twist of lemon peel.

CHI-CHI (FROZEN)

Put some crushed ice in an electric blender and add:

1½ measures vodka
1 measure cream of coconut
3 measures pineapple juice
1 teaspoon lemon juice
1 slice pineapple

Blend well. Pour into a large tumbler containing ice cubes. Garnish with a half slice of pineapple, a cherry and a paper parasol. Serve with straws.

DÉROBADE 🍸

Put some ice cubes in a cocktail shaker and add:

$\frac{3}{10}$ *Moskovskaya vodka*
$\frac{2}{10}$ *poire Williamine*
$\frac{2}{10}$ *Combier triple sec*
$\frac{2}{10}$ *Marie Brizard raspberry liqueur*
$\frac{1}{10}$ *lime juice*

Shake and strain into a cocktail glass. Garnish with a slice of lime and a brandied cherry.

JACKY VIGNAL, BORDEAUX.
ABF, France.

FANTASIA 🍸

Pour into a frosted cocktail glass containing some ice cubes:

1 measure Chartreuse
$\frac{3}{4}$ *measure vodka*
$\frac{1}{4}$ *measure cherry brandy*
$\frac{1}{2}$ *measure grapefruit juice*

Stir to mix. Garnish with a half slice of orange and a cherry.

FESTRUS 🍸

Put some ice cubes in a mixing glass and pour in:

$\frac{1}{2}$ *measure Smirnoff vodka*
$\frac{1}{2}$ *measure Grand Marnier*
$\frac{1}{2}$ *measure Cinzano bitter*

Mix well and strain into a cocktail glass. Garnish with a sliver of orange peel and a cherry.

BJARNE ERIKSEN, 1ST PRIZE,
International Cocktail Competition, Los Angeles, 1973.
NBF, Norway.

FLAMINGO 🍸🍷

Put some ice cubes in a cocktail shaker and add:

$\frac{3}{4}$ *measure vodka*
$\frac{1}{4}$ *measure Campari*

Shake and strain into a champagne flute or tulip glass. Top up with champagne. Garnish with a half slice of orange.

FROSTY AMOUR 🍸

Put some ice cubes in a cocktail shaker and add:

1 measure Smirnoff vodka
1 measure Southern Comfort
1 measure Bols apricot liqueur
1 dash Bols Parfait Amour
1 dash Bols crème de banane

Shake and strain into a tumbler. Top up with Seven Up and serve with straws.

DANIEL STEFANSSON, 1ST PRIZE,
Long Drink Competition, 1974. BCI, Iceland

FROZEN STEPPES 🍷

Pour into an electric blender:

1 measure vodka
1 measure brown crème de cacao
1 scoop vanilla ice cream

Blend for a few seconds. Pour into a balloon glass. Decorate with a cherry.

GIPSY 🍸

Put some ice cubes in a cocktail shaker and add:

1 measure vodka
$\frac{1}{2}$ *measure Benedictine*
1 dash Angostura bitters

Shake and strain into a cocktail glass.

GRAND PRIX 🍷

Half fill a cocktail shaker with ice cubes and pour in:

1 measure vodka
$\frac{3}{4}$ *measure dry vermouth*
$\frac{1}{4}$ *measure Cointreau*
1 teaspoon lemon juice
a few drops grenadine

Shake well and strain into a large balloon glass. Serve with straws.

HARVEY WALLBANGER 🍷

Put three or four ice cubes in a tumbler and pour in:

$1\frac{1}{2}$ *measures vodka*
$2\frac{1}{2}$ *measures orange juice*

Stir to mix. Pour two teaspoons Galliano on top. Garnish with a slice of orange and a cherry on a cocktail stick and serve with straws and a stirrer.

Harvey Wallbanger in a Lalique glass.

LUCKY DIP 🍸

Pour into a cocktail shaker containing several ice cubes:

1 measure vodka
½ measure crème de banane
¼ measure lemon syrup
1 egg white

Shake well and strain into a cocktail glass.

D.J. McLaughlin.
All Ireland Cocktail Competition, 1959.

MOSCOW MULE 🍺

Put plenty of ice cubes in a glass with a handle and squeeze the juice of 1 lime over them. Drop in the squeezed out lime. Pour in 1 measure vodka and top up with ginger ale. Stir gently and garnish with a spiral of cucumber peel.

OMNIA 🍸

Pour into a mixing glass containing some ice cubes:

1 measure Smirnoff vodka
1 measure Stock brandy
¼ measure Martini dry vermouth
¼ measure Isolabella mandarine liqueur
¼ measure Buton orange liqueur

Stir well to mix. Pour into two cocktail glasses and garnish each with a cherry.
Serves 2

Loredano Fortalin, Venice. 1st prize,
Cocktail Competition, 1974. AIBES, Italy.

PANACHÉ 🍸

Put some ice cubes in a mixing glass and pour in:

5/10 Moscovskaya vodka
2/10 Cherry Heering
3/10 Martini dry vermouth

Stir well to mix and strain into a cocktail glass. Garnish with a maraschino cherry.

Roger Souchon, Paris.
ABF, France.

PATRICIA 🍸

Put some ice cubes into a mixing glass and pour in:

½ measure vodka
½ measure triple sec
½ measure sweet vermouth

Stir to mix and strain into a cocktail glass. Garnish with a sliver of lemon peel.

RED LIPS COCKTAIL 🍸

Put some ice cubes in a cocktail shaker and pour in:

1 measure vodka
¼ measure Grand Marnier
¼ measure Campari
1 teaspoon egg white
1 dash Angostura bitters

Shake thoroughly and strain into a cocktail glass.

ROAD RUNNER 🍸

Put some ice cubes in a cocktail shaker and add:

1 measure vodka
½ measure amaretto
½ measure cream of coconut

Shake and strain into a cocktail glass. Sprinkle the top with grated nutmeg.

Al Arteaga, 1st prize,
Guild Competition, 1976. USBG, USA.

ROBERTA 🍸

Pour into a cocktail shaker containing some ice cubes:

½ measure Smirnoff vodka
½ measure Cinzano dry vermouth
½ measure Cherry Heering
2 dashes Campari
2 dashes crème de banane

Shake and strain into a cocktail glass. Garnish with a twist of orange peel.

Pietro Cuccoli. 1st prize,
International Cocktail Competition, Saint-Vincent, 1963.
IBES, Italy.

ROSE OF WARSAW 🍸

Pour into a mixing glass containing some ice cubes:

1 measure Wyborowa vodka
⅔ measure cherry brandy
⅓ measure Cointreau
1 dash Angostura bitters

Stir well to mix and strain into a cocktail glass.

Angélo Biolato, Paris. 1st prize,
Wyborowa Competition. ABF, France.

ROYAL RUSSIAN 🍸

Into a cocktail shaker containing some ice cubes pour:

1 measure vodka
1 measure white crème de menthe
1 dash grenadine
½ measure double cream

Shake thoroughly and strain into a champagne saucer. Garnish with a cherry.

SALTY DOG 🍺

Moisten the rim of a collins glass with lemon juice and dip into salt to frost.

Fill the glass with ice cubes and pour in 1 measure vodka. Fill up with grapefruit juice and stir to mix.

SCANEX ♦ ▼

Pour into a cocktail shaker containing some ice cubes:

1 measure Wyborowa vodka
1 measure bilberry liqueur
1 measure lemon juice
1 measure sugar syrup
1 dash grenadine

Shake and strain into a cocktail glass.

CHARLES NYBERG, 1ST PRIZE,
International Competition, Stockholm, 1972.
EBSK, Finland.

SCOTCH FROG ♦ ▼

Put some ice cubes in a cocktail shaker and add:

1 measure vodka
½ measure Galliano
½ measure Cointreau
juice of 1 lime
1 dash Angostura bitters
1 teaspoon maraschino

Shake and strain into a cocktail glass.

ALBIAN FARLEY,
U.S. (West Coast) Competition, 1957.

SCREWDRIVER ▪

Put three ice cubes in an old fashioned glass and pour in:

1½ measures vodka
2½ measures orange juice

Stir well. Garnish with an orange slice. Serve with a stirrer.

Screwdriver: glass and crystal bowl by Saint-Louis.

SMASH ♦ ▼

Pour into a cocktail shaker containing several ice cubes:

1 measure Stolichnaya vodka
1 measure blackberry liqueur
1 measure Marie Brizard mandarine liqueur
1 measure lemon juice

Shake and strain into a cocktail glass.

PERTTI O. KARL, 1ST PRIZE,
National Cocktail Competition, 1971.
EBSK, Finland.

SNOW FLAKE ♦ ▮

Pour into a cocktail shaker containing several ice cubes:

1 measure vodka
¼ measure Galliano
¼ measure Southern Comfort
½ measure advocaat
2 measures orange juice

Shake thoroughly and strain into a tumbler. Top up with lemonade and stir. Pour a little cream over the top. Garnish with an orange slice and a cherry.

SPRING TIME 🍸🥃

Pour into a cocktail shaker containing several ice cubes:

1½ measures vodka
½ measure Cointreau
1 measure orange juice

Shake and strain into a tumbler filled with ice cubes. Top up with ginger ale and stir to mix. Garnish with spirals of lemon and orange peel, a cherry and a paper parasol. Serve with straws.

SWI 🍸🍸

Put some ice cubes in a cocktail shaker and add:

1 measure vodka
1 measure Campari
1 measure orange juice
1 egg white

Shake vigorously and strain into a cocktail glass.

TROIKA 🍸🍸

Put some ice cubes in a cocktail shaker and pour in:

1 measure orange Chartreuse
½ measure vodka
juice of ½ lime

Shake and strain into a cocktail glass.

TROPICAL STORM 🗑🍷

Put two glassfuls of crushed ice into an electric blender and pour in:

1 measure vodka
3 measures golden rum
2 measures orange juice

1 measure lime juice
1 measure pineapple juice
1 dash Angostura bitters
2 dashes grenadine

Blend for a few seconds and pour into four fancy glasses. Garnish each glass with a piece of pineapple or a slice of orange, a slice of banana and a cherry. Serve with straws.
SERVES 4

TSARINA 🍸🍸

Put some ice cubes in a mixing glass and pour in:

1 measure vodka
½ measure dry vermouth
½ measure apricot brandy
1 dash Angostura bitters

Stir well and strain into a cocktail glass.

VODKA COLLINS 🥃

Fill a tumbler with ice cubes and pour in:

1 measure vodka
juice of ½ lemon
½ measure sugar syrup

Stir well to mix. Squeeze a half lime over the top and drop the shell of the lime into the glass. Top up with soda and stir very gently. Serve with straws.

VODKA GIBSON 🍸🍸

Put some ice cubes in a mixing glass and pour in:

1 measure vodka
1 dash dry vermouth

Stir well and strain into a cocktail glass. Garnish with a cocktail onion or an olive if preferred.

VODKA GIMLET 🍸🍸

Put some ice cubes in a mixing glass and add:

1½ measures vodka
½ measure lime juice
1 teaspoon sugar syrup

Stir well and strain into a cocktail glass. Garnish with a half slice of lime astride the rim of the glass or in the cocktail itself.

VODKA IMPERIAL 🍸

This is a delicious—and powerfully alcoholic!—fruit cocktail. Prepare and cut into pieces any fruit in season such as apples, pears, melon, pineapple, etc, and put them in a bowl. Pour over enough vodka to cover the fruit. Cover the bowl and leave in the refrigerator for 8 hours. Serve in champagne saucers.

VODKATINI 🍸🍸

Put some ice cubes in a mixing glass and add:

1½ measures vodka
1–2 dashes dry vermouth

Stir well to mix and strain into a cocktail glass. Garnish with an olive.

Cocktails based on Bourbon, Rye Whiskey and Canadian Whisky

American and Irish whiskey is spelt with an 'e' and Scotch and Canadian without. There are a great variety of whiskies differing as much by country of origin as by method of manufacture, though experts agree that the local water gives any whisky its character. The best known whisky for this reason is Scotch, which merits a chapter of its own.

Between 1919 and 1933 distilling alcoholic drinks was not allowed in the United States. But despite Prohibition, there was a strong demand for spirits and Canada developed distilleries to meet it. Canadian whisky is still one of the most popular drinks in the United States. It is made by distilling a mash of fermented grain (maize, barley, corn, and rye) in patent stills to a very high strength. It is mostly sold as a blend, is lighter than Bourbon and well suited to cocktails.

American whiskey is the oldest alcohol of the new world, the drink of the pioneers and desperadoes of the western saloons. The first whiskeys of the eighteenth century were strong and rough, but they have gradually become smoother and more respectable. Rye whiskey, made from a mash which contains at least 51 per cent rye, is the oldest whiskey distilled in Pennsylvania and Maryland by immigrants of Irish origin, hence the spelling with an e.

Bourbon was named after Bourbon County, Kentucky, where it was first made in the mid-nineteenth century. It is distilled from a mash containing at least 51 per cent maize to a very high strength (80°), then filtered through charcoal before being aged in charred casks, which gives it its slight smoky flavour. Rye and Bourbon play an important part in cocktails as the great number of recipes demonstrates. Their role might have been greater if Prohibition had not affected the trade.

Happy Blends

Rye whiskey and Canadian whiskies both complement dry and sweet vermouth. Bourbon also blends well with vermouth and adds a note of originality (see table on page 80).

With lemon juice, Bourbon is best known as *Bourbon Sour* and *Rye Sour* is also popular (see table on page 81).

Burning maple wood in Tennessee to produce charcoal for filtration for whiskey, before ageing according to a process introduced by Jack Daniel in the year 1866.

ADRY

Pour into a cocktail shaker containing several ice cubes:

1 measure bourbon
¼ measure curaçao

Shake and strain into a cocktail glass containing crushed ice. Garnish with a cherry.

MICHEL BIGOT, PARIS.
ABF, France.

ALGONQUIN

Pour into a cocktail shaker containing several ice cubes:

1 measure rye
½ measure dry vermouth
½ measure pineapple juice

Shake and strain into an old fashioned glass containing ice cubes.

ARROW HEAD COCKTAIL

Pour into a cocktail shaker containing several ice cubes:

1 measure bourbon
1 teaspoon sweet vermouth
1 teaspoon dry vermouth
1 teaspoon lemon juice
1 egg white

Shake and strain into a cocktail glass.

BLACK HAWK

Put some ice cubes in a mixing glass and pour in:

1 measure bourbon, rye or Canadian whisky
1 measure sloe gin

Stir to mix and strain into a cocktail glass. Garnish with a cherry.

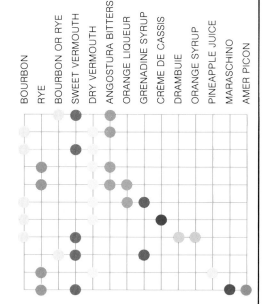

	BOURBON	RYE	BOURBON OR RYE	SWEET VERMOUTH	DRY VERMOUTH	ANGOSTURA BITTERS	ORANGE LIQUEUR	GRENADINE SYRUP	CRÈME DE CASSIS	DRAMBUIE	ORANGE SYRUP	PINEAPPLE JUICE	MARASCHINO	AMER PICON
MANHATTAN			●	●		●								
MANHATTAN DRY			●		●	●								
MANHATTAN PERFECT			●	●	●	●								
RYE AND DRY		●			●									
UP TO DATE		●		●			●	●						
BOURBONELLA	●				●		●	●						
CASSIS COCKTAIL	●								●					
EMBASSY ROYAL	●			●						●	●			
OPENING				●				●						
ALGONQUIN		●			●							●		
BROOKLYN		●		●									●	●

BOSTON FLIP

Put some ice cubes in a cocktail shaker and add:

1 measure rye
1 measure madeira
2 teaspoons sugar syrup
1 egg yolk

Shake well and strain into a small balloon glass. Sprinkle with grated nutmeg.

BOURBON AND SODA

Pour 1 measure bourbon into a collins glass filled with ice cubes. Top up with soda. Stir gently before serving.

BOURBON COLLINS

Put some ice cubes in a collins glass and pour in:

1 measure bourbon
½ measure lemon juice
1 teaspoon sugar

Stir well to mix. Top up with soda. Garnish with a lemon slice and serve with a swizzle stick and straws.

BOURBON COOLER

Put some ice cubes in cocktail shaker and add:

1 measure bourbon
3 dashes white crème de menthe
2 teaspoons grenadine

1 teaspoon sugar syrup
some dashes Angostura bitters

Shake and strain into a tumbler. Add some ice cubes and top up with soda. Garnish with a cherry, a wedge of pineapple and a slice of orange all impaled on a cocktail stick.

BOURBONELLA

Put some ice cubes in a mixing glass and pour in:

1 measure bourbon
⅓ measure triple sec
⅓ measure dry vermouth
1 dash grenadine

Stir well to mix and strain into a cocktail glass.

BOURBON HIGHBALL

Pour 1 measure of bourbon into a tumbler filled with ice cubes. Top up with soda or ginger ale. Stir and garnish with a spiral of lemon peel.

BOURBON MIST

Pour 1 measure of bourbon into an old fashioned glass filled with crushed ice. Garnish with a sliver of lemon peel.

BOURBON SOUR

Put some ice cubes in a cocktail shaker and add:

1 measure bourbon
½ measure lemon juice
1 teaspoon sugar

Shake and strain into a cocktail or fancy glass. Garnish with a cherry.

BROOKLYN

Put some ice cubes in a cocktail shaker and pour in:

1 measure rye
1 measure sweet vermouth
1 dash maraschino
1 dash Amer Picon

Shake and strain into a cocktail glass.

CALIFORNIA LEMONADE

Put some ice cubes in a cocktail shaker and add:

1 measure bourbon, rye or Canadian whisky
juice of 1 lime
juice of 1 lemon
3 teaspoons sugar syrup
2 dashes grenadine

Shake and strain into a collins glass half filled with crushed ice. Top up with soda and garnish with a slice of lemon, a slice of orange and a cherry. Serve with straws.

CAPTAIN COLLINS

Put some ice cubes in a cocktail shaker and pour in:

1 measure Canadian whisky
½ measure lime juice
1 dash grenadine

Shake and strain into a collins glass filled with ice cubes. Top up with soda and stir before serving.

CASSIS COCKTAIL

Pour into a cocktail shaker containing some ice cubes:

1 measure bourbon
½ measure dry vermouth
1 teaspoon crème de cassis

Shake and strain into a cocktail glass.

COMMODORE

Pour into a cocktail shaker containing several ice cubes:

1 measure bourbon
½ measure lemon juice
1 teaspoon sugar
2 dashes Angostura bitters

Shake and strain into a cocktail glass.

	BOURBON	RYE	BOURBON OR RYE	LEMON JUICE	SUGAR/SYRUP	SODA	ANGOSTURA BITTERS	GRENADINE SYRUP	TRIPLE-SEC	GINGER ALE
BOURBON SOUR	●			●	●					
RYE SOUR		●		●	●					
RYE COLLINS		●		●	●	●				
NEW YORK		●		●	●			●		
WAIKIKI									○	
SOUTHERN GINGER	●									●

82

COWBOY 🍶🍸

Pour into a cocktail shaker containing several ice cubes:

1 measure bourbon
½ measure double cream

Shake and strain into a cocktail glass.

DAILY MAIL 🍶🍸

Pour into a cocktail shaker containing several ice cubes:

½ measure rye
½ measure Amer Picon
½ measure orange syrup
3 dashes Angostura bitters

Shake and strain into a cocktail glass.

S. Mitchell, 1st prize,
International Cocktail Competition. London, 1948.

EMBASSY ROYAL 🍶🍸

Put some ice cubes in a cocktail shaker and add:

1 measure bourbon
½ measure Drambuie
½ measure sweet vermouth
2 dashes orange syrup

Shake and strain into a cocktail glass.

ESPRIT CARTÉSIEN ▪

Put 3 ice cubes in an old fashioned glass and pour in:

1 measure bourbon
⅗ measure Pères Chartreux eau de noix
⅕ measure white crème de cacao

Stir to mix before serving.

Jean Biolatto.
ABF, France.

EVANS 🍶🍸

Put some ice cubes in a mixing glass and pour in:

1 measure rye
¼ measure apricot brandy
¼ measure triple sec

Stir well and strain into a cocktail glass.

HUNTER 🍶🍸

Put some ice cubes in a mixing glass and pour in:

1 measure rye
½ measure cherry brandy

Stir and strain into a cocktail glass.

KENTUCKY COLONEL COCKTAIL 🍶🍸

Put some ice cubes in a mixing glass and pour in:

1 measure bourbon
⅓ measure Benedictine

Stir and strain into a cocktail glass. Garnish with a spiral of lemon peel.

KENTUCKY SUNSET 🍶🍷

Put some ice cubes in a mixing glass and pour in:

1 measure bourbon
⅓ measure Strega
⅓ measure anisette

Stir well. Strain into a balloon glass containing ice cubes. Garnish with a sliver of orange peel.

LADIES' COCKTAIL 🍶🍸

Put some ice cubes in a mixing glass and add:

1 measure bourbon, rye or Canadian whisky
½ teaspoon Pernod
½ teaspoon anisette
1 dash Angostura bitters

Stir and strain into a cocktail glass. Garnish with a segment of grapefruit.

LADY'S DREAM 🍶🍸

Put some ice cubes in a cocktail shaker and add:

3/10 Old Grand Dad bourbon
3/10 Cointreau
3/10 Dolfi strawberry liqueur
1/10 double cream

Shake and strain into a cocktail glass.

Sam Sidarith, Paris.
ABF, France.

LOS ANGELES 1 🍶🍸

Put some ice cubes in a cocktail shaker and pour in:

1½ measures bourbon
½ measure lemon juice
1 teaspoon sugar
1 egg

Shake and strain into a champagne saucer. (For variation see p. 90).

MANHATTAN 🍶🍸

Put some ice cubes in a mixing glass and pour in:

1 measure bourbon
½ measure sweet vermouth
1 dash Angostura bitters

Mint Julep in a crystal glass by Daum.

Stir to mix and strain into a cocktail glass. Garnish with a cherry.
N.B. For a change use rye instead of bourbon and add a dash of maraschino.

MANHATTAN DRY

Put some ice cubes in a mixing glass and pour in:

1 measure bourbon or rye
½ measure dry vermouth
1 dash Angostura bitters

Stir and strain into a cocktail glass.

MANHATTAN PERFECT

Put some ice cubes in a mixing glass and pour in:

1 measure bourbon
¼ measure sweet vermouth
¼ measure dry vermouth

Stir well and strain into a cocktail glass. Garnish with a spiral of lemon peel.

MAPLE LEAF COCKTAIL

Put some ice cubes in a cocktail shaker and add:

1 measure bourbon
1 teaspoon maple syrup
juice of ½ lemon

Shake and strain into a cocktail glass.

MINT JULEP

Crush a number of fresh mint leaves in a collins glass with 1 teaspoon sugar using the back of a spoon. Add ½ measure bourbon and stir to mix with the mint and sugar. Half fill the glass with crushed ice and stir until the glass is frosted. Pour in 1 measure of bourbon. Garnish with fresh mint leaves. Serve with straws.

MORNING GLORY 2 🍸 ▪

Put some ice cubes in a mixing glass and pour in:

½ measure rye or bourbon
½ measure cognac
1 teaspoon curaçao
1 teaspoon pastis or Pernod
1 teaspoon sugar syrup
3 dashes Angostura bitters

Stir well to mix and strain into an old fashioned glass containing an ice cube. Add a splash of soda and garnish with a sliver of lemon peel.

NEVINS 🍸 ▪

Put some ice cubes in a cocktail shaker and add:

1 measure bourbon
1 measure grapefruit juice
½ measure apricot liqueur
½ measure lemon juice
2 dashes Angostura bitters

Shake and strain into a tumbler full of ice cubes. Garnish with a slice of lemon fixed on the rim of the glass.

NEW YORK 🍸 ▪

Put some ice cubes in a cocktail shaker and add:

1 measure rye
½ measure lime juice
1 teaspoon sugar
2–3 dashes grenadine

Shake and strain into an old fashioned glass containing several ice cubes. Garnish with a twist of orange peel. N.B. For variation, replace the rye with bourbon, in which case the cocktail is called *New Yorker*.

NIGHT SHADE 🍸 🍸

Put some ice cubes into a cocktail shaker and add:

1 measure bourbon
½ measure sweet vermouth
½ measure orange juice
2–3 dashes yellow Chartreuse

Shake and strain into a cocktail glass.

Old Fashioned in a Baccarat glass, mixer by Hermès.

OLD FASHIONED ▪

Put a cube of sugar in an old fashioned glass and sprinkle with 2 to 3 dashes of Angostura bitters. Add a little water to dissolve the sugar and stir to mix. Put some ice cubes in the glass and add 1 measure bourbon. Garnish with a spiral of lemon peel and a cherry. Serve with a swizzle stick.
N.B. Variations include replacing the bourbon with rye and adding a dash of orange liqueur.

OLD NICK ▪

Put some ice cubes in a cocktail shaker and add:

1 measure rye
½ measure Drambuie
¼ measure orange juice
¼ measure lemon juice
2 dashes Angostura bitters

Shake. Put some ice cubes in an old fashioned glass and pour the cocktail over them. Garnish with a cherry.

OLD PAL ▪

Put some ice cubes in a mixing glass and pour in:

½ measure rye
½ measure dry vermouth
½ measure Campari

Stir to mix and strain into a cocktail glass.

OPENING ▪

Put some ice cubes in a cocktail shaker and pour in:

1 measure bourbon, rye or Canadian whisky

2 teaspoons sweet vermouth
2 teaspoons grenadine

Shake and strain into an old fashioned glass containing some ice cubes.

ORIENTAL ▪

Put some ice cubes in a cocktail shaker and add:

1 measure rye
½ measure sweet white vermouth
½ measure Triple Sec
½ measure lime juice

Shake and strain into a cocktail glass.

ORLEANIAN ▪

Put some ice cubes in a cocktail shaker and add:

1 measure rye
3 dashes Pernod
1 teaspoon sugar syrup
2 dashes Angostura bitters

Shake and strain into a cocktail glass. Garnish with a twist of lemon peel.

PAN AMERICAN ▪

Fill a tumbler with ice cubes and squeeze the juice of half a lemon into it. Pour in:

1 measure rye
1 teaspoon sugar syrup

Stir well and serve.

PORT LIGHT ▪

Put a half glass of crushed ice into an electric blender and pour in:

1 measure bourbon
½ measure lemon juice

2 teaspoons clear honey
1 egg white

Blend for a few seconds at high speed until thoroughly combined. Then pour into a tumbler. Garnish with a fresh mint sprig.

QUEBEC COCKTAIL ▪

Put some ice cubes in a cocktail shaker and pour in:

1 measure Canadian whisky
2 teaspoons dry vermouth
1 teaspoon Amer Picon
1 teaspoon maraschino

Shake and strain into a cocktail glass. Garnish with a cherry.

RATTLESNAKE ▪

Put some ice cubes in a cocktail shaker and pour in:

1 measure bourbon or rye
1 teaspoon sugar syrup
1 egg white
1 teaspoon lemon juice
a few dashes Pernod

Shake well and strain into an old fashioned glass containing crushed ice. Garnish with a half slice of lemon.

RICHELIEU ▪

Pour into a cocktail shaker containing several ice cubes:

1 measure bourbon
1 measure Dubonnet sweet white vermouth
1 teaspoon Vieille Cure

Shake and strain into an old fashioned glass. Add some ice cubes and a sliver of orange peel.

RUBIS 🍸 ▾

Pour into a mixing glass containing several ice cubes:

$\frac{3}{10}$ *Wild Turkey bourbon*
$\frac{3}{10}$ *Cherry Heering*
$\frac{4}{10}$ *Noilly Prat dry vermouth*
2 dashes Angostura bitters
2 dashes lime juice

Stir to mix and strain into a cocktail glass. Garnish with a slice of lime and a cherry.

PHILIPPE GALAS, DIEPPE.
ABF, France.

RYE AND DRY 🍸 ▪

Pour into a cocktail shaker containing several ice cubes:

$\frac{1}{2}$ *measure rye*
1 measure dry vermouth
2 dashes Angostura bitters

Shake and strain into an old fashioned glass. Drop in three ice cubes and serve.

RYE COCKTAIL 🍸 ▾

Put some ice cubes in a cocktail shaker and pour in:

1 measure rye
1 teaspoon sugar syrup
2–3 dashes Angostura bitters

Shake and strain into a cocktail glass.

RYE COLLINS ▪

Put some ice cubes in a collins glass and pour in:

1 measure rye
$\frac{1}{2}$ *measure lemon juice*
1 teaspoon sugar

Stir well to mix and top up with soda. Stir again but lightly and garnish with a lemon slice. Serve with a stirrer and straws.

RYE HIGHBALL ▪

Put an ice cube into a tumbler and pour in 1 measure rye. Top up with soda or ginger ale. Garnish with a lemon slice.

RYE LANE 🍸 ▾

Put some ice cubes in a cocktail shaker and pour in:

1 measure rye
1 measure Triple Sec
1 measure orange juice
2 dashes crème de noyau

Shake vigorously and strain into a cocktail glass.

P. RAZOUVAIEFF.
European Cocktail Competition, Torquay, 1951.

RYE SOUR 🍸 ▾ 🍸

Put some ice cubes in a cocktail shaker and add:

1 measure rye
$\frac{1}{2}$ *measure lemon juice*
1 teaspoon sugar

Shake and strain into a cocktail or fancy glass. Garnish with a maraschino cherry.

RYE WHISKEY COCKTAIL 🍸 ▾

Put some ice cubes in a mixing glass and pour in:

1 measure rye
1 teaspoon sugar syrup
1 dash Angostura bitters

Stir and strain into a cocktail glass. Garnish with a cherry.

SAZERAC 🍸 ▪

Put some ice cubes in a mixing glass and pour in:

1 measure rye
$\frac{1}{3}$ *measure sugar syrup*
1 dash Angostura bitters

Stir well. Put a dash of Pernod into an old fashioned glass. Turn the glass until the inside is coated with the Pernod. Pour in the rye mixture. Serve with a chaser of chilled water.

SOUTHERN BELLE 🍸 ▾

Put some ice cubes in a cocktail shaker and add:

1 measure bourbon
1 measure double cream
1 teaspoon green crème de menthe
1 teaspoon white crème de cacao

Shake and strain into a cocktail glass.

SOUTHERN GINGER 🍸 ▪

Put some ice cubes in a cocktail shaker and add:

1 measure bourbon
$\frac{1}{2}$ *measure lemon juice*

Shake and strain into a tumbler containing ice cubes. Top up with ginger ale.

TEMPTATION 🍸 ▾

Put some ice cubes in a cocktail shaker and add:

1 measure rye
2 dashes triple sec
2 dashes Dubonnet
2 dashes Pernod

Shake and strain into a cocktail glass.
Squeeze the zest of some lemon and
orange peel over the top and then
drop in the peel.

UP-TO-DATE

Pour into a mixing glass:

½ measure rye
½ measure dry vermouth
¼ measure Grand Marnier
1 dash Angostura bitters

Stir well and strain into a cocktail
glass. Squeeze the zest of some lemon
over the top.

WAIKIKI

Put a half glass of crushed ice into an
electric blender and pour in:

1 measure bourbon
½ measure lemon juice
¼ measure triple sec
1 teaspoon grenadine

Blend and pour into a champagne
saucer.

WARD EIGHT

Put some ice cubes in a cocktail
shaker and add:

1 measure rye
½ measure orange juice
½ measure lemon juice
1 teaspoon grenadine

Shake and strain into a cocktail glass.

WESTMINSTER

Put some ice cubes into a mixing glass
and pour in:

½ measure bourbon or rye
½ measure dry vermouth
3 dashes aurum
1 dash Angostura bitters

Stir and strain into a cocktail glass.

WHISKY TODDY

Put some ice cubes in an old
fashioned glass and pour in:

1 measure bourbon, rye or Canadian
   whisky
½ teaspoon sugar
2 teaspoons water

Stir well to mix. Add a twist of lemon
peel.

Cocktails based on Scotch and Irish

'A torchlight procession marching down your throat' was how one devotee, G.W.E. Russell, once described drinking whisky. Its ability to add courage and colour to a person's body are of long-standing renown. Scotch is the oldest of whiskies. Since the fifteenth century fermented barley has been distilled on the farms in the Scottish Highlands to make aquavitae, in Gaelic 'usquebaugh' the name from which whisky derived.

Whisky is made in the traditional manner from malted barley which has been dried in peat smoke to give the characteristic aroma of Scotch. Pure malt whisky is double distilled in pot stills. You can drink a pure malt whisky with a little water as they do in Scotland. But it would be a pity to use it for cocktails; that would turn an excellent drink into a poor cocktail, because malt whiskies are strong, full bodied, well rounded and do not mix easily with other flavours.

It is better to use blended Scotch whiskies which consist of 20 to 50 per cent malt whisky mixed with grain whisky distilled to a high strength in patent stills. Lighter than malts, blended whiskies go well with a number of spirits. Like Bourbon, Scotch combines handsomely with dry and sweet vermouth.

Irish whiskey is made principally from barley to which is added wheat, oats, rye and maize. It is triple distilled in very large pot stills to a high strength (90°) before being aged. Very different from Scotch whiskies in flavour, Irish whiskey is traditionally drunk with a little water. It is used in some cocktails but particularly in *Irish Coffee* (see Hot Drinks), for a smooth, warming and digestive end to any fine dinner.

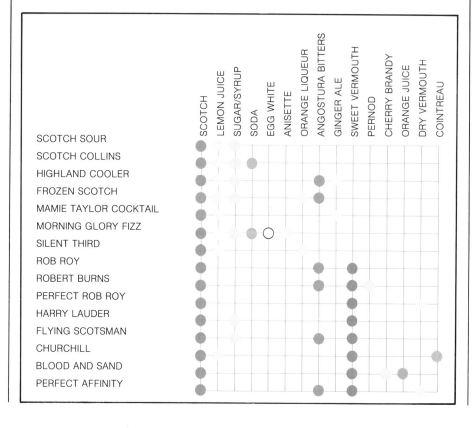

	SCOTCH	LEMON JUICE	SUGAR/SYRUP	SODA	EGG WHITE	ANISETTE	ORANGE LIQUEUR	ANGOSTURA BITTERS	GINGER ALE	SWEET VERMOUTH	PERNOD	CHERRY BRANDY	ORANGE JUICE	DRY VERMOUTH	COINTREAU
SCOTCH SOUR	●	●	●												
SCOTCH COLLINS	●	●	●	●											
HIGHLAND COOLER	●	●	●						●						
FROZEN SCOTCH	●	●						●							
MAMIE TAYLOR COCKTAIL	●	●							●						
MORNING GLORY FIZZ	●	●	●		○										
SILENT THIRD	●	●													●
ROB ROY	●							●		●					
ROBERT BURNS	●							●		●					
PERFECT ROB ROY	●							●		●				●	
HARRY LAUDER	●		●							●					
FLYING SCOTSMAN	●		●					●		●					
CHURCHILL	●									●					●
BLOOD AND SAND	●									●		●	●		
PERFECT AFFINITY	●							●		●				●	

(see Hot Drinks)

AFFINITY COCKTAIL

Put some ice cubes in a cocktail shaker and pour in:

½ measure scotch
½ measure ruby port
½ measure dry sherry
2 dashes Angostura bitters

Shake and strain into an old fashioned glass containing ice cubes.

BARBARY COAST COCKTAIL

Put some ice cubes in a cocktail shaker and add:

½ measure scotch
½ measure gin
½ measure crème de cacao
½ measure double cream

Shake and strain into a cocktail glass. N.B. You may also add a ½ measure of white rum.

BARBICAN

Put some ice cubes in a cocktail shaker and pour in:

1 measure scotch
⅓ measure passion fruit juice
2 dashes Drambuie

Shake and strain into a cocktail glass.

BENEDICT COCKTAIL

Put some ice cubes in an old fashioned glass and pour in:

¾ measure scotch
¾ measure Benedictine

Stir well and top up with ginger ale. Stir again lightly and serve.

BLACK WATCH ▪

Put some ice cubes in an old fashioned glass and pour in:

1 measure scotch
½ measure Kahlúa

Add a splash of soda and stir to mix. Garnish with a twist of lemon peel.

BLOOD AND SAND ⬥ 🍷 ✓

Put some ice cubes in a cocktail shaker and pour in:

½ measure scotch
½ measure sweet vermouth
½ measure cherry brandy
½ measure orange juice

Shake and strain into a balloon glass. Add 2 ice cubes and garnish with a half slice of orange and a cherry.

CHANCELLOR ⬥ 🍸

Pour into a cocktail shaker containing several ice cubes:

1 measure scotch
¼ measure dry vermouth
¼ measure ruby port
2 dashes Angostura bitters

Shake and strain into a cocktail glass. Garnish with a cherry.

CHURCHILL ⬥ 🍸

Pour into a cocktail shaker containing several ice cubes:

1 measure scotch
⅓ measure sweet vermouth
⅓ measure Cointreau
2 teaspoons lemon juice

Shake and strain into a cocktail glass.

Poster by Richard Claverie (1981) for Johnnie Walker.

FLYING SCOTSMAN 🍸

Put some ice cubes in a mixing glass
and pour in:

$\frac{3}{4}$ *measure scotch*
$\frac{3}{4}$ *measure sweet vermouth*
$\frac{1}{2}$ *teaspoon sugar*
1 *dash Angostura bitters*

Stir and strain into a cocktail glass.

FROZEN SCOTCH 🍹

Put a half glass of crushed ice into an
electric blender and pour in:

1 *measure scotch*
1 *measure lemon juice*
$\frac{1}{2}$ *teaspoon sugar*
   dash Cointreau
1 *dash Angostura bitters*
1 *slice pineapple*

Blend for a few seconds. Pour into an
old fashioned glass and garnish with a
wedge of pineapple.

HAIR OF THE DOG 🍸

Put some ice cubes in a cocktail
shaker and add:

1 *measure scotch*
$\frac{1}{2}$ *measure double cream*
$\frac{1}{2}$ *measure clear honey*

Shake and strain into a cocktail glass.

HARRY LAUDER 🍸

Put several ice cubes in a mixing glass
and pour in:

$\frac{3}{4}$ *measure scotch*
$\frac{3}{4}$ *measure sweet vermouth*
1 *teaspoon sugar syrup*

Stir and strain into a cocktail glass.

HIGHLAND COOLER 🍺

Put 2 ice cubes in a tumbler and pour
in:

1 *measure scotch*
juice of $\frac{1}{2}$ lemon
1 *teaspoon sugar syrup*
2 *dashes Angostura bitters*

Stir and top up with ginger ale. Stir
again and serve.

IRISH CHEER 🍸

Put some ice cubes in a mixing glass
and pour in:

1 *measure Irish whiskey*
$\frac{1}{4}$ *measure sweet vermouth*

Mix and strain into a cocktail glass.

KING GEORGE V 🍸

Put some ice cubes in a cocktail
shaker and pour in:

$\frac{1}{3}$ *measure scotch*
$\frac{1}{3}$ *measure gin*
$\frac{1}{3}$ *measure Cointreau*
$\frac{1}{3}$ *measure white crème de cacao*
$\frac{1}{3}$ *measure lemon juice*

Shake and strain into a cocktail glass.

LINSTEAD 🍸

Put some ice cubes in a cocktail
shaker and add:

1 *measure scotch*
1 *measure grapefruit juice*
1 *dash pastis*

Shake and strain into a large cocktail
glass. Squeeze the zest of some lemon
on top and drop in the peel.

LOCH LOMOND COCKTAIL 🍹

Put some ice cubes in a cocktail
shaker and add:

1 *measure scotch*
1 *measure sugar syrup*
a few dashes Angostura bitters

Shake and strain into an old fashioned
glass containing ice cubes.

LOS ANGELES 2 🍸

Put some ice cubes in a cocktail
shaker and add:

1 *measure scotch*
$\frac{1}{2}$ *measure lemon juice*
1 *egg*
1 *dash sweet vermouth*

Shake and strain into a large cocktail
glass. (For variation see p. 82).

MAMIE TAYLOR 🍺

Fill a collins glass with ice cubes and
pour in:

1 *measure scotch*
juice of $\frac{1}{2}$ lime

Stir and top up with ginger ale. Stir
again before serving.

MIAMI BEACH 🍸

Put some ice cubes in a cocktail
shaker and add:

1 *measure scotch*
1 *measure dry vermouth*
$\frac{1}{2}$ *measure grapefruit juice*

Shake and strain into a champagne
saucer. Garnish with a half slice of
lemon and a cherry.

Bienvenue

Bénédictine FÉCAMP.

MORNING GLORY 2

Put some ice cubes in a cocktail shaker and add:

1 measure scotch
1 egg white
1 teaspoon sugar

Shake and strain into a tumbler containing ice cubes. Top up with soda.

MORNING GLORY FIZZ

Put some ice cubes in a cocktail shaker and add:

1 measure scotch
juice of 1 lemon
1 egg white
1 dash anisette
1 teaspoon sugar

Shake thoroughly. Strain into a tumbler containing ice cubes and top up with soda. Garnish with a cherry and a slice of lemon.

ONE IRELAND

Pour into an electric blender:

1 measure Irish whiskey
1 teaspoon green crème de menthe
1 scoop vanilla ice cream

Blend for a few seconds and pour into a champagne saucer. Decorate with a cherry and serve with straws.

PADDY COCKTAIL

Pour into a cocktail shaker containing several ice cubes:

1 measure Irish whiskey
½ measure sweet vermouth
1 dash Angostura bitters

Shake and strain into an old fashioned glass. Drop in a few ice cubes.

PALMER COCKTAIL

Pour into a cocktail shaker containing several ice cubes:

1 measure scotch
1 dash lemon juice
1 dash Angostura bitters

Shake vigorously and strain into a cocktail glass. Decorate with a slice of lemon if desired.

PERFECT AFFINITY

Put some ice cubes in a mixing glass and pour in:

1 measure scotch
¼ measure sweet vermouth
¼ measure dry vermouth
2 dashes Angostura bitters

Shake and strain into a cocktail glass. Garnish with a sliver of lemon peel. N.B. For a sweeter cocktail replace the Angostura bitters with two dashes of Benedictine.

PERFECT ROB ROY

Put some ice cubes in a mixing glass and pour in:

1 measure scotch
¼ measure sweet vermouth
¼ measure dry vermouth

Stir well and strain into a cocktail glass. Garnish with a spiral of lemon peel.

(Left): Benedictine and Scotch inseparable in the Benedict Cocktail (poster by F. Burel, 1981).

Vermouth and Whisky get on well together. Poster designed for Martini & Rossi.

ROBERT BURNS

Put some ice cubes in a mixing glass and pour in:

1 measure scotch
½ measure sweet vermouth
1 dash Angostura bitters
1 dash Pernod

Stir and strain into a cocktail glass.

ROB ROY

Put some ice cubes in a mixing glass and pour in:

1 measure scotch
½ measure sweet vermouth
1 dash Angostura bitters

Stir and strain into a cocktail glass. Garnish with a cherry.

RUSTY NAIL

Put some ice cubes in an old fashioned glass and pour in:

1 measure scotch
1 measure Drambuie

Stir well and serve.

SCOTCH COLLINS

Put some ice cubes in a tumbler and add:

1 measure scotch
1 measure lemon juice
½ measure sugar syrup

Top up with soda and stir lightly. Serve with straws.

SCOTCH FRAPPÉ

Pour 1 measure scotch into an old fashioned glass half filled with crushed ice. Garnish with a sliver of lemon peel.

Rob Roy in a Lalique crystal glass.

SCOTCH SOUR

Put some ice cubes in a cocktail shaker and pour in:

1 measure scotch
½ measure lemon juice
1 teaspoon sugar syrup

Shake and strain into a cocktail glass. Garnish with a cherry on a cocktail stick.

SHAMROCK

Put some ice cubes in a mixing glass and pour in:

½ measure Irish whiskey
½ measure dry vermouth
3 dashes green Chartreuse
3 dashes green crème de menthe

Stir well and strain into a cocktail glass.

SILENT THIRD

Pour into a cocktail shaker containing some ice cubes:

1 measure scotch
1 measure Cointreau
1 measure lemon juice

Shake and strain into a cocktail glass. Garnish with a sliver of lemon peel.

WEMBLEY

Pour into a cocktail shaker containing some ice cubes:

½ measure scotch
½ measure dry vermouth
½ measure pineapple juice

Shake and strain into a cocktail glass. Garnish with a cube of pineapple impaled on a cocktail stick.

SCOTCH MIST

Pour 1 measure scotch and 1 glassful of crushed ice into a cocktail shaker. Shake and pour without straining into an old fashioned glass. Garnish with a twist of lemon peel. Serve with short straws.

SCOTCH OLD FASHIONED

Put a cube of sugar in an old fashioned glass. Moisten it with a few dashes of Angostura bitters. Pour in just enough water to dissolve the sugar. Drop in 2 or 3 ice cubes and pour in 1 measure scotch. Stir.

WHISKY COBBLER ♥

Fill a balloon glass with ice cubes and add:

1 measure scotch
1 teaspoon sugar
a few dashes triple sec

Stir to mix. Garnish with fresh fruit. Serve with straws.

WHISKY COCKTAIL ⬚ ¥

Put some ice cubes in a mixing glass and pour in:

1 measure scotch
¼ measure triple sec
2 dashes Angostura bitters

Stir well and strain into a cocktail glass. Garnish with a cherry.

WHISKY-MINT COCKTAIL ⬚ ¥

First infuse 2 sachets mint tea in 225 ml/8 fl oz boiling water. Allow to cool and discard the sachets. Pour the infusion into a cocktail shaker and put in some ice cubes. Add:

4 measures scotch
juice of 2 limes

Shake well and strain into four cocktail glasses. Garnish with mint leaves.
SERVES 4

WHISKY SANGAREE ◧

Fill an old fashioned glass with crushed ice and pour in:

1 measure scotch
1 measure water

Stir to mix. Sprinkle grated nutmeg over the top and serve with short straws.

WHIZZ BANG ⬚ ¥

Put some ice cubes in a mixing glass and pour in:

1 measure scotch
⅓ measure dry vermouth
2 dashes Pernod
2 dashes grenadine
2 dashes Angostura bitters

Stir vigorously and strain into a cocktail glass.

Tequila-based Cocktails

Tequila is a Mexican spirit distilled from the fermented sap of the American aloe. Its name comes from the town in southern Mexico where it was first made at the beginning of this century. Tequila was little known outside of Mexico for a long time, until its use in cocktails established its international reputation. It is now manufactured in a number of countries other than Mexico, including the United States. Drunk straight, Mexican-style, however, tequila is an experience not to be missed—but not to be overdone (see *Tequila Straight*). Diluted by a variety of fruit juices, it gives the mixture the strength of an original spirit and an uncommon flavour. The best-known cocktail, on which its fame was based, is the *Margarita*, served in a glass rimmed with salt. Sipping the lemony alcohol through the salt is a tangy, heady pleasure. The other internationally famous cocktail is the *Tequila Sunrise*, as lovely to behold as it is delicious to drink. Tequila is softened by the addition of orange liqueur but enlivened by lemon juice.

	TEQUILA	LEMON JUICE	COINTREAU	SALT	GRENADINE SYRUP	CRÈME DE CASSIS	SODA	ORANGE JUICE	ORANGE FLOWER WATER	GRAPEFRUIT JUICE
MARGARITA	●		●	●						
AMERICAN LEGION MARGARITA	●		●	●						
TEQUILA SUNSET	●				●	●	●			
TEQUILA SUNRISE	●				●			●		
CHAPALA	●					●		●		
ICE-BREAKER	●				●	●				●
CONCHITA	●									●
MOCKINGBIRD	●									
TEQUILA DAISY	●				●		●			
TEQUILA STRAIGHT	●									

ACAPULCO

Put some crushed ice in a cocktail shaker and add:

1 measure tequila
1 measure white rum
2 measures pineapple juice
1 measure grapefruit juice
1 measure coconut milk

Shake and strain into a collins glass filled with ice cubes. Garnish with a pineapple wedge and a cherry.

AMBASSADOR

Put some ice cubes in a collins glass and pour in:

1 measure tequila
1 teaspoon sugar syrup

Top up with orange juice and stir to mix. Decorate with an orange slice and a cherry. Serve with a swizzle stick and straws.

AMERICAN LEGION MARGARITA

Put some ice cubes in a cocktail shaker and pour in:

1 measure tequila
½ measure Cointreau
¼ measure lemon juice
¼ measure lime juice

First dampen the rim of a cocktail glass with lemon juice and dip it into fine salt to frost. Shake the cocktail and pour it into the glass.

AZTECA

Put a half glass of crushed ice into an electric blender and add:

1 measure tequila
juice of ½ lime
½ teaspoon sugar
1 small slice mango

Blend for a few seconds and strain into a champagne saucer. Decorate with a half slice of lime and serve with short straws.

BLOODY BULL

Put 2 to 3 cubes of ice in an old fashioned glass and add:

1 measure tequila
1 dash lemon juice
2 measures tomato juice
2 measures cold beef bouillon

Stir to mix. Garnish with a lemon slice and celery leaves.

CHAPALA

Put some ice cubes in a cocktail shaker and add:

1 measure tequila

$\frac{1}{2}$ *measure lemon juice*
$\frac{1}{2}$ *measure orange juice*
$\frac{1}{2}$ *measure grenadine*
2 drops orange flower water

Shake and strain into a balloon glass containing 1 or 2 ice cubes. Garnish with a slice of lemon and a slice of orange. Serve with straws.

COCONUT TEQUILA

Put a half glass of crushed ice into an electric blender and add:

1 measure tequila
$\frac{1}{2}$ *measure lemon juice*
$\frac{1}{2}$ *measure coconut milk*
3 dashes maraschino

Blend for a few seconds and pour into a collins glass. Garnish with a lemon slice.

CONCHITA

Pour into a cocktail shaker containing several ice cubes:

1 measure tequila
1 measure grapefruit juice
2 dashes lemon juice

Shake and strain into a cocktail glass. Add 2 ice cubes and serve.

DURANGO

Pour into a cocktail shaker containing several ice cubes:

1 measure tequila
3 measures grapefruit juice
1 teaspoon orgeat syrup

Shake and strain into collins glass filled with ice cubes. Top up with soda and garnish with fresh mint leaves, a segment of grapefruit and a cherry. Serve with straws.

Peruvian vessel used for alcohol in the pre-Columbian era.

EARTHQUAKE

Put a half glass of crushed ice into an electric blender and add:

1 measure tequila
$\frac{1}{2}$ *measure grenadine*
2–3 strawberries
2–3 dashes Angostura bitters

Blend for several seconds. Pour into a champagne saucer and garnish with a lemon slice and a strawberry.

EL DIABLO

Squeeze the juice of $\frac{1}{2}$ lime into a tumbler filled with ice cubes and drop in the shell. Then add:

1 measure tequila
$\frac{1}{2}$ *measure crème de cassis*

Top up with ginger ale and stir. Serve with straws.

EVERGREEN

Put some ice cubes in a mixing glass and add:

1 measure tequila
$\frac{1}{2}$ *measure green crème de menthe*
$\frac{1}{4}$ *measure Galliano*
3 measures pineapple juice

Stir and strain into a balloon glass. Garnish with a mint sprig.

FROSTBITE

Put some ice cubes in a cocktail shaker and add:

1 measure tequila
1 measure double cream
1 measure white crème de cacao

Shake and strain into a cocktail glass. Sprinkle with grated nutmeg.

FROZEN STRAWBERRY 🍷 🍸

Put a half glass of crushed ice into an electric blender and pour in:

1 measure tequila
1 measure strawberry liqueur
4 ripe strawberries
1 dash lemon juice

Blend for a few seconds. Pour without straining into a champagne saucer and garnish with a lemon slice and a strawberry.

ICE-BREAKER 🍶 🍹

Pour into a cocktail shaker containing several ice cubes:

1 measure tequila
½ measure Cointreau
1 measure grapefruit juice
2 teaspoons grenadine

Shake and strain into a tumbler filled with ice cubes. Serve with fancy straws.

MARGARITA 🍶 🍸

Pour into a cocktail shaker containing several ice cubes:

1 measure tequila
1 measure lemon or lime juice
½ measure Cointreau

First dampen the rim of a champagne saucer with lemon juice and dip it into fine salt to frost. Shake the cocktail and strain it into the glass. N.B. There are many variations but this is one of the commonest. Reduce the amount of lemon juice, if you prefer.

Margarita in a Lalique crystal glass.

MARIA THERESA ♦ ♟

Put some ice cubes in a cocktail shaker and add:

1 measure tequila
½ measure lime juice
½ measure bilberry juice

Shake and strain into a champagne saucer.

MATADOR ♦ ♟

Put some crushed ice into a cocktail shaker and add:

1 measure tequila
2 measures pineapple juice
1 teaspoon lemon juice

Shake and strain into a balloon glass. Add some ice cubes and serve with short straws.

MOCKINGBIRD ▪

Fill an old fashioned glass with ice cubes and pour in:

1 measure tequila
2 measures grapefruit juice
1 dash lime juice

Stir to mix. Garnish with a cherry.

CBMA, Mexico.

PANCHO VILLA ♦ ♟

Put some ice cubes in a cocktail shaker and pour in:

1 measure Cuervo tequila
½ measure Tía Maria
1 teaspoon Cointreau

Shake and strain into a cocktail glass. Decorate with a lemon slice, a brandied cherry and a coffee bean.

Jean-Francois Saurin, Monte Carlo. ABF, France.

PICADOR COCKTAIL ▨ ♟

Put some crushed ice into a mixing glass and add:

1 measure tequila
1 measure kahlúa

Stir well and strain into a cocktail glass. Garnish with a sliver of lemon peel.

SILK STOCKINGS ▨ ♟

Put a half glass of crushed ice into an electric blender and add:

1 measure tequila
⅓ measure white crème de cacao
⅓ measure grenadine
2 measures powdered milk

Blend for a few seconds and pour into a balloon glass. Sprinkle some cinnamon on top and garnish with a cherry.

CBMA, Mexico.

TEQUILA COCKTAIL ▨ ♟

Put a half glass of crushed ice into an electric blender and add:

1 measure tequila
juice of 1 lime
1 dash sugar syrup
1 dash grenadine

Blend well and strain into a cocktail glass. Garnish with a slice of lime.

TEQUILA DAISY ♦ ♟

Put some ice cubes in a cocktail shaker and add:

1 measure tequila
juice of ½ lime
2 teaspoons grenadine

Shake and strain into a balloon glass half full of crushed ice. Top up with soda and stir lightly before serving.

TEQUILA ORANGE ▯

Put 1 measure of tequila into a tumbler full of ice cubes. Top up with orange juice.

TEQUILA SUNRISE ♟

Put some ice cubes in a goblet and pour in 1 measure tequila. Top up with orange juice and stir well to mix. Add ½ measure grenadine, and when it sinks to the bottom the shaded colours will resemble a sunrise. Place an orange slice on the rim of the glass and serve with 2 straws and a stirrer.

TEQUILA SUNSET ▯

Put some ice cubes in a tumbler and add:

1 measure tequila
½ measure lemon juice

Top up with soda and stir to mix. Now add with a light hand:

2 dashes grenadine
2 dashes crème de cassis

These will sink slowly giving a splendid effect. Place a lemon slice on the rim of the glass. Serve with straws and a stirrer.

TEQUILA STRAIGHT ▮

Pour 1 measure of tequila into a liqueur glass. Suck a quarter lemon, put a little salt on your tongue and drink down the tequila in one gulp.

N.B. Another way is to put a pinch of salt on the back of the hand (in the hollow between the thumb and the first finger), lick the salt, suck juice out of a lemon quarter, and finally toss back the tequila at a gulp.

TEQUINI

Put some ice cubes in a mixing glass and pour in:

1 measure tequila
⅓ measure dry vermouth

Stir and strain into a cocktail glass. Squeeze the zest of some lemon over the top and drop in the peel. Drop in a green olive and serve.

TNT (TEQUILA AND TONIC)

Squeeze the juice of ½ lime into a tumbler. Drop in the shell. Add some ice cubes and 1 measure tequila. Top up with tonic and stir well before serving.

Tequila Sunrise in a Lalique crystal glass.

Cocktails based on Apéritifs and Cocktail Apéritifs

The word apéritif is applied to all drinks which stimulate the appetite, so it would follow that apéritifs are supposed to make you want to eat. It is not really so: many spirits produce the opposite effect. But dieticians agree that sugar, bitter mixtures and a moderate amount of alcohol do rouse the appetite.

Sweet or flavoured wines and spirits based on plant extracts are the ones most commonly classed as apéritifs. These are either made from unfermented grape juice mixed with brandy (such as Pineau des Charentes) or from grape juice to which brandy has been added during fermentation (like port, sherry, or madeira). Vermouth and other wine-based apéritifs could be classed in the same family if they were made in a less complicated way, for they are indeed wines to which fermented extracts of plants and herbs have been added. Spirits based on plant extracts are obtained by macerating or distilling herbs or other plants: bitters such as Gentiane and Campari and aniseed-flavoured drinks like pastis and Pernod belong to this category.

With all the contrasting flavours of these apéritifs it would be natural to assume that there are a great many cocktails with a wide range of colours and tastes in this class. But in fact very few have achieved popularity. Most of the apéritifs are themselves sophisticated cocktails and do not mix readily with other drinks. Pineau of Charentes, for example, is a cocktail of grape juice and brandy. The flavoured wines are already complex mixtures of wines from various regions, with different herbs.

Happy Blends

Campari is traditionally drunk with soda, but because of its original taste and colour it is one of the bitters most frequently used in cocktails: *Americano* is the best known example and there are a number of successful variants (see table opposite below).

There are numerous recipes based on absinthe substitutes and pastis, the best known being *Absinthe Drip*, *Parrot*, *Tomato* and *Mauresque* (see table oppo-

Poster produced at the end of the nineteenth century for Cusenier's Sherry Vermouth.

site) A number of cocktails are based on sherry mixed with flavoured wines (*Adonis, Amontillado Cocktail*), bitters and even Tequila (see table opposite above).

Dry vermouth can be the basis of certain cocktails whose sweetness varies according to the other ingredients.

PIMM'S NO 1

James Pimm ran an oyster bar in the City of London and in 1840 he invented a gin sling for his customers. It was so successful that his successors started to bottle and sell it commercially.

ABSINTHE COCKTAIL

Put some ice cubes in a mixing glass and pour in:

1 measure Pernod
1 dash anisette
1 dash orgeat syrup
2 dashes Angostura bitters

Mix well and strain into a cocktail glass.

ABSINTHE DRIP

Pour 1 measure of absinthe substitute (Pernod) into an old fashioned glass. Put a lump of sugar into a strainer and balance the strainer over the glass. Put a good tablespoon of shaved ice over the sugar. Pour over some cold water. When the sugar and water have dripped on to the Pernod the drink is ready to serve.

ABSINTHE SPECIAL

Put some ice cubes in a cocktail shaker and add:

½ measure Pernod
½ measure gin
1 dash grenadine
1 dash Angostura bitters

Shake and strain into a cocktail glass.

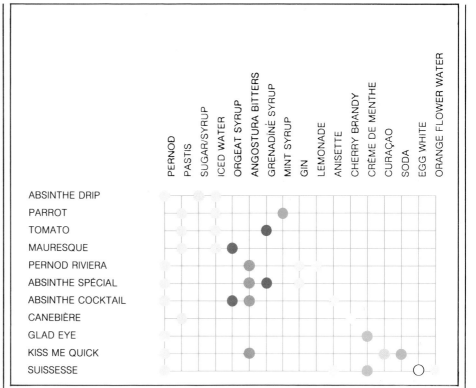

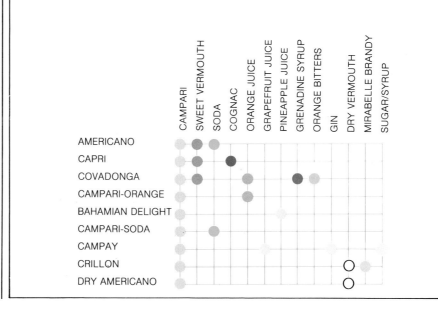

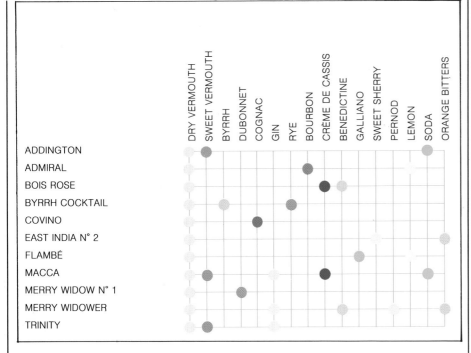

Poster designed by Guydo

ST. RAPHAËL QUINQUINA

ADDINGTON

Put some ice cubes in a mixing glass and pour in:

1 measure dry vermouth
1 measure sweet vermouth

Stir well and strain into a small tumbler. Add 2 ice cubes and top up with soda.

ADMIRAL

Put some ice cubes in a cocktail shaker and pour in:

1 measure dry vermouth
½ measure bourbon

Shake and strain into a small tumbler. Squeeze the juice of ½ lemon over the top and drop in the squeezed out shell. Add some ice cubes and serve.

ADONIS

Pour into a mixing glass containing some ice cubes:

1 measure dry sherry
½ measure sweet vermouth
1–2 dashes Angostura bitters

Stir and strain into a cocktail glass. Garnish with a sliver of orange peel. N.B. For a sweeter cocktail use sweet sherry instead of dry.

AMERICANO

Put 2 or 3 ice cubes in an old fashioned glass and pour in:

1 measure Campari
1 measure sweet vermouth

Stir well and top up with soda. Garnish with a half slice of orange and serve with a swizzle stick.

N.B. You can vary the proportions of Campari to vermouth try $1\frac{1}{2}$ to $\frac{1}{2}$ or $1\frac{1}{4}$ to $\frac{3}{4}$ according to taste. John Doxat in *Stirred, Not Shaken* suggests using a cocktail shaker.

AMER PICON COCKTAIL

Put some ice cubes in a cocktail shaker and pour in:

1 measure Amer Picon
1 measure sweet vermouth

Shake and pour into a cocktail glass.

AMER PICON COOLER

Put some ice cubes in a cocktail shaker and pour in:

1 measure Amer Picon
$\frac{2}{3}$ measure gin
1 dash lemon juice
1 dash sugar syrup

Shake and strain into a tumbler filled with ice cubes. Top up with soda.

AMER PICON HIGHBALL

Pour into a mixing glass containing several ice cubes:

1 measure Amer Picon
$\frac{1}{2}$ measure grenadine

Stir and strain into a collins glass filled with ice cubes. Top up with soda.

AMONTILLADO COCKTAIL

Pour into a tumbler filled with ice cubes:

$\frac{1}{2}$ measure Amontillado sherry
$\frac{1}{2}$ measure Dubonnet

Stir to mix. Add a twist of lemon.

Poster by Tamagno, 1900, extolling the virtues of Cusenier absinthe.

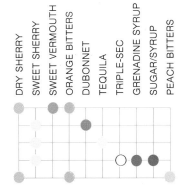

	DRY SHERRY	SWEET SHERRY	SWEET VERMOUTH	ORANGE BITTERS	DUBONNET	TEQUILA	TRIPLE-SEC	GRENADINE SYRUP	SUGAR/SYRUP	PEACH BITTERS
ADONIS		●	●	●						
AMONTILLADO COCKTAIL	○				●					
MEXICO Y ESPAÑA	○					●				
SHERRY COBBLER	○							○	●	●
SHERRY COCKTAIL	●			●						●

ANGOSTURA FIZZ 🍾▮

Pour into a cocktail shaker containing several ice cubes:

1 measure Angostura bitters
1 teaspoon grenadine
1 teaspoon cream
1 egg white
juice of 1 lime

Shake and strain into a tumbler filled with ice cubes. Top up with soda and garnish with a twist of lemon peel.

ANTOINE 🍸

Put 2 ice cubes in a balloon glass. Add:

1 measure Monin triple lime liqueur
2 dashes crème de cassis

Top up with orange juice, stir to mix and garnish with an orange slice.

AQUAVIT FIZZ 🍾▮

Pour into a cocktail shaker containing several ice cubes:

1 measure aquavit
$\frac{1}{4}$ measure cherry brandy
$\frac{1}{4}$ measure lemon juice
1 egg white
2–3 teaspoons sugar syrup

Shake and strain into a collins glass containing some ice cubes. Top up with soda.

ARAK COOLER 🍾▮

Put some ice cubes in a cocktail shaker and add:

1 measure arak
$\frac{1}{3}$ measure white rum
1 teaspoon lemon juice
1 teaspoon sugar syrup

Shake and strain into a tumbler filled with ice cubes. Top up with soda and stir before serving.
N.B. For a deadlier drink top up with champagne instead of soda.

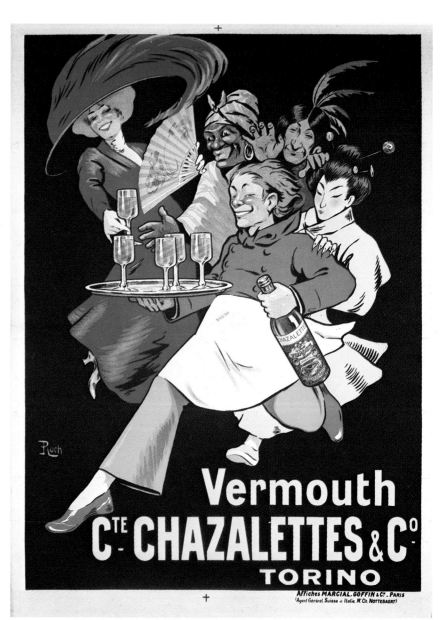

Poster designed by Roch for Vermouth from Cte Chazalettes & Co, Turin.

ATTILA

Put some ice cubes in a mixing glass
and pour in:

1 measure Banyuls
½ measure vodka

Stir and strain into a cocktail glass.
Dilute with the same quantity of soda.
Garnish with a sliver of lemon peel.

AURUM

Put some ice cubes in a mixing glass
and pour in:

½ measure aurum
½ measure gin
1 measure sweet vermouth

Stir well and strain into a large
cocktail glass. Drop in an ice cube.

Americano in a Baccarat glass. (See p.102)

AVIATION

Put some ice cubes in a mixing glass
and pour in:

1 measure Dubonnet
1 measure sweet sherry

Stir and strain into a cocktail glass.
Garnish with a twist of orange peel.

BAHAMIAN DELIGHT

Put some ice cubes in a mixing glass
and pour in:

1½ measures Campari
1½ measures pineapple juice

Stir and strain into a balloon glass
containing 3 ice cubes. Garnish with a
cherry.

BITTER HIGHBALL

Put 2 to 3 ice cubes in a tumbler and
pour in 1 measure Angostura bitters.
Top up with soda or ginger ale and
garnish with a twist of lemon peel.
Stir before serving.

BOIS ROSE

Put some ice cubes in a mixing glass
and pour in:

1 measure dry vermouth
½ measure crème de cassis
½ measure Benedictine

Stir well and strain into a cocktail
glass. Garnish with a cherry.

BYRRH-CASSIS

Put 2 or 3 ice cubes in an old
fashioned glass and pour in:

1 measure Byrrh
3 dashes crème de cassis

Stir and serve.

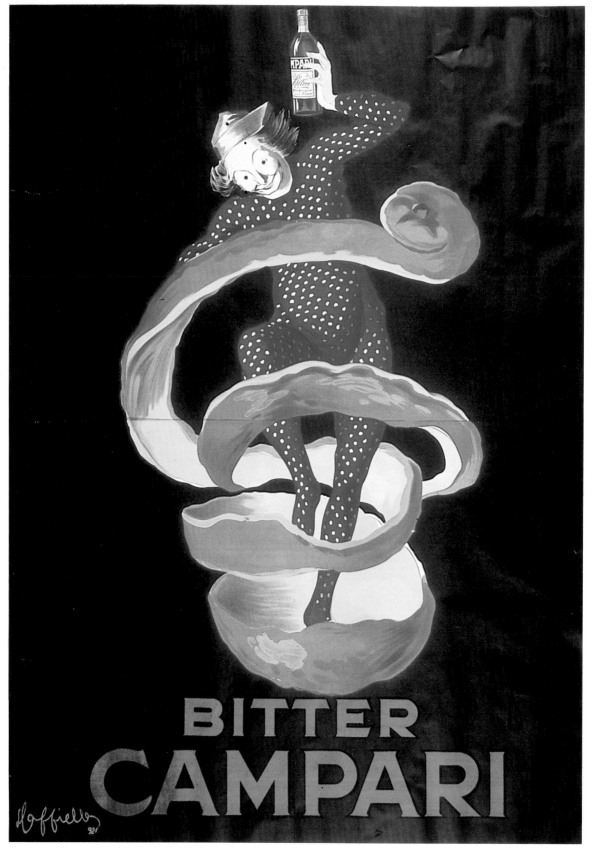

*Cappiello
lithograph,
Devambez Studio,
1921.*

BYRRH COCKTAIL 🍶 🍸

Put some ice cubes in a cocktail shaker and add:

½ measure Byrrh
½ measure dry vermouth
½ measure rye

Shake and strain into a cocktail glass. N.B. There are many similar recipes that replace the rye with gin or brandy, but rye is best.

CAMPARI ORANGE ▮▮

Put 1 measure Campari in a tumbler filled with ice cubes. Top up with orange juice.

CAMPARI SHAKERATO 🍶 🍸

Put 1 measure Campari into a cocktail shaker with several ice cubes. Shake and strain into a cocktail glass.

CAMPAY 🍶 🍷

Put some ice cubes in a cocktail shaker and add:

1 measure gin
1 measure Campari
2 measures grapefruit juice
1 teaspoon sugar

Shake well and strain into a balloon glass. Decorate with a fine spiral of lemon peel. Serve with straws.

CANEBIÈRE 🍶 🍸

Put some ice cubes in a cocktail shaker and add:

1 measure pastis
⅔ measure cherry brandy

Shake well and strain into a cocktail glass.

CAPRI 🍶 🍸

Put some ice cubes in a mixing glass and add:

½ measure Campari
½ measure sweet Martini
½ measure cognac

Stir and strain into a cocktail glass. Drop in some ice cubes and a twist of lemon peel.

ROGER LABET, Lugano.

COVADONGA 🍶 🍸

Put some ice cubes in a cocktail shaker and add:

1½ measures Campari
1 measure sweet vermouth
1 measure orange juice
½ measure grenadine
4–5 dashes Angostura bitters

Shake and strain into a large cocktail glass. Garnish with a half slice of orange.

COVINO 🍶 🍸

Pour into a mixing glass containing several ice cubes:

1 measure Noilly Prat
1 measure Martell cognac

Stir vigorously and strain into a cocktail glass. Add a twist of lemon peel.

ANDRÉ PEUTEUIL, Paris.

CRILLON 🍶 ▮

Pour into a cocktail shaker containing several ice cubes:

⅓ measure Campari
⅓ measure mirabelle eau-de-vie
1 measure Noilly Prat

Shake and strain into an old fashioned glass. Add some ice cubes and garnish with an orange slice and a sliver of lemon peel.

MARCEL PACE, Paris.

DRY AMERICANO 🍶 🍸

Pour into a mixing glass containing several ice cubes:

1 measure Campari
1 measure Noilly Prat

Stir and strain into a cocktail glass. Drop in 2 ice cubes and garnish with a slice of orange.

DUBONNET FIZZ 🍶 ▮

Put some ice cubes in a cocktail shaker and pour in:

2 measures Dubonnet
1 teaspoon cherry brandy
juice of ½ orange
juice of ¼ lemon

Shake and strain into an old fashioned glass containing ice cubes. Top up with soda and stir before serving.

EAST INDIA 2 🍶 🍸

Pour into a cocktail shaker containing several ice cubes:

1 measure Noilly Prat
1 measure sweet sherry
1 dash Angostura bitters

Shake and strain into a cocktail glass.

FLAMBÉ ♈

Fill a champagne saucer with crushed ice and pour in:

1 measure dry vermouth
1 measure lemon juice

Place a ¼ lemon on top. Heat 1 measure Galliano. Set it alight and pour it over the top. Serve immediately.

FOND DE CULOTTE ♈

Put 2 or 3 ice cubes in a balloon glass and add:

1 measure Suze
¼ measure crème de cassis

Top up with water, if you like.

Still life, painted in the twenties for Suze.

GLAD EYE ♊ ♈

Put several ice cubes in a cocktail shaker and add:

1 measure Pernod
½ measure white crème de menthe

Shake and strain into a cocktail glass.

KISS ME QUICK ♊ ▮

Put several ice cubes in a cocktail shaker and add:

1 measure Pernod
a few dashes curaçao
a few dashes Angostura bitters

Shake and strain into a tumbler. Drop in 2 or 3 ice cubes and top up with soda.

MACCA ▮

Put some ice cubes in a tumbler and add:

½ measure sweet vermouth
½ measure dry vermouth
½ measure gin
1 dash crème de cassis

Top up with soda and stir to mix. Squeeze some lemon peel to extract the zest over the top and drop in the peel.

MAURESQUE ▮

Pour into a tumbler:

1 measure pastis
⅓ measure orgeat syrup

Top up with iced water and stir before serving.

MERRY WIDOW 1 ▯ ♈

Pour into a mixing glass containing several ice cubes:

1 measure dry vermouth
1 measure Dubonnet

Stir well and strain into a cocktail glass. Squeeze some lemon peel over the top to extract the zest and drop in the peel.

MERRY WIDOW 2 ▯ ♈

Put some ice cubes in a mixing glass and pour in:

1 measure Byrrh
1 measure gin

Stir well and strain into a cocktail glass.

MERRY WIDOWER 🍸 ❢

Put some ice cubes in a cocktail shaker and add:

1 measure dry vermouth
1 measure gin
2 dashes Pernod
2 dashes Benedictine
1 dash Angostura bitters

Shake and strain into a cocktail glass.

MEXICO Y ESPAÑA ❢ ❢

Put some ice cubes in a mixing glass and pour in:

1 measure amontillado sherry
1 measure tequila

Stir and strain into a cocktail glass. Garnish with a green olive.

MICHEL ❢ ❢

Put several ice cubes in a mixing glass and pour in:

1 measure Monin triple lime liqueur
½ measure gin
1 dash strawberry syrup

Stir and strain into a cocktail glass. Drop in a twist of lemon peel.

MICHEL BIGOT, PARIS.

MORNING GLORY DAISIES ❢ ❢

Put several ice cubes in a cocktail shaker and add:

1½ measures rum, gin, whisky, brandy or calvados
3 teaspoons egg white
2 teaspoons Pernod
1 teaspoon sugar

Shake thoroughly. Strain into a tumbler filled with ice cubes. Top up with soda or tonic.

Mauresque, Parrot and Tomato, three colourful cocktails made with pastis.

MOUNT FUJI 🗑 ❢

Put some crushed ice into an electric blender and add:

1 measure calvados
1 measure white rum
1 measure Southern Comfort
juice of ½ lime
3 teaspoons sugar

Blend for a few seconds and pour without straining into an old fashioned glass.

ORANGE BLOOM ❢ ❢

Put several ice cubes into a cocktail shaker and add:

1 measure gin
⅓ measure Cointreau
⅓ measure sweet vermouth

Shake and strain into a cocktail glass.

ORANGE FIZZ ❢ ❢

Put several ice cubes in a cocktail shaker and add:

1 measure gin
2 teaspoons Cointreau
2 teaspoons lemon juice
1 teaspoon sugar syrup
2 dashes Angostura bitters

Shake and strain into a tumbler. Top up with soda. Squeeze the juice of a quarter orange over the top. Garnish with a half slice of orange.

PARROT ❢

Pour into a large tumbler:

1 measure pastis
3 dashes mint syrup

Top up with iced water. Decorate with a cucumber slice and a mintsprig.

PERNOD BITTER LEMON ♀

Put 2 or 3 ice cubes in a balloon glass and add:

1 measure Pernod
4 measures bitter lemon

Stir before serving.

PERNOD RIVIERA ▮

Pour into a large tumbler containing 2 or 3 ice cubes:

1 dash Angostura bitters
½ measure gin
1 measure Pernod

Top up with lemonade and garnish with a lemon slice.

PIMM'S NO 1 ▮

Put a few ice cubes in a tumbler and pour in 2 measures Pimm's No 1. Top up with soda or lemonade. Garnish with cucumber peel, a mint sprig, a slice of orange, a slice of lemon and a cherry. Serve with straws.
N.B. The original Pimm's No 1 was topped up with lemonade and served ungarnished.

PINK EXPLOSION ❶ ♈

Put some ice cubes in a cocktail shaker and add:

¾ measure Grand Marnier
½ measure Pernod
¾ measure Noilly Prat
1½ measures double cream
1 dash grenadine
1 dash Angostura bitters

Shake well and strain into a champagne saucer. Decorate with a strawberry fixed on to the rim of the glass and a small paper parasol.

PINK PUSSY ▮

Pour into a collins glass:

1 measure Campari
½ measure peach liqueur

Add some ice cubes and top up with bitter lemon.

PRELUDE ❶ ♈

Put several ice cubes in a cocktail shaker and pour in:

4⁄10 Noilly Prat
2⁄10 Combier peach liqueur
1⁄10 Gordon's gin
3⁄10 peach juice
1 dash raspberry juice
½ teaspoon clear honey

Shake and strain into a cocktail glass. Decorate with peach slices that have been macerated in grenadine and a sprig of mint.

J-F. Sestillange, Rennes.
ABF, France.

ROSE 2 ▽ ♈

Put several ice cubes in a mixing glass and add:

1 measure dry vermouth
¼ measure cherry brandy
¼ measure kirsch

Stir well and strain into a cocktail glass. Garnish with a cherry.

SHERRY COBBLER ♀

Pour into a large goblet filled with crushed ice:

1 teaspoon sugar syrup
1 dash grenadine

1 dash triple sec
2 measures amontillado sherry

Stir well with a spoon until the outside of the glass becomes frosted. Add slices of fruit in season and serve with straws.

SHERRY COCKTAIL ❶ ♈

Put several ice cubes in a cocktail shaker and add:

3 measures dry sherry
2 dashes orange bitters
1 dash peach bitters

Shake and strain into a cocktail glass.

SINGAPORE SLING ❶ ▮

Put some ice cubes in a cocktail shaker and pour in:

1 measure cherry brandy
1 measure gin
1 measure lemon juice

Shake and strain into a tumbler. Top up with iced soda.

SUISSESSE ❶ ♈

Put some ice cubes in a cocktail shaker and add:

1 measure Pernod
1 dash anisette
1 dash white crème de menthe
1 egg white
a few drops orange flower water

Shake thoroughly and strain into a cocktail glass.

TAMPICO ▽ ♀

Put several ice cubes in a mixing glass and pour in:

1 measure Campari
1 measure Cointreau
¼ measure lemon juice

Stir well and strain into a balloon glass. Top up with tonic and stir to mix. Garnish with an orange slice and a cherry.

RAOUL SONDREZ AND RUDOLPF SLAVICK.

TOMATO

Pour into a tumbler:

1 measure pastis
3 dashes grenadine

Top up with iced water. Decorate with a cherry.

TRINITY

Put several ice cubes in a mixing glass and add:

½ measure dry vermouth
½ measure sweet vermouth
½ measure gin

Stir and strain into a cocktail glass.

Anis from Pernod Fils (now Pernod), product of the famous firm founded at Couvet in Switzerland in 1798, and moved to Pontarlier in 1805.

Cocktails based on Digestives and Cocktail Digestives

Whilst it is true that certain substances and plant extracts are aids to digestion, unfortunately there are a great variety of alcoholic drinks which, with the passing of time or as a result of legislation, have lost some or all of their important digestive qualities.

Nowadays the pre-dinner drink seems to have replaced the ritual after-dinner drink, be it a liqueur, a fine brandy or a 'little something'. Quite rightly people are cautious about their alcoholic intake. But the true epicure is careful to leave room at the end of the meal for the pleasure of savouring a final treat for the palate. The classic after dinner drink is a great brandy—a Grande Champagne cognac, a vintage armagnac, or a noble fruit brandy. Alternatively, many people choose fine vintage port. However, there are also some delicious and sophisticated mixtures:
- with mint, table below right
- with cream, table opposite
- with apricot, table on page 114
- with orange, table below left

AFTER DINNER

Put several ice cubes in a cocktail shaker and add:

1 measure curaçao
1 measure apricot brandy
1 measure lime juice

Shake and strain into a cocktail glass.

AFTER DINNER COCKTAIL

Put several ice cubes in a mixing glass and add:

1 measure maraschino
1 measure kirsch
2 dashes curaçao
2 dashes Angostura bitters

Stir and pour into a balloon glass. Top up with pineapple juice to taste. Squeeze the zest from one or two pieces of lemon peel on top and drop in the peel.

ALMOND EYE

Put some ice cubes in a cocktail shaker and add:

1 measure marsala
1 measure crème de cacao
1 measure double cream

Shake and strain into a cocktail glass.

AMABILE BEONE

Put some ice cubes in a cocktail shaker and add:

½ measure Drambuie
1 measure green crème de menthe
1 dash Pernod
a little sugar

Dampen the rim of a cocktail glass with Pernod and dip into fine sugar to frost. Shake the cocktail and strain it into the glass.

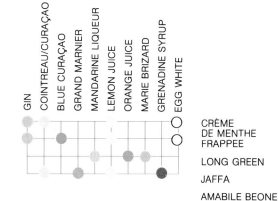

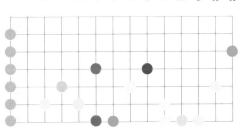

ANGEL'S DELIGHT (POUSSE-CAFÉ) ❗

A pousse-café is composed of several different coloured liqueurs poured carefully into a liqueur glass one by one so that they float on top of each other. Use the back of a spoon to help you pour in order:

½ measure grenadine
½ measure crème d'Yvette
½ measure double cream

ANGEL'S DREAM (POUSSE-CAFÉ) ❗

Pour carefully into a liqueur glass one after the other and in the order given:

½ measure maraschino
½ measure crème d'Yvette
½ measure cognac

ANGEL'S KISS (POUSSE-CAFÉ) ❗

Pour carefully into a liqueur glass one after the other and in the order given below:

½ measure brown crème de cacao
½ measure crème d'Yvette
½ measure cognac
½ measure double cream

ANGEL'S TIP (POUSSE-CAFÉ) ❗

Pour carefully into a liqueur glass one after the other and in the order given below:

¾ measure crème de cacao
¼ measure double cream

ANGEL'S TIT (POUSSE-CAFÉ) ❗

Pour carefully into a liqueur glass one after the other:

1 measure maraschino
⅓ measure double cream

Place a cherry in the centre of the cream.

ANGEL'S WING (POUSSE-CAFÉ) ❗

Pour carefully into a liqueur glass one after the other and in the order given:

1 measure crème de cacao
1 measure cognac
1 measure double cream

ANTICIPATION 🗑 🍸

Put some crushed ice in an electric blender and add:

2 measures Irish Velvet
1 scoop vanilla (or other flavour) ice cream

Blend for 1 minute. Pour into a champagne saucer and sprinkle with grated dark chocolate.
N.B. Other flavour ice creams that blend well are coffee, chocolate and orange.

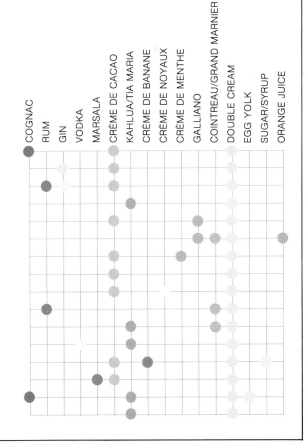

APRICOT BRANDY COLLER

Blanch 4 apricots in boiling water and remove their skins. Crush the apricots to a purée with a fork. Put the purée in a mixing glass with a few ice cubes and add:

juice of 2 lemons
4 measures apricot brandy
4 measures sugar syrup

Stir well to mix and pour into four tumblers or balloon glasses.
SERVES 4

APRICOT LADY

Put a glassful of crushed ice into an electric blender and pour in:

1 measure rum
1½ measures apricot juice
¼ measure curaçao
1 egg white

Blend for a few seconds and pour without straining into a fancy glass.

ATHOLL BROSE COCKTAIL

Pour into a bowl:

1 measure scotch
1 measure clear honey
1 measure double cream

Stir well to mix. Strain into a champagne saucer. Leave to chill in the refrigerator before serving.

BANSHEE

Put a half glass of crushed ice in an electric blender and add:

1 measure crème de banane
1 measure crème de cacao
1 measure double cream
1 dash sugar syrup

Blend for a few seconds and pour without straining into a cocktail glass.

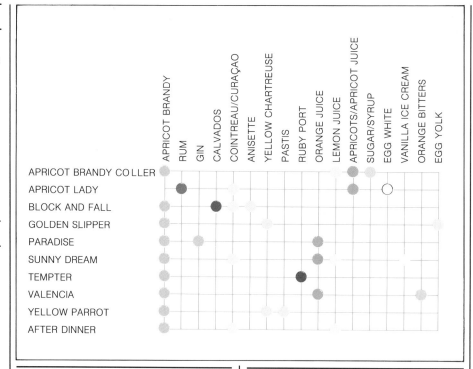

	APRICOT BRANDY	RUM	GIN	CALVADOS	COINTREAU/CURAÇAO	ANISETTE	YELLOW CHARTREUSE	PASTIS	RUBY PORT	ORANGE JUICE	LEMON JUICE	APRICOTS/APRICOT JUICE	SUGAR/SYRUP	EGG WHITE	VANILLA ICE CREAM	ORANGE BITTERS	EGG YOLK
APRICOT BRANDY COLLER	●											●	●				
APRICOT LADY		●			●							●		○			
BLOCK AND FALL	●			●	●												
GOLDEN SLIPPER	●						●										
PARADISE	●		●							●		●					
SUNNY DREAM	●									●		●					
TEMPTER	●								●	●							
VALENCIA	●									●		●				●	
YELLOW PARROT	●					●		●									
AFTER DINNER	●																

BAYOU

Put some ice cubes in a cocktail shaker and add:

1 measure cognac
2 teaspoons lime juice
1 teaspoon mango juice
a few dashes peach liqueur

Shake well and strain into a cocktail glass. Decorate with a slice of lime, if obtainable.

BENEDICTINE COCKTAIL

Put some ice cubes in a cocktail shaker and add:

1 measure cognac
½ measure Benedictine
½ measure lemon juice

Shake well and strain into a cocktail glass.

BENEDICTINE SCAFFA

Pour into a small liqueur glass:

1 measure Benedictine
1 measure whisky
1 dash Angostura bitters

And serve.
N.B. You may replace the whisky with gin or rum. Both these spirits give an equally good result.

BLACKTHORN

Put several ice cubes in a mixing glass and pour in:

1 measure sloe gin
1 measure sweet vermouth
2 dashes orange bitters

Stir well and strain into a cocktail glass. Garnish with a twist of lemon peel.

BLOCK AND FALL

Put several ice cubes in a mixing glass and pour in:

$\frac{1}{2}$ *measure apricot brandy*
$\frac{1}{2}$ *measure Cointreau*
$\frac{1}{4}$ *measure calvados*
$\frac{1}{4}$ *measure anisette*

Stir and strain into a cocktail glass.

BLUE LADY

Put some ice cubes in a cocktail shaker and add:

1 measure blue curaçao
$\frac{1}{2}$ *measure gin*
$\frac{1}{2}$ *measure lemon juice*
1 dash egg white

Shake and strain into a cocktail glass.

BRUNETTE

Put some ice cubes in a cocktail shaker and add:

1 measure Kahlúa
1 measure bourbon
1 measure double cream
$\frac{1}{2}$ *teaspoon sugar*

Shake and strain into a tulip glass.

CÂLIN COCKTAIL

Put some ice cubes in a cocktail shaker and add:

$\frac{4}{10}$ *orange juice*
$\frac{3}{10}$ *Marie Brizard anisette*
$\frac{3}{10}$ *Mandarine Imperiale*

Shake and strain into a cocktail glass. Garnish with a slice of lime, a mint leaf and a brandied cherry.

DANIÈLE WOJCIK.
ABF, France.

Poster by Jean Mercier for Cointreau, 1950.

CAFÉ CURAÇAO

Put 3 ice cubes in an old fashioned glass and add:

1 measure Kahlúa
1 measure triple sec

Add a twist of orange peel and serve with short straws.

CARIOCA

Put some crushed ice into an electric blender and pour in:

1 measure cognac
$\frac{1}{2}$ *measure Kahlúa*
$\frac{3}{4}$ *measure double cream*
1 egg yolk

Blend for a few seconds and pour into a champagne saucer. Sprinkle a little ground cinnamon over the top and serve.

CHAMPERELLE (POUSSE-CAFÉ)

Pour into a liqueur glass very carefully in the order given so that they float one on top of the other:

$\frac{1}{2}$ *measure curaçao*
$\frac{1}{2}$ *measure anisette*
$\frac{1}{2}$ *measure Chartreuse*
$\frac{1}{2}$ *measure cognac*

CHERRY BLOSSOM

Pour into a cocktail shaker containing several ice cubes:

1 measure cognac
$\frac{1}{2}$ *measure cherry liqueur*
a few dashes curaçao
a few dashes grenadine
$\frac{1}{2}$ *measure lemon juice*

Shake and strain into a frosted fancy glass.

CHARTREUSE TONIC

Put 2 ice cubes in an old fashioned glass and pour in:

1 measure green Chartreuse
juice of 1 lime

Stir well to mix and top up with tonic. Garnish with a half slice of lime.

COOL CARIBBEAN

Put some ice cubes in a tumbler and pour in:

1 measure Malibu
½ measure crème de banane

Top up with orangeade. Garnish with an orange slice and a cherry.

COOL BANANA

Pour into a cocktail shaker containing several ice cubes:

1 measure crème de banane
¾ measure curaçao
1 measure double cream
1 dash egg white

Shake and strain into a cocktail glass. Garnish with a cherry.

COQUITO

Put some crushed ice in an electric blender and pour in:

1 measure white rum
½ measure Cherry Heering
½ measure cream of coconut
3 measures double cream

Blend at high speed and pour into a tumbler (or into a ceramic coconut shell). Serve with straws.

Corpse Reviver No 3 makes effective use of Fernet-Branca. (Above): A calendar designed for this brand in 1909.

CORPSE REVIVER 4

Pour into a cocktail shaker containing several ice cubes:

1 measure Fernet-Branca
1 measure crème de menthe

Shake and strain into a cocktail glass.

CORSICAN BOUNTY

Pour into a cocktail shaker containing several ice cubes:

1 measure Malibu
½ measure Mandarine Imperiale
1 measure lemon juice
1 dash orgeat syrup
1 dash egg white

Shake and strain into a cocktail glass. Decorate with a lemon slice and a cherry.

CRÈME DE MENTHE FRAPPÉ

Pour 1 measure of green crème de menthe into a brandy snifter or cocktail glass full of crushed ice. Serve with two straws.

CUBA LIBRE SUPREME

Put 3 or 4 ice cubes in a collins glass. Squeeze over the juice of ½ lime on top and drop in the squeezed-out shell. Add 1 measure Southern Comfort and stir to mix. Top up with Coca-Cola.

DRAMBUIE SWIZZLE ▮

Pour into a tumbler half filled with crushed ice:

1 measure Drambuie
½ measure lime juice
1 teaspoon sugar

Stir well to mix and top up with soda. Garnish with a mint sprig and serve with a swizzle stick.

DUKE ♦ ♉

Pour into a cocktail shaker containing several ice cubes:

1 measure Drambuie
½ measure orange juice
½ measure lemon juice
1 egg

Shake and strain into a tulip glass. Add a splash of champagne.

EL METRAYA ♦ ♉

Pour into a cocktail shaker one third full of ice cubes:

½ measure rum
1 measure Tía Maria
3 measures cane syrup

Shake well and pour the lot (ice cubes as well) into a fancy glass.

FROSTY DAWN ♦ ♉

Put some ice cubes in a cocktail shaker and add:

½ measure white rum
½ measure orange juice
¼ measure maraschino
¼ measure Falernum

Shake and strain into a cocktail glass.

A. CARILLO,
Competition 1954, West Coast, U.S.A.

FROZEN SOUTHERN COMFORT ♦ ♉

Put a half glass of crushed ice into an electric blender and pour in:

1 measure Southern Comfort
1 dash maraschino
juice of ½ lime
½ teaspoon sugar

Blend for a few seconds and pour into a champagne saucer. Serve with short straws.

GIN ALEXANDER ♦ ♉

Put some ice cubes in a cocktail shaker and add:

1 measure gin
½ measure brown crème de cacao
½ measure double cream

Shake and strain into a cocktail glass. Grate some nutmeg over the top.

GLOOM CHASER ♦ ♉

Put some ice cubes in a cocktail shaker and add:

½ measure curaçao
½ measure Grand Marnier
½ measure lemon juice
½ measure grenadine

Shake and strain into a cocktail glass.

GOLD COCONUT ♦ ♉

Put some ice cubes in a cocktail shaker and add:

1 measure Malibu
1 measure cognac
2 measures orange juice
1 dash egg white
1 dash grenadine

Shake and strain into a cocktail glass. Garnish with a cherry.

GOLDEN CADILLAC ♦ ♉

Put some ice cubes in a cocktail shaker and add:

1 measure Galliano
1 measure white crème de cacao
1 measure double cream

Shake well and strain into a cocktail glass.

GOLDEN DREAM ♦ ♉

Pour into a cocktail shaker containing several ice cubes:

1 measure Galliano
1 measure Cointreau
1 measure orange juice
1 measure double cream

Shake and strain into a cocktail glass.

LE ROY CHANON,
Competition 1959, West Coast, U.S.A.

Golden Cadillac served in a Habitat glass.

GRAND NORD ▪

Put 2 ice cubes in an old fashioned glass and pour in:

1 measure green Chartreuse
1 measure vodka

Stir before serving.
N.B. For a sweeter cocktail, substitute yellow Chartreuse for the green.

GRASSHOPPER ❡ ⍦

Half fill a cocktail shaker with ice cubes and pour in:

1 measure white crème de cacao
1 measure green crème de menthe
1 measure double cream

Shake well and strain into a cocktail glass.

GREEN DRAGON ❡ ⍦

Half fill a cocktail shaker with ice cubes and pour in:

1 measure gin
½ measure green crème de menthe
¼ measure kummel
¼ measure lemon juice

Shake and strain into a cocktail glass. Garnish with a sliver of lemon peel.

GOLDEN SLIPPER ❡ ⍦

Pour into a cocktail shaker containing several ice cubes:

1 measure yellow Chartreuse
1 measure apricot brandy
1 egg yolk

Shake and strain into a cocktail glass. Garnish with a cherry impaled on a cocktail stick.

JAFFA ▮

Put some ice cubes in a tumbler and pour in:

1 measure Cointreau
1 measure white crème de menthe

Stir well to mix thoroughly and top up with Coca-Cola. Garnish the cocktail with a long spiral of orange peel and a cherry.

JAMAICA JOE ❡ ⍦

Put some ice cubes in a cocktail shaker and pour in:

½ measure Lemon Hart white rum
½ measure Tía Maria
½ measure advocaat

Shake and strain into a cocktail glass. Add a dash of grenadine and grate a little nutmeg over the top.

ALLAN CLARKE,
Jamaica Rum Cocktail Competition, London, 1948.

KAHLUA ALEXANDER ❡ ⍦

Put some ice cubes in a cocktail shaker and pour in:

1 measure gin
1 measure Kahlúa
1 measure double cream

Shake well and strain into a cocktail glass.

KING ALFONSE ❗

Pour 1 measure brown crème de cacao into a liqueur glass. Very carefully pour in a little double cream over the back of a spoon so that it floats on top. Serve without stirring.

LENINGRAD ▪

Half fill an old fashioned glass with crushed ice and pour in:

1 measure yellow Verveine du Velay
1 measure vodka

Stir and garnish with a yellow cherry impaled on a cocktail stick.

LONG GREEN ▮

Put a few ice cubes in a tumbler and pour in 1 measure green crème de menthe. Top up with soda and garnish with a mint sprig. Serve with straws.
N.B. For Royal Green, substitute chilled sparkling white wine for the soda.

Grasshopper served in a Habitat glass.

MAZEL TOV ❶ ⍦

Pour into a cocktail shaker containing several ice cubes:

$\frac{3}{10}$ Gordon's gin
$\frac{3}{10}$ Sabra liqueur
$\frac{3}{10}$ double cream
$\frac{1}{10}$ raspberry liqueur

Shake and strain into a cocktail glass. Decorate with a raspberry and a slice of kiwi fruit.

CHRISTIAN SIMON, PARIS.
ABF, France.

MERRY WIDOW 3 ❶ ⍦

Pour into a cocktail shaker containing several ice cubes:

1 measure cherry brandy
1 measure maraschino

Shake and strain into a cocktail glass. Garnish with a cherry.

MONA LISA ⍦

Put some crushed ice into a large goblet and pour in:

1 measure orange Chartreuse
$\frac{1}{3}$ measure Campari
$\frac{1}{3}$ measure gin

Stir and top up with ginger ale. Decorate with an orange slice and a sliver of lemon peel. Serve with a straw.

GABY WILLEMS, PARIS.
ABF, France.

MORNING DEW ❶ ⍦

Pour into a cocktail shaker containing several ice cubes:

$\frac{3}{10}$ Irish whiskey
$\frac{2}{10}$ Marie Brizard crème de banane
$\frac{1}{10}$ Bols blue curaçao
$\frac{4}{10}$ grapefruit juice
1 egg white

Shake and strain into a cocktail glass. Garnish with an orange slice and a red and a green cherry.

M.MACLOUGHLIN, DUBLIN.
BAI, Eire.

PARADISE ❶ ⍦

Pour into a cocktail shaker containing several ice cubes:

1 measure gin
$\frac{1}{2}$ measure apricot brandy
1 teaspoon orange juice

Shake and strain into a cocktail glass.

PINK SQUIRREL ❶ ⍦

Put some ice cubes in a cocktail shaker and add:

1 measure white crème de cacao
1 measure crème de noyaux
1 measure double cream

Shake and strain into a champagne saucer.

PISCO PUNCH ❶ ⍦

Put some ice cubes in a cocktail shaker and add:

1 measure pisco
$\frac{1}{2}$ measure pineapple juice
$\frac{1}{2}$ measure lime juice
2 dashes maraschino
2 dashes sugar syrup

Shake and strain into a balloon glass. Garnish with a piece of pineapple and two cherries.

PLATINUM BLONDE ❶ ⍦

Put some ice cubes in a cocktail shaker and add:

1 measure Grand Marnier
1 measure rum
$\frac{1}{2}$ measure double cream

Shake and strain into a cocktail glass. Garnish with a half slice of orange on the rim of the glass.

PORT AND STARBOARD (POUSSE-CAFÉ) ❗

Very carefully pour into a liqueur glass in the order given so that they float one on top of the other:

1 measure grenadine
1 measure green crème de menthe

And serve.

POUSSE L'AMOUR (POUSSE-CAFÉ) ❗

Very carefully pour into a liqueur glass in the order given so that they float one on top of the other:

$\frac{1}{2}$ measure maraschino
1 beaten egg yolk
$\frac{1}{2}$ measure Benedictine
$\frac{1}{2}$ measure cognac

RAINBOW 1 (POUSSE-CAFÉ) ❗

Very carefully pour into a liqueur glass in the order given so that they float one on top of the other:

$\frac{1}{4}$ measure grenadine
$\frac{1}{4}$ measure anisette
$\frac{1}{4}$ measure green crème de menthe
$\frac{1}{4}$ measure blue curaçao
$\frac{1}{4}$ measure violet liqueur
$\frac{1}{4}$ measure goldwasser
$\frac{1}{4}$ measure cognac

RAINBOW 2 ♀ ▮

Put some ice cubes in a balloon glass or tumbler and add:

1 measure advocaat
a squeeze of orange juice

Stir and then very carefully, so that they do not mix, pour in:

½ measure blue curaçao
½ measure cherry brandy

Serve with straws.
N.B. You get a very pretty effect with this mixture of colours.

RUM ALEXANDER ♦ ▾

Put some ice cubes in a cocktail shaker and add:

1 measure rum
1 measure crème de cacao
1 measure double cream

Shake and strain into a cocktail glass.

SAINT GERMAIN ♦ ▮

Put some ice cubes in a cocktail shaker and add:

1 measure green Chartreuse
1 measure lemon juice
1 measure grapefruit juice
1 egg white

Shake and strain into a tumbler containing a few ice cubes.

SAVOY 90 ♦ ▾

Put some ice cubes in a cocktail shaker and add:

1 measure amaretto
1 measure lime juice
1 dash orange flower water
Dampen the rim of a tulip glass and

dip into fine sugar to frost. Shake the cocktail and pour it into the glass. Top up with chilled dry champagne.

SCARLET O'HARA ♦ ▾

Put some ice cubes in a cocktail shaker and add:

1 measure Southern Comfort
juice of ½ lime
½ measure bilberry juice

Shake and strain into a lager glass.

SHANNON SHANDY ▮

Put some ice cubes in a tumbler and pour in:

1 measure Irish Mist
1 dash Angostura bitters

Stir and top up with ginger ale.

SLOE GIN COCKTAIL ▿ ▾

Pour into a mixing glass containing some ice cubes:

1 measure sloe gin
½ measure dry vermouth
½ measure sweet vermouth

Stir and strain into a cocktail glass. Garnish with a twist of lemon peel.

SNAKE IN THE GRASS ♦ ▾

Pour into a cocktail shaker containing several ice cubes:

½ measure Cointreau
½ measure dry vermouth
½ measure gin
½ measure lemon juice

Shake and strain into a cocktail glass. Garnish with a twist of lemon peel.

SNOWBALL ♦

Put some ice cubes in a fancy glass and pour in:

1 measure advocaat
1 dash lime juice
1 dash sugar syrup

Stir and top up with lemonade.

SUMMER MINT ▭ ▾

Put some crushed ice into an electric blender and pour in:

⅓ measure green crème de menthe
⅓ measure Cointreau
⅓ measure Galliano
1 measure pineapple juice
1 measure lemon juice
1 measure grapefruit juice

Blend for a few seconds and pour into a champagne flute. Garnish with a mint sprig and a cherry. Serve with a straw.

SUNNY DREAM ▭ ♀

Put into an electric blender:

1 measure apricot liqueur
½ measure Cointreau
3 measures orange juice
1 dash lemon juice
1 scoop vanilla ice cream

Blend and pour into a balloon glass. Garnish with an orange slice and a cherry.

TEMPTER ▭

Put 3 ice cubes in an old fashioned glass and pour in:

1 measure apricot liqueur
1 measure ruby port

Stir and serve.

Creation Septembre 1922

AFFICHES **EDIA** 44, Rue Letellier **PARIS**

Cherry Rocher

LIQUEUR

*Poster designed by
Paul Mohr, 1922, for
Cherry Rocher
Liqueur.*

TIDAL WAVE ▮▮

Put some ice cubes in a tumbler and pour in:

1 measure mandarine liqueur
1 dash lemon juice

Top up with bitter lemon. Stir to mix and garnish with a slice of lemon or orange.

VALENCIA ♦ ♈

Put some ice cubes in a cocktail shaker and add:

1 measure apricot brandy
½ measure orange juice
a few dashes Angostura bitters

Shake well and strain into a cocktail glass.

VELVET HAMMER ♦ ♈

Put some ice cubes in a cocktail shaker and add:

1 measure Cointreau
1 measure Tía Maria
1 measure double cream

Shake well and strain into a cocktail glass.

WHITE RUSSIAN ▬

Put some ice cubes in an old fashioned glass and pour in:

1 measure vodka
½ measure Kahlúa

Stir to mix. Pour in a little double cream over the back of a spoon to cover the top.

WHITE SATIN ♦ ♈

Put some ice cubes in a cocktail shaker and add:

1 measure Cointreau
½ measure gin
1 dash lemon juice

Shake well and strain into a cocktail glass.

XOCHIMILCO ▮

Pour 1 measure of Kahlúa into a liqueur glass. Cover with a thin layer of double cream, pouring it carefully over the back of a spoon.

YELLOW PARROT ⋈ ♈

Put some ice cubes in a mixing glass and pour in:

½ measure pastis
½ measure yellow Chartreuse
½ measure apricot brandy

Stir well and strain into a cocktail glass.

Punches

'. . . *To dispel his sorrow he had three hounds, punch and a mistress.'*

Voltaire

Traditionally punch was a mixture of rum or brandy, tea, lemon juice and sugar. But current fashion has turned it into a mixture of many ingredients. Tea is often replaced by infusions of orange flower, verbena or camomile. Most punches are rum based, but other spirits can be used with various fruit juices.

Punches and cups are favourite drinks for parties and receptions. They can be made in advance in large bowls and kept for several hours. Just before serving, fresh fruit and ice should be added.

Poster designed by Stephano for Rhum Black.

A1 PICK ME UP

12 lemons
12 eggs
600 ml/1 pint golden rum
500 g/1 lb sugar

Squeeze the lemons and put the juice in a bowl. Break the eggs into the bowl and stir to mix. Crush the egg shells into tiny pieces and add them to the mixture. Cover with a clean piece of damp muslin and leave in a cool place for several days or until the egg shells have completely dissolved. Strain the mixture through a double layer of scalded muslin.

Put the rum and sugar into a saucepan with 2.25 litres/4 pints water over a low heat and stir continuously until the sugar has dissolved. Take the pan off the heat and allow to cool slightly before mixing in the egg and lemon juice. Bottle and store until required.

Makes about 2·8 litres/5 pints

ARTILLERY PUNCH

6 pineapples
1 kg/2 lb strawberries
2·75 kg/6 lb oranges
5 litres/9 pints dry cider
1 bottle bourbon
1 bottle golden rum
12 bottles champagne

Peel and cut the pineapples into slices. Remove the cores and then process to extract the juice. Put the juice in a large bowl. Press the strawberries through a strainer and add to the pineapple juice along with the juice from the oranges. Stir in the cider, bourbon and rum. Cover and refrigerate overnight.

When you are ready to serve pour in the champagne and plenty of ice cubes.

Serves 150

AZTEC PUNCH

Prepare 425 ml/¾ pints tea and when cold pour into a punch bowl and put in a block of ice. Then pour in:

1 bottle tequila
4 litres/7 pints grapefruit juice
1 measure lemon juice
4 measures sugar syrup

Stir well to mix. Serve on ice cubes.
Serves 30

BRANDY PUNCH

700 g/1½ lbs sugar
juice of 20 lemons
1 bottle cognac
6 measures Cointreau
4 measures white rum
2 measures maraschino
1 litre/1¾ pints chilled soda
Fruit in season

Put the sugar and lemon juice in a large punch bowl and stir to dissolve the sugar. Put in a block of ice and pour in the remaining ingredients except the soda and fruit. Leave to get cold. When you are ready to serve pour in soda and garnish with the fruit.
Serves 15

BUCCANEER

1½ bottles white rum
600 ml/1 pint dry white wine
juice of 6 oranges
juice of 4 lemons
300 g/10 oz can pineapple chunks
2 vanilla pods
250 ml/8 fl oz sugar syrup
1 cinnamon stick
1 nutmeg, grated
1 orange, cut into slices
1 lemon, cut into slices

Into a large punch bowl pour the rum, wine, orange juice, lemon juice and pineapple chunks along with syrup in the can. Split the vanilla pods and add them with the cinnamon stick and the grated nutmeg. Stir to mix and refrigerate for 3 to 4 hours. Just before serving add the fruit.
Serves 15

CAMOMILE AND WINE

1 bottle dry white wine
16 sachets camomile tea
20 g/¾ oz bitter orange peel
1 vanilla pod
30 sugar lumps
250 ml/8 fl oz white rum

Put the wine and camomile sachets into a jug. Crumble the orange peel and split the vanilla pod and add them to the jug with the sugar. Stir to mix and set aside, covered, for 48 hours. Pour the mixture through a paper filter. Stir in the rum. Bottle and keep for a month before drinking.
Makes 1 litre/1¾ pints

CECEMA PUNCH

1 litre/1¾ pints pineapple juice
1 litre/1¾ pints orange juice
juice of 4 lemons
2 bottles white rum
450 ml/¾ pint sugar syrup
2 litres/3½ pints lemonade, chilled
3 oranges cut into slices

Mix the fruit juices, rum and syrup in a large punch bowl. Just before serving pour in the lemonade, 20 or so ice cubes and the orange slices.
Serves 30

COFFEE AND BITTER ORANGE PUNCH

3 sachets orange tea
4 tablespoons instant coffee
4 tablespoons vanilla sugar
4 tablespoons curaçao
4 orange slices

Bring 700 ml/1¼ pints of water to the boil and pour it over the orange tea sachets. Leave for 5 minutes then discard the sachets. Immediately stir in the instant coffee and the sugar. Allow to cool and then chill in the refrigerator.

Put a large glassful of crushed ice into a mixing glass. Strain the infusion on to the ice and stir in the curaçao. Strain into 4 glasses and garnish each glass with an orange slice astride the rim.
Serves 4

FRUIT PUNCH

300 g/10 oz fresh fruit (pears, peaches, pineapple, strawberries)
350 g/12 oz brown sugar
⅔ bottle white rum

Peel the fruit, cut into pieces and put into a 1 litre/2 pint jar. Add the sugar and rum and stir well to mix. Close the jar tightly and leave for 5 days. Serve on ice cubes.
Makes 1 litre/1¾ pints

GOLDEN RUM PUNCH 1

50 g/2 oz sugar
1 litre/1¼ pints pineapple juice
juice of 6 oranges
juice of 6 lemons
1 bottle golden rum
1 litre/1¾ pints ginger ale or soda
fruit in season

In a punch bowl dissolve the sugar in the pineapple juice. Add the orange and lemon juice and pour in the rum. Stir to mix. Put a large block of ice in the middle and leave the punch to get really cold. When you are ready to serve, pour in the ginger ale or soda. Garnish with slices of pineapple and orange, cherries, strawberries and any other fruit in season.
Serves 20

GOLDEN RUM PUNCH 2

1 bottle golden rum
200 ml/7 fl oz apricot liqueur
600 ml/1 pint grapefruit juice
300 ml/½ pint pineapple juice
juice of 2–3 lemons
soda
orange slices
pineapple chunks

Put a large block of ice in the middle of a large punch bowl. Pour in all the ingredients except the soda and fruit. Mix well. When you are ready to serve pour in soda (between 600 ml/1 pint and 1 litre/1¾ pints, to taste) and add some orange slices and pineapple chunks.
Serves 30

A Kava Bowl from Trader Vic's.

KAVA BOWL

6 measures Puerto Rico golden rum
1 measure Siegerts Bouquet rum
1 measure orgeat syrup
1 measure grenadine
4 measures lemon juice
2 measures pineapple juice

Put 3 glassfuls of crushed ice into an electric blender and pour in all the ingredients. Blend for a few seconds and pour into a punch bowl.
Serves 4

MATOUBA

2 glassfuls of fresh raspberries or wild
  blackberries
350 g/12 oz brown sugar
1 bottle white rum

Put all the ingredients in a jar and stir well to mix. Cover the jar tightly and leave in a dark cool place for 2 months. Serve on ice accompanied by fresh fruit.
Makes 1 litre/1¾ pints

ORANGE PUNCH

1 litre/1¾ pints vodka
1 litre/1¾ pints orange juice
1 litre/1¾ pints ginger ale
1 litre/1¾ pints soda
orange slices

Put a large block of ice in a punch bowl. Pour in all the ingredients and stir well to mix. Float orange slices on top.
Serves 20–25

RUM ORANGE PUNCH

4–5 oranges, washed
700 ml/1¼ pints white rum
300 ml/½ pint sugar syrup

Peel the oranges and put the peel in the sun or in a low oven (with the door open) until it is quite dry and brittle. Put the dried peel in a jar and pour the rum over the top. Cover the jar tightly and set aside for 6 weeks. After that time pour in the syrup, cover again and leave for another 6 weeks. Strain the punch and store in bottles.
Makes 1 litre/1¾ pints

SANS SOUCI

2 measures Lemon Hart rum
2 measures Grand Marnier
2 measures Tía Maria
juice of ½ lime
600 ml/1 pint orange juice

Fill a jug one-third full of ice cubes and pour in all the ingredients. Stir well to mix. Serve in large glasses with straws.
Serves 4

TOBAGO PUNCH

1½ bottles white rum
300 ml/½ pint sugar syrup
juice of 2 lemons
8 bananas, cut into slices
300 g/10 oz can pineapple chunks
250 g/9 oz can litchis

Put all the ingredients in a punch bowl and stir to mix. Put in 10 or more ice cubes, stir again and serve.
Serves 12

Milk-based Cocktails

The nutritional value of milk makes it a good ingredient for some cocktails. Milk sweetens the taste and reduces alcoholic strength. Its blandness helps to lessen the impact of the cocktail on the digestive system too. When combined with eggs, for *Eggnog* for instance, it makes an excellent tonic. Milk-based cocktails used to be very popular; they were drunk hot, as in *Auld Man's Milk*, or *Lait de Poule*, perhaps to keep out the cold in poorly-heated homes. Dickens captures the good feeling of this in a simple sentence in *The Holly Tree Inn*: 'I got up to The Peacock where I found everybody drinking hot punch in self-preservation. . .'

AULD MAN'S MILK

Pour into a heated cocktail shaker:

1 measure cognac
1 measure rum
1 egg
1 teaspoon sugar
1 glassful boiling milk

Put a napkin round the shaker to avoid burning yourself and shake. Pour into a heatproof handled glass or a champagne saucer. Grate a little nutmeg over the top and serve.

BALTIMORE EGGNOG

Put some ice cubes in a cocktail shaker and add:

1½ measures madeira
1 measure cognac
½ measure rum
1 fresh egg
4 measures fresh milk
2 measures double cream
2 teaspoons sugar

Fill 4 tumblers with ice cubes. Shake the eggnog well and pour into the glasses. Top up with more fresh milk and grate some nutmeg or dark

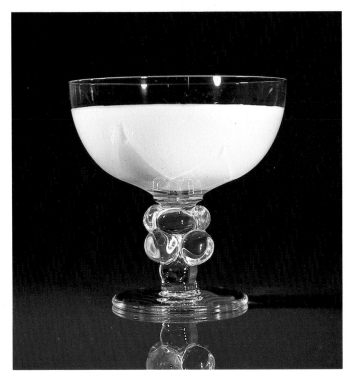
Auld Man's Milk in a Lalique crystal glass.

chocolate over the top or garnish with a sprig of mint.
SERVES 4

BANANA COW

Put a half-glassful of crushed ice into an electric blender and add the following ingredients:

1 measure white Puerto Rico rum
3 measures chilled milk
1 banana
1 teaspoon sugar
1 dash mint essence
1 dash Angostura bitters

Blend for a few seconds and pour without straining into a tumbler. Grate a little nutmeg or dark chocolate on top if liked, or garnish with a sprig of mint.

BOSTON EGGNOG

Put a glassful of crushed ice in an electric blender and add:

2 measures madeira
¼ measure cognac
⅛ measure rum
1 teaspoon sugar
2 measures fresh milk

Blend and strain into a tumbler. Top up with chilled milk and grate a little nutmeg on top.

BRANDY ALEXANDER MILK PUNCH

Put some ice cubes in a cocktail shaker and add:

1 measure cognac
½ measure crème de cacao
6 measures fresh milk

Shake well and strain into a tumbler.
Grate some nutmeg over the top and
serve with straws.

BRANDY EGGNOG 🍶🍺

Pour into a cocktail shaker containing
several ice cubes:

1 measure cognac
1 egg yolk
1 teaspoon sugar
5 measures fresh milk

Shake thoroughly and strain into a
tumbler. Grate nutmeg on top.
N.B. For a Brandy Milk Punch leave
out the egg yolk.

DRAMBUIE EGGNOG 🍸

6 eggs, separated
2 teaspoons sugar
6 measures Drambuie
3 measures sherry
1 litre/1¾ pints milk
300 ml/1 pint vanilla ice cream
½ teaspoon grated nutmeg

Put the egg yolks into a bowl and beat
with the sugar until smooth and
creamy. Stir in all the other
ingredients except the egg whites. Mix
well. Just before serving, whip the egg
whites until white and snowy. Mix it
into the other ingredients. Pour into a
punch bowl, mix well and serve in
goblets.
Serves 12

HIGHLAND MILK PUNCH 🍶🍷

Put some ice cubes in a cocktail
shaker and add:

1 measure scotch

3 measures fresh milk
1 teaspoon sugar

Shake and strain into a balloon glass.
Grate some nutmeg on top.
N.B. For an American version,
substitute bourbon for the scotch.

JAMAICAN COW 🍸

Put three-quarters of a glass of cold
milk into a bowl and whisk in 1 egg.
Put some ice cubes in a fancy glass.
Pour in the egg and milk and add 1
measure Tía Maria. Mix thoroughly
and serve.

LAIT DE POULE 2 🍶🍺

Put some ice cubes in a cocktail
shaker and pour in:

1 measure rum or brandy
1 egg yolk
1 teaspoon sugar
3 measures milk

Shake thoroughly and strain into a
tumbler.
N.B. Add ½ measure of any liqueur
you like, such as Tía Maria, Curaçao,
crème de banane, white crème de
cacao or white crème de menthe and
serve it hot if you prefer.

MILK PUNCH 🗑🍸

Put a glassful of crushed ice into an
electric blender and add:

4 measures fresh milk
1 teaspoon sugar
1 measure white rum

Blend for a few seconds and strain
into a chilled fancy glass. Grate some
nutmeg on top.
N.B. You may replace the rum with
brandy, calvados, bourbon or rye. For
a more sophisticated taste add a dash

or two of curaçao or maraschino.

RAMOS FIZZ 🍶🍺

Put some crushed ice into cocktail
shaker and add:

1½ measures gin
2 measures milk
2 measures double cream
1 egg white
juice of ½ lemon
2 teaspoons sugar
1 teaspoon orange flower water

Shake thoroughly and pour into a
tumbler.

SHERRY EGGNOG 🍶🍺

Put some ice cubes in a cocktail
shaker and add:

2 measures sweet sherry
1 teaspoon sugar
4 measures fresh milk
1 egg

Shake well and strain into a collins
glass. Grate some nutmeg on top.
N.B. Omit the egg for a Sherry Milk
Punch.

TÍA EGGNOG 🍶🍺

Put a half glass of crushed ice into a
cocktail shaker and add:

1 measure Tía Maria
1 measure milk
½ measure cognac
1 egg
1 teaspoon sugar

Put some ice cubes in a tumbler.
Shake the eggnog and pour it over the
ice cubes. Grate some nutmeg over
the top.

Cocktails based on Wine and Beer

Wine is as good as life to men, if thou drink it in its measure: What life is there to a man that is without wine?

ECCLESIASTICUS XXXI, 27

Wine is produced by fermenting grape juice to convert its sugar into alcohol. If the skins of black grapes are present during fermentation, red wine results: if only the juice of black or white grapes is fermented, white wine results. Wines are distinguished by the grape varieties from which they are made as well as the areas in which they are produced. In addition, fine wines are classified by the châteaux which produce them. However, these are less suitable for cocktails.

The same grape variety can produce very different wines: the pinot noir grape used exclusively in red burgundies also produces champagne and Sancerre rosé, and is used in wines from Alsace and Provence. The Cabernet franc is the only grape used in the red wines of Chinon and Bourgeuil, and it is also a basic grape in Médoc (in association with cabernet sauvignon) and in St Emilion (in association with merlot). While some wines are made from a single grape variety (riesling, sylvaner, gewürztraminer, burgundy, beaujolais etc), others are skilful mixtures of several varieties.

All bordeaux wines are made from three or four varieties, sometimes more. Each year every cellar master in Bordeaux makes his blend of wines from different grape varieties and vines of different ages to produce his vintage wine. This activity, frequently misunderstood, has an obvious parallel in the art of mixing drinks.

Champagne itself could also be described as a skilfully made 'cocktail': a blend of white wines undergoes a secondary fermentation in the bottle encouraged by adding sugar and yeast to produce carbon dioxide and ultimately the sparkle. After the sediment caused by the yeast is removed, the bottle is topped up and recorked.

Wine and champagne cocktails are ideal party-openers: wine in particular is less expensive to use than spirits and is easier on the palate and the head.

Cappiello Poster for St Dizier, a Fort-Carré beer.

(Opposite): Ateliers Cheret poster for Mumm Cordon Rouge Champagne

Taverne Olympia
Restaurant
OUVERT TOUTE LA NUIT
ORCHESTRE
DE DAMES
MONTAGNES RUSSES
28, Boul^d. des Capucines & 6, Rue Caumartin
IMPRIMERIE CHAIX (Ateliers Chéret) Rue Bergère 20, PARIS

ALE FLIP ▮

2 egg whites
4 egg yolks
2 teaspoons sugar syrup
750 ml/1¼ pints pale or brown ale

Beat the egg whites until they are frothy. Mix in the egg yolks, syrup and ale. Pour into a saucepan and place over low heat. Bring the mixture to just under boiling point, stirring constantly with a wooden spoon. Heat 2 jugs and pour the mixture from one to the other until it becomes frothy. Pour into handled glasses and sprinkle grated nutmeg on top.
SERVES 4

AMOUR COCKTAIL ▮ ▾

Pour into a cocktail shaker containing several ice cubes:

1 measure sweet sherry
1 measure dry vermouth
2 dashes Angostura bitters

Shake and strain into a cocktail glass. Squeeze some orange peel over the top to extract the zest and drop in the peel.

ARCHBISHOP PUNCH ▮

1 orange
4 cloves
1 bottle claret
sugar

Wash and dry the orange. Stick the cloves in the orange and put it on a baking sheet. Put in a moderately hot oven. When the orange turns brown remove it and cut it into slices. Discard the pips. Put the orange slices in a saucepan. Pour in the wine and 1 or 2 tablespoons sugar. Put the pan over low heat and bring to just under boiling point. Serve in handled glasses.

N.B. For a Brandy Bishop put a peg of brandy into each glass before serving.
SERVES 6

ARGENTINE JULEP ▮ ▾

Put some ice cubes in a cocktail shaker and add:

1 measure claret
1 measure cognac
1 measure orange juice
1 measure pineapple juice
1 dash Cointreau

Shake and strain into a tulip glass one-third full of crushed ice. Garnish with an orange slice and a mint sprig.

BAMBOO COCKTAIL ▯ ▾

Pour into a mixing glass containing several ice cubes:

1 measure dry sherry
½ measure dry vermouth
2 dashes orange bitters

Stir to mix and strain into a cocktail glass. Garnish with a green olive.

BARBOTAGE ▮ ▾

Pour into a cocktail shaker containing several ice cubes:

3 measures orange juice
1 measure lemon juice
1 teaspoon grenadine

Shake and strain into a tulip glass. Top up with chilled champagne.

BELLINI ▾

Peel 3 or 4 cold, ripe peaches and purée the flesh. Put the purée in a bowl with 2 or 3 teaspoons sugar. Pour in a bottle of cold champagne. Stir well and strain into 6 tulip glasses.
SERVES 6

BISHOP ▮

Half fill a tumbler with crushed ice and pour in:

2 measures orange juice
1½ measures lemon juice
1 teaspoon sugar

Top up with red burgundy and stir well. Pour a teaspoon of rum over the top and serve.

BLACK AND TAN ▮ ▾

Pour into a cocktail shaker containing several ice cubes:

1 measure sweet vermouth
½ measure crème de cassis
½ measure Pernod

Shake and strain into a cocktail glass. Decorate with a thin slice of lemon.

BLACK PEARL ▾

Put 2 spoons of crushed ice into a tulip glass and add:

½ measure Tía Maria
½ measure cognac

Top up with cold champagne and garnish with a black cherry.

BLACK VELVET ▾

Pour into a lager glass:

150 ml/¼ pint cold stout
150 ml/¼ pint dry champagne

Serve without stirring.

BORDEAUX COOLER ▾

Put 3 ice cubes in a large balloon glass and pour in:

4 measures claret
1 measure orange juice
½ measure brandy
½ measure lemon juice
1 teaspoon sugar

Stir well to mix. Garnish with a long spiral of lemon peel.

BROKEN SPUR COCKTAIL ♦ ▼

Pour into a cocktail shaker containing several ice cubes:

1 measure white port
1 measure gin
1 dash anisette
1 egg yolk

Shake and strain into a cocktail glass.

BUCK'S FIZZ ♥

Pour into a champagne flute the juice of 1 orange (cold from the refrigerator). Top up with cold champagne.

BURGUNDY COCKTAIL ▽ ♥

Put some ice cubes in a mixing glass and pour in:

3 measures red burgundy
1 measure cognac
3 dashes maraschino

Stir well and strain into a goblet. Garnish with a slice of lemon or orange and a maraschino cherry.

BURGUNDY PUNCH ♥

Put 10 or more ice cubes in a punch bowl and pour in:

1 bottle red burgundy
100 ml/3 fl oz ruby port
80 ml/2½ fl oz orange juice

2 teaspoons lemon juice
1 litre/1¾ pints iced water
3 tablespoons sugar

Stir very well and garnish with half slices of orange and cherries. Serve in goblets.
SERVES 10

CHABLIS CUP ♥

Put into a punch bowl:

3 ripe peaches, peeled and sliced
1 orange, cut into thin slices
cherries
3 teaspoons sugar

1 bottle chablis
4 measures Grand Marnier
4 measures kirsch

Stir to mix and leave in the refrigerator for 1 hour. Garnish with 4 mint sprigs and serve in goblets.
SERVES 6

CHAMPAGNE COCKTAIL ♥

Put 1 sugar lump in a champagne flute and add a few dashes of Angostura bitters. Pour in ½ measure cognac and fill up with cold champagne. Garnish with an orange slice and a cherry.

Buck's Fizz in a Lalique crystal glass.

Champagne Cocktail in Daum champagne glasses.

CHAMPAGNE JULEP ❦

Crush some mint leaves with 1 teaspoon sugar and put in the bottom of a champagne flute. Top up with cold champagne. Garnish with a mint sprig.

CHAMPAGNE VERBENA ❦

Infuse 3 sachets of verbena tea in 600 ml/1 pint boiling water. Allow to get cold and discard the sachets. Add some ice cubes and stir. Half fill 4 champagne flutes with cold champagne then pour in the verbena infusion. Stir lightly. Add a slice of peach to each glass and serve.
SERVES 4

CLARET PUNCH ❦

Pour into a punch bowl:

4 bottles claret
250 ml/8 fl oz brandy
250 ml/8 fl oz curaçao
1 litre/1¾ pints soda
3 oranges, cut into thin slices

Twenty minutes before serving put in 20 to 30 ice cubes. Serve in tulip glasses.
SERVES 25

CLOUD BUSTER ❦

Put 1 measure vodka in a tulip glass and drop in 3 ice cubes. Top up with champagne and garnish with a spiral of lemon peel.

DRUNKEN APRICOT PUNCH ❦

In a large jar put a layer of ice cubes, then a layer of apricots, peeled and sliced. Repeat the layers, ending with a layer of ice cubes. Then pour in:

4 measures Southern Comfort
1 bottle cold dry champagne

Serve in tulip glasses.
SERVES 8

DYNAMITE 🍸🍸

Put some ice cubes in a cocktail
shaker and add:

1 measure Grand Marnier
1 measure brandy
2 measures orange juice

Shake and strain into a champagne
flute. Top up with chilled champagne.
Garnish with a slice of orange astride
the rim of the glass and a cherry.

EAGLET 🍸

Put 1 measure Mandarine Imperiale in
a champagne flute. Top up with
chilled dry champagne.

KIR 8 🍷🍸

Pour into a balloon or tulip glass ¼ or
⅓ measure (according to taste) crème
de cassis. Top up with chilled dry
white wine, preferably a white
burgundy.

KIR ROYAL 🍸

Pour into a champagne flute ¼ or
⅓ measure (according to taste) crème
de cassis. Top up with cold
champagne.

MONIN 1 🍷

Pour into a tulip glass:

1 measure Monin triple lime liqueur
¼ measure Campari

Top up with chilled champagne.

Kir in a Daum glass.

POMPIER DAISY ▪

Put 2 ice cubes in an old fashioned glass and add:

1½ measures dry vermouth
1 measure crème de cassis

Stir to mix and top up with soda.

PORT FLIP ▮ ▼

Pour into a cocktail shaker containing several ice cubes:

1½ measures ruby port
½ measure cognac
1 teaspoon sugar
1 egg yolk

Shake thoroughly and strain into a cocktail glass. Grate some nutmeg on top.

POUSSE-RAPIÈRE ▮

Pour 1 measure armagnac into a tulip glass. Top up with cold pink or white sparkling wine or champagne.

SANGRIA ▮

Pour into a 2 litre/3½ pint jug:

1 bottle red wine
4 teaspoons sugar
2 measures cognac
2 measures Cointreau
juice of 1 orange
juice of ½ lemon
1 spiral of orange peel
1 spiral of lemon peel

Set aside until ready to serve then add 10 or more ice cubes. Top up with soda to taste (about 300 ml/½ pint). Garnish with half slices of orange and thin slices of lemon, peaches and apricots, if in season. Stir well and serve in balloon glasses.
SERVES 4–6

SHERRY FLIP ▮!

Put some ice cubes in a cocktail shaker and pour in:

1 measure sherry
1 egg
½ teaspoon sugar

Shake thoroughly and strain into a liqueur glass. Grate some nutmeg on top.

Port flip in a glass of Saint-Louis crystal.

SMILING ▼

Fill a champagne saucer with crushed ice to chill the glass. Throw away the ice, wipe the glass and pour in:

¼ measure brandy
2½ measures chilled dry white wine
1 measure ginger ale

Garnish with a half slice of orange and a cherry. Serve with a swizzle stick.

SPRITZER ♀

Pour into a balloon glass:

3 measures cold dry white Rhine wine
2 measures soda

Serve immediately.

WESTERN ELECTRIC 🍸🍷

Put some ice cubes in a cocktail shaker and add:

½ measure cognac
½ measure red Médoc wine
½ measure Cointreau

Shake and strain into a tulip glass. Top up with champagne and serve without stirring.

XERES COCKTAIL ♈

Put some ice cubes in a mixing glass and add:

1 dash orange bitters
1 dash peach bitters
1 glass sherry

Stir well and strain into a cocktail glass.

Sangria served in a glass by Cristal d'Arques and in a pitcher of Saint-Louis Crystal.

Hot Drinks

Hot drinks are the ancestors of today's cocktails. Until the middle of this century it was much easier to heat a mixture on a winter evening than to chill a drink on a hot summer's day. Electric refrigerators were not widely available till after the Second World War; ice was rare and expensive. Grog was the best remedy against a cold, taken before going to bed. If the prescription had not worked by next morning, the patient went to the chemist for advice, or if the cold got worse, to the doctor. Now the world has changed and so have drinks. Instead of *Grog*, *Hot Buttered Rum*, *Bishop* and the famous *Tom and Jerry*, people prefer coffee mixed with spirits or liqueurs—*Irish Coffee*, *Coffee Calypso* etc. On the other hand, at a time when people are returning to natural foods, the pleasure in age-old methods of preparing infusions of plants is due for a revival, making possible a variety of hot drinks as delicious as they are invigorating.

How to make an infusion

You need:
○ plants gathered at the right time, dried thoroughly and stored away from light, damp and smells;
○ boiling water with little or no mineral content (Evian or Volvic, for example);
○ a suitable container—an infuser, a pot made of porcelain, earthenware or glazed pottery, or a teapot used only for this purpose.

Always:
○ scald the pot;
○ put the sachet or the right amount of loose dried herbs in the pot;
○ cover and leave the herbs to give off their scent;
○ pour on boiling water;
○ cover again and leave to infuse for 3 to 5 minutes;
○ stir, take out the sachet before pouring, or pour the liquid and leaves through a fine strainer.

Do not reheat.

DECOCTION

Decoction is the process of boiling plants in order to extract the essence of the roots, stems or fruits to the full. It is not recommended for flowers or delicate leaves if the extract is intended for a drink.

Ruby Port, an ingredient of Bishop. Poster by Jean d'Ylen for Quindto's Port.

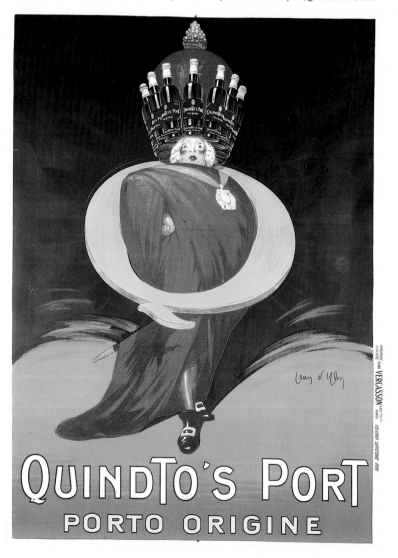

AMERICAN GROG ⬚

Put into a heatproof glass with a handle:

1 measure golden rum
1–2 teaspoons sugar
1–3 cloves
1 piece cinnamon
juice of ½ lemon
1 slice lemon

Top up with boiling water. Stir and serve.

APHRODISIAC ⬚

1 glass of port
1 dash curaçao

Put a good glassful of port into a small pan and add a dash of curaçao. Put over low heat and when it comes to just under boiling point pour into a heatproof glass with a handle. Garnish with a lemon slice and grate nutmeg over the top.

APPLE TODDY ⬚

4 cooking apples
200 ml/7 fl oz brandy
100 ml/3 fl oz peach liqueur
8 lemon slices, each stuck with a clove
1 cinnamon stick

Bake the apples in the oven. When they are cool peel them and purée the flesh. Put the apple purée in a jug or bowl and pour in the brandy and peach liqueur. Stir, cover and leave for 3 days. When you are ready to serve put 2 teaspoons of the mixture in each of 8 handled glasses and top up with boiling water. Garnish with a lemon slice with clove and a piece of the cinnamon stick.
SERVES 8

BILBERRY GROG ⬚

Poach 2 tablespoons of fresh bilberries and put them with 2 pieces sugar candy in a handled glass. Put into a small pan:

100 ml/3 fl oz bilberry juice
100 ml/3 fl oz whisky
100 ml/3 fl oz water

Put the pan over low heat and stirring constantly, bring to just under boiling point. Pour into the glass and garnish with a cinnamon stick and an orange slice astride the rim of the glass. Serve hot.

BISHOP ⬚

2 lemons
20 cloves
1 teaspoon ground mixed spice
1 cinnamon stick
3 tablespoons sugar
1 bottle ruby port
3 dashes cognac

Stick the lemons with the cloves and put them in a medium oven. While they are baking put a glass of water into a small saucepan with the mixed spice, cinnamon stick and sugar. Stir to dissolve the sugar then boil until reduced by half. Add the port, reduce the heat to low and stir constantly. Just before the mixture comes to the boil pour it into a preheated punch bowl. Drop in the baked lemons and stir in the cognac. Serve very hot.
SERVES 6

BLUE BLAZER ⬚

Put some very hot black coffee in a handled glass. Stir in 2 teaspoons sugar and grate some orange peel over the top. Heat 2 measures Irish whiskey and quickly set it alight. Pour it flaming on to the coffee and serve.

CAMOMILE AND WHITE WINE ⬚

Infuse 1 camomile tea sachet in 150 ml/¼ pint boiling water. Leave for 5 minutes and remove the sachet. Then heat a ½ glass white wine with 1 tablespoon rum and 2 teaspoons honey. Pour into a heatproof glass with a handle with the camomile infusion. Stir to mix. Serve hot.

CHOCOLATE PUNCH ⬚

Heat in a small pan:

300 ml/½ pint fresh milk
3 teaspoons cocoa powder
1 teaspoon instant coffee powder
1 teaspoon sugar
1 measure Kahlúa

Whisk until well mixed. Just before it comes to the boil pour into a heatproof glass with a handle. Spoon some whipped cream on top and sprinkle with ground cinnamon.
SERVES 2

CIDER GROG ⬚

Pour into a small pan:

200 ml/7 fl oz cider
100 ml/3 fl oz rum

Put over low heat and before the mixture comes to the boil pour it into a heatproof glass with a handle. Stir in sugar to taste and garnish with a lemon slice stuck with 2 cloves.

COFFEE AMARETTO ⬚

Put some very hot black coffee into a heatproof glass with a handle and add the following:

½ measure amaretto
½ measure Tía Maria or Kahlúa

Stir and spoon some whipped cream on top. Serve with amaretti biscuits.

COFFEE CALYPSO ◐

Make enough coffee for four and add:

4 measures Tía Maria
3 measures Lambs Navy rum

Put in a small pan over low heat. When hot, pour into heatproof glasses with handles. Add sugar to taste and top with whipped cream.
SERVES 4

COFFEE DIABLO ◐

Make enough hot black coffee to fill a handled glass three-quarters full. Pour into a small saucepan:

1 measure cognac
½ measure Cointreau
2 cloves
1 piece orange peel
1 piece lemon peel

Put the pan over low heat. Just before the mixture comes to the boil set it alight and pour it flaming over the coffee and serve.

GOLDEN TEA ◐

Beat 2 egg yolks with 3 teaspoons sugar until pale and thick. Make some strong tea and put 100 ml/3 fl oz of it in a small pan with 1 measure arak and 3 measures double cream. Heat gently stirring constantly. Stir in the egg yolk mixture. Pour into a heatproof glass with a handle and serve with a cinnamon stick to garnish.

GROG ◐

Put into a heatproof glass with a handle:

1 measure golden rum
1 sugar lump
2 cloves
½ measure lemon juice
1 cinnamon stick

Top up the mixture with boiling water and garnish with a sliver of lemon peel or a lemon slice.

HOT BULLSHOT ◐

Heat gently a cupful of beef bouillon or consommé and add to it:

1 measure vodka
½ measure lemon juice
1 teaspoon Worcestershire sauce
1 dash Tabasco sauce

Stir the mixture gently and pour into a heatproof glass with a handle. Serve while still warm.

Grog, the most widely popular of hot drinks.

Irish Coffee. Glass and accessories from the Danish Boutique, Paris.

MARTINO TEA ⅏

Into a heatproof glass with a handle pour:

300 ml/½ pint hot mint tea
2 measures arak
1 teaspoon clear honey

Add sugar to taste. Stir well to mix and serve.

NIGHT CAP ⅏

Beat 3 egg yolks and 4 teaspoons sugar until pale and thick. Put into a small pan:

600 ml/1 pint beer
3 measures whisky
2 teaspoons cocoa powder

Put the pan over low heat and bring to just under boiling point. Pour it very slowly over the beaten egg yolks stirring constantly until the mixture is smooth. Pour into heatproof glasses with handles. Sprinkle powdered cinnamon on top and serve with cinnamon sticks.
SERVES 2

PEPPERMINT PICK ME UP ⅏

Make 200 ml/7 fl oz strong black coffee and pour it into a heatproof glass with a handle. Add 1 measure crème de menthe and stir to mix. Cover the top with whipped cream and sprinkle the cream with several dashes of green crème de menthe. Serve immediately.

RUM ORANGE GROG ⅏

Infuse 1 sachet orange tea in 200 ml/7 fl oz boiling water. After a few minutes remove the sachet. Add:

1 tablespoon rum
1 teaspoon vanilla sugar

Stir and garnish with a slice of orange.

HOT BUTTERED RUM ⅏

Put into a heatproof handled glass:

1½ measures rum
1 sugar lump
2 cloves

Top up with boiling water. Float a pat of butter on top. Stir gently and serve.

HOT JAMAICAN COW ⅏

Heat a glassful of milk in a small pan. Just before it comes to the boil pour it into a handled glass. Pour in 1 measure Tía Maria and serve.

IRISH COFFEE ⅏

Heat a handled glass. Then fill it three-quarters full of hot strong coffee. Add:

1 teaspoon sugar (or more to taste)
1 measure Irish whiskey

Stir to mix. Then carefully pour in some double cream over the back of a spoon so that it floats on top.

ISLAND CREAM GROG ⅏

Heat a heatproof glass with a handle and pour in:

3 measures rum
200 ml/7 fl oz boiling water

Sweeten to taste and stir to mix. Put some whipped cream on top and sprinkle with grated nutmeg.

KLABAUTER MAN ⅏

Put some sugar candy (to taste) in a heated handled glass. Pour into a small pan:

200 ml/7 fl oz ruby port
3 measures arak
2 teaspoons lemon juice

Put the pan over low heat. Just before the mixture comes to the boil pour it into the glass.

Tea, rum and Cointreau combine well together in Sunset Tea.

SKI BUNNY 🍷

Heat in a small pan:

300 ml/½ pint beer
½ measure rum
1 measure Steinhäger gin
1 pinch ground cardamom
1 pinch ground cinnamon
1 pinch ground ginger

Beat 3 egg yolks in a bowl with a whisk. Gradually add the hot liquid whisking all the time until you have a smooth mixture. Serve in a large heatproof glass with a handle. Garnish with a cinnamon stick and a piece of lemon peel.

SUNSET TEA 🍷

Make 200 ml/7 fl oz tea and pour it into a heatproof glass with a handle. Pour into a small pan:

½ measure golden rum
1 measure Cointreau
2 measures orange juice

Put the pan over low heat and bring the mixture to just under boiling point, stirring constantly. Pour immediately into the glass with the tea. Garnish with a slice of orange stuck with 3 cloves, a spiral of orange peel and a cinnamon stick.

TOM AND JERRY 🍷

Separate 1 egg and mix the yolk with:

1 measure golden rum
1 teaspoon sugar
1 pinch pepper
1 pinch ground cinnamon
1 pinch grated nutmeg

Mix well until smooth. Beat the egg white until stiff and mix it into the egg yolk mixture. Pour it into a large heatproof glass with a handle. Top up with boiling water, stirring well to mix. Add ¼ measure brandy and sprinkle grated nutmeg on top.
N.B. If you prefer top up with boiling milk instead of the water.

VALLÉE D'AUGE 🍷

Beat an egg yolk with 1 teaspoon sugar until pale and thick. Heat in a small pan:

200 ml/7 fl oz milk
1 measure calvados

Just before the mixture comes to the boil pour it over the egg yolk, stirring until smooth. Pour into a heated heatproof glass with a handle. Garnish with a slice of apple astride the rim of the glass. Sprinkle ground cinnamon over the top.

VERBENA CREOLE 🍷

Infuse 1 sachet verbena in 200 ml/7 fl oz boiling water. After 5 minutes remove the sachet and add to the infusion:

juice of 1 lemon
1 dash rum
a little ground cinnamon
2 dessertspoons sugar

Stir and serve in a handled glass.

WHISKY-LIME GROG 🍷

Infuse 1 sachet lime tea in 300 ml/½ pint boiling water. After 5 minutes remove the sachet and add:

1 tablespoon whisky
1 dash vanilla essence
2 teaspoons sugar

Serve in a handled glass. Garnish with a slice of lemon.

WINTER WARMER 🍷

Beat an egg yolk with 1 teaspoon sugar until pale and thick. Heat in a small pan:

300 ml/½ pint milk
1½ measures whisky

Before the mixture comes to the boil pour it over the egg yolk and beat until smooth. Serve in a handled glass.

Non-alcoholic Cocktails and Drinks

savoir boire...

peu et bon

Is temperance the greatest of the virtues? Plutarch thought so. Many religions forbid the consumption of alcohol and it can also be banned by law as happened in the United States earlier this century during the infamous 'Prohibition' period. Even one stiff drink can have a ruinous effect on certain people's mood or complexion. There are also occasions when even the most enthusiastic wine- and spirit-drinker will feel like sampling what William Cowper called 'the cups that cheer but not inebriate.' (Cowper was speaking of a particular beverage, tea, but there are many delicious and refreshing recipes in this chapter to which the description could apply equally well.)

It is neither shameful nor ridiculous to abstain from alcohol and in these health-conscious days an increasing number of drinkers are reducing their alcohol intake, even if they do not choose to give up entirely. There are many cocktail recipes to please lovers of good food who do not like or cannot take alcoholic drinks. The rules are just the same as for other cocktails, the only difference being that the sole ingredients are fruit juices, soda, herbal infusions, syrups and non-alcoholic essences. The results are amazing if you take some care with the preparation and presentation of the cocktails.

"Learn to drink a little of the best. . . ." and learn to appreciate non-alcoholic cocktails. Poster issued by the French National Committee against Alcoholism.

ANGEL SPECIAL 🍶❗

Pour into an electric blender:

200 ml/7 fl oz orange juice
½ measure grenadine
1 egg yolk
2 dashes Angostura bitters
3–4 tablespoons crushed ice

Blend for 30 seconds and pour into a champagne flute. Garnish with a cherry on a cocktail stick.

BARBARELLA 🍷

Put 2 ice cubes in a balloon glass. Add:

4–5 dashes Angostura bitters
2 teaspoons strawberry syrup

Top up with grape juice and stir well.

CATHERINE BLOSSOM 🍶▯

Put into an electric blender:

200 ml/7 fl oz orange juice
2 teaspoons maple syrup
2 scoops orange sorbet

Blend for 15 seconds and pour into a collins glass. Top up with soda.

CHOCOLATE WITH TWO FLAVOURS ▯

70 g/2½ oz bitter chocolate
1 glass hot milk
2 teaspoons sugar
1 sachet lime tea

Melt the chocolate very gently in a little water. Very gradually stir in the hot milk. Add the sugar and heat for a few minutes. Drop in the lime sachet and leave for 5 minutes. Remove the sachet and serve very hot in a handled glass.

CINDERELLA 🍶▯

Put some ice cubes in a cocktail shaker and add:

2 measures lemon juice
2 measures orange juice
2 measures pineapple juice

Blend and strain into a whisky tumbler. Garnish with a half slice pineapple, half slice orange and half slice lemon all impaled on a cocktail stick.

COCO-OCO 🍶🍷

Put some crushed ice into an electric blender and add:

4 teaspoons cream of coconut or coconut syrup
2 teaspoons lemon juice
1 teaspoon maraschino syrup
100 ml/3 fl oz fresh milk
4 dashes Angostura bitters

Blend for a few seconds and strain into a balloon glass or into a coconut shell. Garnish with a cherry.

CONCLAVE 🍶▯

Fill a cocktail shaker one-third full of crushed ice and add:

½ glass orange juice
¼ glass fresh milk
⅛ glass raspberry syrup

Shake and pour into a tumbler. Garnish with an orange slice and serve with a straw.

DOU DOU FIZZ 🍶🍷

Put 3 or 4 tablespoons of crushed ice into an electric blender and add:

1 egg white
3 teaspoons sugar
4 teaspoons lemon juice
2 teaspoons cream of coconut or coconut syrup 6 dashes rum essence

Blend for a few seconds and pour into a fancy glass. Top up with soda and garnish with a lemon slice impaled on a cocktail stick.

DUMMY DAISY 🍶🍷

Put some crushed ice in a cocktail shaker and add:

4 teaspoons raspberry syrup
2 teaspoons lime juice
1 teaspoon sugar

Shake and pour without straining into a cocktail glass. Garnish with fresh raspberries.
N.B. For variation, replace the raspberry syrup with strawberry syrup and garnish with two fresh strawberries impaled on a cocktail stick.

FARMER'S JOY 🍶▯

Put some ice cubes in a cocktail shaker and add:

1 egg yolk
3 measures tomato juice
1 dash lemon juice
Worcestershire sauce, celery salt and
*   black pepper, to taste*

Shake and strain into an old fashioned glass. Garnish with a piece of celery.

FELICITATION 🍶🍷

Put 2 or 3 tablespoons of crushed ice into an electric blender and add:

1 measure orange juice
1 measure tomato juice
1 measure blackcurrant juice
1 egg yolk

Blend well at high speed until the ice has melted. Pour into a fancy glass and serve. Garnish with a half slice orange fixed on the rim of the glass.

FROSTY LIME

Put in an electric blender:

1 scoop lime sorbet
4 teaspoons grapefruit juice
4 teaspoons mint syrup

Blend at high speed for 30 seconds and strain into a champagne saucer. Garnish with a fresh mint sprig and a slice of lemon fixed on the rim of the glass. Serve with short straws.

FRUIT CUP

Put some ice cubes in a mixing glass and add:

1 measure raspberry syrup
1 measure strawberry syrup
1 measure pineapple juice
1 measure lemon juice
1 measure orange juice
1 measure grape juice

Stir well to mix and strain into a large tumbler. Garnish with banana slices.

FRUIT PUNCH

Pour into a goblet:

1½ measures pineapple juice
1½ measures lemon juice
2 measures orange juice
a few dashes grenadine

Mix well. Add two or three ice cubes and garnish with a slice of orange, a slice of lemon, a cube of pineapple and a cherry. Serve with decorative straws.

Frosty Lime in a glass from the Danish Boutique,.Paris. Accessory by Habitat.

GRENADINE SHAKE

Put 3 tablespoons of crushed ice into an electric blender and add:

4 teaspoons grenadine
4 teaspoons pineapple juice
2 teaspoons lemon juice
1 egg white

Blend for 10 seconds and pour without straining into a goblet. Add some soda or lemonade and garnish with a mint sprig and a cherry on a cocktail stick.

HONEYMOON

Put some crushed ice into a cocktail shaker and add:

1 measure maple syrup or clear honey
4 teaspoons lime juice
1 measure orange juice
1 measure apple juice

Shake and strain into a tulip glass. Garnish with a twist of orange peel and a cherry on a cocktail stick.

INCORRUPTIBLE CHAMPAGNE

Put some ice cubes in a cocktail shaker and add:

1 measure grapefruit juice
½ measure orange juice

Shake and strain into a champagne flute. Top up with chilled lemonade.

JACK'S SPECIAL

Put some crushed ice into an electric blender and add:

50 g/2 oz strawberries
200 ml/7 fl oz pineapple juice
1–2 dashes lemon juice

Blend and pour into a balloon glass. Decorate with a strawberry halved and impaled on a cocktail stick.

KENTUMI

Pour into an electric blender:

1 measure passion fruit syrup
1 scoop vanilla ice cream
2 teaspoons lime juice

Blend and pour without straining into a goblet. Top up with soda or lemonade and garnish with a cherry on a cocktail stick.

LAIT DE POULE WITH LIME

4 glasses milk
3 sachets lime tea
3 fresh eggs
4 level tablespoons sugar

Bring the milk to the boil. Take the pan off the heat and drop in the lime sachets. Infuse for 5 minutes and remove the sachets. Beat the eggs with the sugar and add gradually to the milk stirring all the time. Pour into handled glasses and serve hot.
SERVES 4

LEMON MINT

Infuse 1 mint tea sachet in 250 ml/ 8 fl oz boiling water in a heatproof handled glass for 5 minutes. Rub 2 sugar lumps over a lemon until they absorb the zest. Add the sugar to the infusion. Serve hot.

LIME AND BLACKCURRANT TEA

Infuse 2 sachets of lime tea in 350 ml/ 12 fl oz boiling water. Remove the sachets after 5 minutes and leave to cool. Pour the infusion into a jug and add 100 ml/3 fl oz blackcurrant syrup and a large glass of crushed ice. Stir and serve in fancy glasses.
SERVES 4

LIME MARTINIQUE

Infuse 3 sachets lime tea in 600 ml/ 1 pint boiling water. Leave until cold. Discard the sachets and pour the infusion into a large jug. Add 3 small (individual) bottles pineapple juice and some ice cubes. Pour into goblets. Garnish with a piece of pineapple and a cherry on a cocktail stick.
SERVES 4

MAI-TAI MIX

Mai-Tai Mix is an ingredient in many cocktails. To make it mix:

250 ml/8 fl oz sugar syrup
300 ml/½ pint orange juice
a few dashes Angostura bitters
a few dashes bitter almond essence

MEXICAN GRANDMA

Infuse a sachet of camomile tea in 200 ml/7 fl oz boiling water for 5 minutes. Discard the sachet and add 1 clove. Squeeze the juice of half an orange and half a lemon and put in a small pan with 2 teaspoons of honey. Heat gently and mix with the infusion. Remove the clove and serve hot in a handled glass.

MINT TOMATO

3 sachets mint tea
3 small (individual) bottles tomato juice
1 lime, cut into slices

Infuse the mint sachets in 300 ml/ 12 fl oz boiling water and allow to cool. Discard the sachets. Add the tomato juice and stir well to mix. Strain into tulip glasses and add some ice cubes. Garnish with the lime slices.
SERVES 4

NONALC MAI TAI ♀♟

Put some ice cubes in a cocktail shaker and add:

10 dashes rum essence
*2 measures Mai-Tai Mix**
1 measure lime juice
1 measure pineapple juice

Shake and strain into a balloon glass one-third full of crushed ice. Top up with soda. Stir to mix and garnish with a half slice of pineapple and a mint sprig.
*See recipe on page 144.

ORANGE-PEPPERMINT SHAKE ♟♟

Put 3 tablespoons of crushed ice into an electric blender and add:

1 egg white
2 teaspoons sugar
2 mint sprigs

Blend until the mint is finely chopped. Add 200 ml/7 fl oz orange juice and blend for a few seconds. Pour into a balloon glass and garnish with a slice of orange and a mint sprig.

PARSON'S SPECIAL ♟♟

Put some ice cubes in a cocktail shaker and add:

2 measures orange juice
4 dashes grenadine
1 egg yolk

Shake and strain into a champagne saucer. Top up with soda.

PIÑA COLADA ♟♟

Put a little crushed ice into an electric blender and add:

2 measures cream of coconut (Coco Lopez)
1 measure pineapple juice
1 dash orgeat syrup

Blend and pour into a fancy glass. Garnish with a piece of pineapple and a cherry impaled on a cocktail stick. Serve with 2 straws.

PINEAPPLE COBBLER ♟♟

Put some ice cubes in a cocktail shaker and pour in:

200 ml/7 fl oz pineapple juice
1 dash lime juice
5 dashes Angostura bitters

Shake and strain into a goblet. Top up with bitter lemon. Garnish with a quarter slice of fresh pineapple, a cherry and a paper parasol. Serve with decorative straws.

PINEAPPLE COOLER ♟♟

Put some ice cubes in a cocktail shaker and pour in:

200 ml/7 fl oz pineapple juice
2 teaspoons lime juice
100 ml/3 fl oz bitter lemon
5 dashes Angostura bitters

Shake and strain into a large tulip glass. Garnish with a slice of pineapple, a cherry and a paper parasol. Serve with straws.

PINK MELON DELIGHT ♟♟

60 g/2½ oz melon, cut into dice
60 g/2½ oz strawberries
1 scoop orange sorbet
150 ml/¼ pint ginger ale

Put the melon, strawberries and orange sorbet into an electric blender and blend at high speed for 15 seconds. Gently stir in the ginger ale

and pour into a large cocktail glass. Garnish with a piece of fresh melon and a hulled strawberry impaled on a cocktail stick and a paper parasol.

PINK PANTHER FLIP ♟♟

Put 3 tablespoons of crushed ice in an electric blender and add:

200 ml/7 fl oz orange juice
4 teaspoons grenadine
1 egg yolk
2 dashes Angostura bitters

Blend at high speed for 10 seconds and pour into a tulip glass. Garnish with a cherry on a cocktail stick and a paper parasol.

PLUM SHAKE ♟♟

Put in an electric blender:

150 ml/¼ pint plum juice
100 ml/3 fl oz orange juice
2 scoops vanilla ice cream

Blend and pour into a large goblet. Serve with two decorative straws.
N.B. For variation, try other flavours of ice cream, such as orange or pistachio.

PUSSY CAT ♟♟♟

Put some crushed ice into a cocktail shaker or an electric blender and add:

2 measures orange juice
2 measures pineapple juice
2 tablespoons grapefruit juice
3 dashes grenadine

Blend or shake and pour into a cocktail glass. Garnish with a half slice of orange and a quarter slice of grapefruit.

Pussy Foot in a glass by Cristal d'Arques.

PUSSY FOOT 2 🍸 🍷

Pour into a cocktail shaker:

2 measures orange juice
2 measures lemon juice
2 measures lime juice
1 dash grenadine
1 egg yolk

Shake well and strain into a tulip glass. Garnish with a cherry impaled on a cocktail stick and a slice of lemon or orange fixed on the rim of the glass.

RED LIGHT 🍸 🍷

Put some ice cubes in a cocktail shaker and pour in:

1 measure lemon juice
1 measure strawberry juice
1 measure orange juice
1 measure pineapple juice
a few dashes grenadine

Shake well and strain into a balloon glass. Garnish with an orange slice and a flower. Serve with 2 short straws.

RED SOMBRERO COCKTAIL 🍸 🍶

Put some ice cubes in a cocktail shaker and pour in:

1 measure pineapple juice
1 measure orange juice
1 measure lemon juice
1 measure grenadine

Shake thoroughly and strain into a large tumbler. Top up with cold ginger ale and garnish with a lemon slice, a cherry and a paper parasol. Serve with a straw.

RIVIERA ♦ ▮

Put some ice cubes in a cocktail shaker and pour in:

200 ml/7 fl oz orange juice
4 teaspoons blackcurrant syrup
10 dashes Angostura bitters

Shake and strain into a tumbler containing several ice cubes. Garnish with a kumquat and an orange slice. Serve with straws.
N.B. For variation, substitute redcurrant syrup.

SCARLET COCKTAIL WITH ORANGE ▯ ▮

Infuse 3 sachets of orange tea in 1 litre/1¾ pints boiling water. Allow to cool and discard the sachets. Put some ice cubes in a mixing glass and add:

the cold infusion
2 tablespoons strawberry syrup
2 tablespoons raspberry syrup
2 tablespoons blackcurrant syrup

Mix well and strain into four tumblers, each containing two or three ice cubes. Add a few fresh raspberries and strawberries and serve with decorative straws.
SERVES 4

SKI WASSER ▮

Fill a tumbler with ice cubes and pour in:

1 measure lemon juice
1 measure raspberry juice

Top up with soda. Garnish with a half slice of lemon and a half slice of orange. Serve with straws.
N.B. For variation, try different fruit syrups, such as strawberry, blackcurrant or redcurrant.

SORBET AND TEA PUNCH ▥ �

Put into an electric blender:

2 scoops orange sorbet
1 measure orange juice
2 measures cold tea
1 tablespoon sugar
2 teaspoons lemon juice

Blend and pour into a tulip glass.

SPICY GINGER TANTALIZER ▥ �!

Put some crushed ice in an electric blender and add:

100 ml/3 fl oz orange juice
15 g/½ oz stem ginger (in syrup)
2 teaspoons ginger syrup

Blend and pour into a cocktail glass. Garnish with a slice of stem ginger and serve with straws.

SUMMER COOLER ♦ �C

Put some ice cubes in a cocktail shaker and pour in:

4 teaspoons blackcurrant syrup
200 ml/7 fl oz orange juice
10 dashes Angostura bitters

Shake and strain into a large tulip glass. Drop in 2 ice cubes and serve.

SWINGER ♦ ▮

Put some crushed ice in a cocktail shaker and pour in:

200 ml/7 fl oz grapefruit juice
1 measure pineapple juice
4 teaspoons sugar syrup

Shake and strain into a tumbler. Add a few frozen cubes of grapefruit juice. Garnish with a grapefruit segment and a cherry on a cocktail stick.

TEA WITH MINT ▥

Put 4 teaspoons green tea in a heated teapot with 4 mint leaves and 5 to 8 sugar lumps. Pour in 1 litre/1¾ pints boiling water, infuse for 5 minutes and serve in handled glasses.
SERVES 4

TENDERFOOT MINT ♦ �C

Fill a cocktail shaker one third full of ice cubes and add:

1 measure mint syrup
½ measure lemon juice
2 teaspoons sugar syrup
1 dash lime juice

Shake and pour without straining into a champagne saucer.

TIPSY GUAVA ▥ �C

Put some crushed ice in an electric blender and add:

200 ml/7 fl oz guava juice
2 teaspoons lime juice
4 teaspoons blackcurrant syrup
5 dashes rum essence

Blend and strain into a tulip glass. Decorate with 3 melon balls.

TOMATO CUCUMBER COOLER ▥

Put a little crushed ice in an electric blender and add:

150 ml/¼ pint tomato juice
25 g/1 oz peeled cucumber
2 dashes lemon juice
2 dashes Worcestershire sauce
1 pinch salt
a little black pepper

Blend well. Frost a balloon glass with salt. Pour in the mixture and garnish with a slice of cucumber on the rim of the glass.

Tomato Cucumber Cooler in a Daum glass.

TOMATO MINT COCKTAIL

3 sachets mint tea
600 ml/1 pint tomato juice
pepper
celery salt
4 slices lemon

Infuse the mint sachets in 3 cups boiling water for 5 minutes and remove the sachets. Allow to cool. Put some ice cubes in a mixing glass and pour in the infusion and the tomato juice. Mix well and pour into tumblers containing ice cubes. Season to taste with pepper and celery salt and garnish with the lemon slices.

SERVES 4

TRAPICHE SYRUP

1 litre/1¾ pints orange juice
500 g/1 lb cane sugar
1 teaspoon ground cloves
1 teaspoon ground cinnamon

In a saucepan heat the orange juice over low heat. When moderately hot add the sugar and stir to dissolve completely. Add the spices. Turn off the heat and let the mixture cool slowly on the hob. When cold strain into bottles.

TUTTI FRUTTI VERBENA COCKTAIL

Infuse 3 sachets verbena tea in 600 ml/1 pint boiling water. Leave to cool. Remove the sachets. Strain into a mixing glass and add:

juice of 2 oranges
juice of 2 lemons
1 glass apricot juice
1 glass pineapple juice
a few ice cubes

Mix well and strain into goblets. Add 2 ice cubes to each goblet and garnish with a slice of lemon or orange.
SERVES 4

VIRGIN MARY ∎

Put 2 ice cubes in an old fashioned glass and add:

150 ml/¼ pint tomato juice
2 dashes Tabasco sauce
2 dashes lemon juice
2 dashes Worcestershire sauce
celery salt and pepper to taste

Stir well and garnish with a sprig of celery leaves.

YELLOW DWARF 🍹 🍸

Put some crushed ice into a mixing glass and add:

1 egg yolk
100 ml/3 fl oz double cream
4 teaspoons passion fruit syrup
1 dash bitter almond essence
a splash of soda

Stir well and strain into a champagne saucer.

Glossary

A

Absinthe banned in its original form because its main ingredient, wormwood, was considered dangerous to health. There are many popular substitutes flavoured with aniseed and other herbs. See Anis, Pastis, Pernod.

Advocaat a Dutch liqueur, yellow in colour and thick in consistency, made of brandy, egg yolks and herbs.

Aguardiente a generic Spanish term for brandy-like spirits and particularly applied to marcs.

Allasch a kind of kummel flavoured with almonds.

Amaretto an Italian liqueur made from apricot kernels. BN Amaretto di Amore, Amaretto di Sarronno.

Amaro the Italian word for bitters.

Ambassadeur (BN) an apéritif made of wine flavoured with quinine, and orange peel (16°).

Amer Picon (BN) an apéritif flavoured with quinine, gentian and orange essence (21°).

Amontillado see sherry.

Amoroso see sherry.

Anesone an Italian aniseed-flavoured drink similar to Pastis (45°).

Angostura (BN) the best-known aromatic bitters used in cocktails. Made in Trinidad with gentian and orange peel as its dominant ingredients (44°).

Anis term used to cover a number of alcoholic drinks flavoured with aniseed.

Anisette a sweet aniseed-flavoured liqueur (25°). BN Marie Brizard.

Apéritif the French word for a drink taken before meals to stimulate the appetite. Also used specifically to describe those brand-name drinks like Dubonnet, St Raphael, Pernod, Campari, Punt e Mes etc.

Aperol an orange-coloured Italian bitter of low alcoholic strength (6°).

Apple brandy see Applejack and Calvados.

Applejack an apple brandy made in the United States with a strong rough taste. Calvados can be used as a substitute.

Apricot brandy an apricot-flavoured brandy made by the infusion of apricots in spirit.
BN Abricotine, Apry.

Aquavit a spirit produced in Scandinavian countries from grain or potatoes and redistilled with flavourings (35°–50°).

Armagnac a brandy or eau-de-vie based on wine produced in the vineyards of the departments of Gers and part of Les Landes and Lot et Garonne (40°–43°). It is made from some of the grape varieties used for Cognac. The finest armagnac with excellent bouquet comes from Bas-Armagnac while Ténarèze produces a more strongly flavoured drink.

Arak a spirit distilled in the east and usually flavoured with aniseed.

Aurum (BN) a golden-coloured Italian liqueur tasting of orange (40°).

B

B & B (BN) a ready-prepared liqueur combining Benedictine and brandy (43°).

Bacardi (BN) a famous Caribbean firm of rum producers best known for its light white rums.

Baileys Irish Cream (BN) a cream liqueur based on Irish whiskey flavoured with chocolate.

Banane, crème de a liqueur made from spirit and bananas.

Banyuls a sweet red wine (vin doux naturel) from Roussillon in the southwest of France.

Benedictine (BN) a liqueur flavoured with a number of herbs and essences prepared at Fecamp (Normandy) according to an old recipe belonging to the local Benedictine abbey (43°).

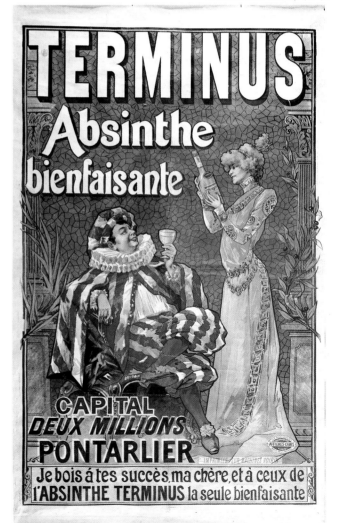

Poster by Tamagno, 1914, for Terminus Absinthe.

Bilberry (myrtille) liqueur or crème based on bilberry and spirit (not much used in cocktails).

Bitters concentrated essences or drinks made from roots, fruits and peel, commonly gentian, quinine and orange, macerated in spirits. Concentrated bitters include (BN) Angostura, Peychaud, Underberg, and bitter apéritifs include Amer Picon, Campari, Fernet Branca.

Blackberry (mûre) liqueur based on ripe fruit and spirit and very popular in northern Europe (Kroatzbeere in Germany and Jerzyvowka in Poland).

Blend applied particularly to whisk(e)y on both sides of the Atlantic. It describes Scotch which is a mixture of a malt and a grain whisky; and American whiskey which is a mixture of straight whiskeys or of whiskey and a neutral spirit. Blended rye is a mixture of whiskeys coming from several distilleries.

Borovicka a kind of gin from eastern Europe (40°).

Boukha a brandy made from figs in Tunisia.

Bourbon American whiskey originally made in Bourbon County, Kentucky. BN Barclay's, Four Roses, IW Harper, Jim Beam, Kentucky Gentleman, Old Charter, Old Forester etc.

Brandy a spirit distilled from any fruit but particularly the grape.

Byrrh (BN) an apéritif based on red wine and flavoured with quinine and orange peel (17°).

C

Cacao, crème de a chocolate liqueur made from roasted cocoa beans; there is a brown and a white version.

Calvados a brandy made from apple cider in the Calvados region of Normandy (40°–45°). The finest comes from the pays d'Auge.

Camomile its dried flowers are used in herbal tea. It can rouse appetite, help digestion, calm a fever, cure a headache. Its bitter flavour is found in vermouths and in some liqueurs.

Campari (BN) an Italian bitter apéritif, crimson in colour, and essential base for the Americano and the Negroni.

Canadian whisky distilled in Canada from a mash of fermented cereals including rye, malted rye etc (32.5°–43.5°). BN Black Velvet, Canadian Club, Crown Royal, Seagram's VO.

Cassis, crème de a sweet liqueur made from blackcurrants; the best comes from Dijon.

Chambéry dry white French vermouth made in the Chambéry region of France. BN Boissière, Dolin, Gaudin.

Champagne a sparkling white wine produced in the Champagne region of France; its special sparkle is produced by secondary fermentation in the bottle.

Chartreuse (BN) a liqueur based on herbs and made by the Carthusian fathers at Voiron in France. The green variety is very scented and strong (55°) and the yellow is sweeter (40°).

Cherry brandy a liqueur produced by macerating cherries in alcohol. BN Cherry Marnier, Peter Heering, see also Kirsch and Maraschino.

Chocolate many liqueurs are flavoured with chocolate: the best known are the crèmes de cacao, BN Chocolat Suisse, Royal Mint Chocolate, Royal Orange Chocolate.

Cinzano (BN) Italian vermouth available as sweet

Poster designed by Mucha in 1899 for Moet & Chandon Champagne.

red (rosso), dry white (secco) and sweet white (bianco).

Coffee liqueur made from roasted coffee beans; there are many examples on the market including Kahlúa and Tía Maria.

Cognac brandy (eau-de-vie) obtained from two distillations of white wine made from grapes grown in the Charente region (40°). The best is Fine Champagne which describes a brandy distilled from wines from both the Grande and Petite Champagne but containing more than half the former.

Cointreau (BN) an orange liqueur based on the peel of bitter oranges, the best known of the triple-sec curaçaos.

Cordial the name for a fruit liqueur in the United States.

Corn whiskey American whiskey made from a mash containing not less than 80 per cent maize (40°).

Crème de designation of sweet liqueurs containing more than 400 g (14 oz) sugar per litre (1¾ pint), not to be confused with cream liqueurs actually containing cream.

Cuarante y Tres (BN) a very sweet Spanish liqueur with a vanilla flavour (34°).

Curaçao a Caribbean island which grows the small bitter oranges the peel of which is used in making orange liqueurs like triple-sec (25°). Curaçao is available in various colours including blue.

Cynar (BN) Italian apéritif based on artichokes (17°). Served as a bitter apéritif with ice and soda.

D

Danziger Goldwasser originally made in Danzig (Gdansk, Poland) and nowadays in Berlin (30°). It is related to Kummel, is flavoured with caraway and anis and contains flecks of gold leaf, hence its name.

Drambuie (BN) a liqueur based on Scotch whisky, heather honey and herbs (40°).

Dubonnet (BN) a wine-based apéritif of three kinds—red flavoured with quinine, dry rather like a dry white vermouth, and white which is sweeter.

F

Falernum a syrup made in the Caribbean mainly of limes and ginger and containing very little alcohol.

Fernet-Branca (BN) an Italian bitter made of roots and herbs (40°). Recommended as a hang-over cure.

Fine a brandy: the term to use when ordering an unspecified brandy in France.

Fino see sherry.

Floc a mixture of armagnac and grape juice.

French shorthand for dry vermouth. French vermouths used to be dry eg Chambéry, Noilly Prat, and Italian sweet, but now both countries produce both kinds.

G

Galliano (BN) a straw-coloured Italian liqueur flavoured with herbs and spices which is well known because of its contribution to Harvey Wallbanger and Golden Cadillac.

Genever Dutch gin frequently sold in stoneware bottles; also known as Hollands and in the past as Schiedam (an old centre of gin distillery near Rotterdam). Genever is distilled from fermented rye, barley and maize and flavoured with juniper, coriander, caraway and aniseed (40°).

Gentiane an apéritif liqueur with a bitter-sweet taste based on gentian root and alcohol.

Gin a grain spirit flavoured with juniper and coriander (40°). Its name comes from Genever (see above). The best-known gin today is London Dry Gin, very dry and lightly flavoured, an essential ingredient in many cocktails. Plymouth Gin is sweeter and lighter. BN Beefeater, Booth, Burnett's, Coates (Plymouth Gin), Gilbeys, Gordons, Greenalls, Squires, Tanqueray.

Glayva Scotch liqueur based on whisky, honey and herbs (40°).

Grand Marnier (BN) a liqueur based on cognac and orange (40°). Like many orange-flavoured liqueurs it is made from orange peel of the curaçao type.

Grappa an Italian brandy distilled from grape skins (40°).

Grenadine a red syrup flavoured with pomegranate.

H

Highland malt pure malt whisky distilled in the Scottish Highlands north of an imaginary line running from Greenock to Dundee.

Hollands see Genever.

I

Irish Mist (BN) a liqueur based on Irish whiskey and heather honey (40°).

Irish Velvet (BN) an Irish liqueur based on whiskey and coffee.

Irish whiskey distilled from a mash of fermented barley and other cereals; its method of distillation and the cereals used give it the clear and light flavour typical of this whiskey.

izarra (BN) a French Basque liqueur based on armagnac flavoured with herbs and plants. Yellow Izarra (40°) is sweeter and less strong than the green variety (50°).

J

Jack Daniel's (BN) an American whiskey similar to bourbon made in Tennessee by the sour mash process (45°).

Advertisement for Gordon's Gin by Malinowski, 1981.

K

Kabänes (BN) a German liqueur with a bitter taste made in Cologne (35°).

Kahlúa (BN) a coffee liqueur originating in Mexico (26.5°).

Kirsch a French brandy double-distilled from fermented cherries (40°–45°).

Korn a grain spirit from northern Germany (35°–40°).

Kummel a north European liqueur flavoured with caraway, cumin, fennel and orris root (30°–40°). BN Allasch, Bols, Fockink, Mentzendorff, Wolfschmidt.

L

Lillet (BN) a French dry white vermouth; there is also a sweeter red variety.

Lowland malt a pure malt whisky distilled in the south of Scotland.

M

Madeira a fortified wine produced in the island of that name. There are four types: Bual and Malmsey, fruity and sweet dessert wines; Verdelho and Sercial, lighter and drier apéritifs.

Malibu (BN) a liqueur based on rum and coconut.

Malt whisky a Scotch whisky made exclusively from fermented malted barley. A single malt comes from one distilling and a vatted malt is a blend of single malts.

Mandarine a liqueur made with tangerine peel and cognac; it is best known under various brand names: Cartron, Mandarin, Mandarine Imperiale, Mandarine Pages, Monin.

Maraschino an Italian cherry liqueur much used in cocktails, made from small acid cherries grown in the Trieste region. BN Casoni, Drioli, Luxardo.

Marc the French name for a brandy distilled from the by-products of winemaking (40°).

Marie Brizard French producer of Anisette, Apry and other liqueurs.

Marsala a Sicilian fortified wine.

Martini & Rossi (BN) producers of Italian vermouth—red (rosso), sweet white (bianco) and dry white (secco).

Menthe, crème de a sweet liqueur flavoured with mint available in a green or white version (25°). BN Bols, Cartron, Cusenier, Peppermint, Pippermint etc.

Mezcal a Mexican spirit

Poster by Nevy for Cusenier Mandarin.

distilled from the fruit of the agave (40°). It is sometimes sold with an agave worm in the bottle. Cortés is supposed to have called it the nectar of the Aztec gods. Tequila can be used as a substitute. BN Gusano.

Midori (BN) a Japanese sweet green liqueur tasting of melon.

Mirabelle a very sweet small yellow plum from which an excellent fruity brandy is distilled.

Mistelle a mixture of brandy and fresh grape juice; examples are Pineau from the Charentes, Ratafia from Champagne and Floc from Gascony.

Monin (originally Triple Lime) (BN) a liqueur based on lemon peel and cognac (33°).

N

Noilly Prat (BN) a vermouth made in France; the dry white is much the better known, but there is also a red.

Noyaux, crème de an almond-flavoured liqueur based on the kernels of peach, apricot etc crushed in spirit.

O

Oloroso see sherry.

Orange liqueurs better known under their brand names, such as Cointreau and Grand Marnier, or under their generic names of triple-sec and curaçao. See Triple-sec and Curaçao.

Orgeat syrup originally made from barley, but now made with ground almonds steeped in orange water and sweetened.

P

Parfait Amour a purple coloured sweet liqueur made from a variety of ingredients including orange, lemon etc. Every liqueur producer has his own recipe.

Pastis a generic term in France for spirit flavoured with aniseed and liquorice (45°). When diluted with water pastis becomes cloudy and releases a strong scent of aniseed. BN Alise, Berger, Casanis, Duval, Pastis 51, Pecanis, Ricard.

Peach liqueur based on peaches and spirit. Peach is the dominant flavour in Southern Comfort (BN).

Pear brandy made by distilling the fermented juice of the William pear; liqueurs are obtained by mixing pear brandy with sugar.

Pernod (BN) the most famous of the aniseed-flavoured drinks; it is drier than pastis. It is used in cocktails as a substitute for absinthe.

Peter Heering brand name of cherry brandy (also known as Cherry Heering).

Pimm's No 1 (BN) a ready-prepared gin sling.

Pineau des Charentes a mixture of fresh grape juice and cognac (16°–22°).

Pisco a brandy made from wine in Chile and Peru.

Plum brandy produced by fermenting the juice and crushed kernels of plums; those best known in France are based on Mirabelle and Quetsche (Switzen) plums. Plum brandy from Yugoslavia is called Slivovitz.

Plymouth gin see Gin.

Port a sweet wine from Portugal fortified by adding brandy during fermentation. There are two main types: wood and vintage. Wood port is matured in cask and is normally a blended wine; its three main varieties are ruby, tawny and white, the last being popular as an apéritif. Vintage port is wine of a single year matured in bottle and sold for laying down. Vintage character ports are blended wines almost as smooth as but less rich than vintage ports. BN Cockburn, Croft, Delaforce, Dows, Feuerheerd, Fonseca, Graham, Martinez, Offley, Quinta do Noval, Smith Woodhouse, Warres.

Prunelle brandy based on the sloe berry. Sloe berries are also used to flavour gin.

Pulque a Mexican spirit obtained from fermenting the fruit and sap of the agave plant.

Punt e Mes (BN) bitter red Italian vermouth.

Q

Quinquina name of apéritifs made from wine flavoured with quinine. BN Ambassadeur, Byrrh, Dubonnet, St. Raphael.

R

Raspberry (framboise) liqueur made by macerating raspberries in spirit. If the spirit is a grape brandy and the mixture is distilled twice, the result is a raspberry brandy.

Ratafia a mixture of fresh grape juice and brandy from the Champagne area.

Ricard (BN) aniseed-flavoured spirit; see Pastis.

Rock and Rye (BN) an American liqueur based on rye whiskey and lemon or orange flavouring. It is sold with a lump of candy rock in the bottle.

Royal Mint Chocolate and **Royal Orange Chocolate** see Chocolate.

Rum spirit distilled from sugar cane juice or from molasses (40°) and imported mainly from the Caribbean. There are many different styles of rum ranging from the light bodied white through golden to dark heavily flavoured. BN Appleton Special, Bacardi, Carta Blanca, Carta Oro, Lambs Navy, Lemon Hart, Mount Gay, Myer's Planters Punch, Old Oak, Rhum Negrita.

Rye American whiskey made in Pennsylvania and Maryland from rye (minimum 51%) and other grains. Canada also makes a rye on the same principles. A straight rye comes from a single distillery and blended rye is a blend of several straight ryes.

S

Sabra (BN) Israeli liqueur flavoured with orange and chocolate.

Sambuca an Italian liqueur strongly flavoured with aniseed.

Schnapps a brandy made from grain or potato with a strong taste and little flavour. It resembles Aquavit and Korn.

Scotch whisky a grain spirit made only in Scotland and distilled from a mash of fermented cereals in patent stills, to be distinguished from malt whisky which is made exclusively from fermented malted barley distilled twice in a pot still. Two types of Scotch are sold:
*Blended Scotch whiskies which are 50 to 80 per cent grain whisky, the balance being made up of malt whisky. BN Ballantine's, Bell's, Black & White, Buchanan's, Chivas Regal.
*Pure malt whisky BN Aberlour Glenlivet, Bladnoch, Cardhu, Glenfiddich.

Sherry a blended wine made from white grapes grown in the Jerez district of Spain and fortified with brandy. The principal types are fino, pale, delicate and dry; amontillado medium dry; oloroso and amoroso rich and sweet. Manzanilla is a special very dry sherry with a salty character due to its being made and stored by the sea. BN Domecq, Garvey, Gonzalez Byass, Harveys of Bristol, Sandeman.

Single malt see Malt whisky.

Sloe gin gin flavoured with sloe berries.

Southern Comfort (BN) an American liqueur based on bourbon and peaches and produced in St Louis, Missouri.

St Raphael (BN) an apéritif flavoured with quinine. It comes in a red and white variety.

Steinhager a type of German gin (generic name wacholder). BN Schlichte, Konig, Tashe.

Stock (BN) brand of Italian brandy.

Straight used to describe American whiskeys coming

from a single distillery; synonymous with single when applied to Scotch whisky.

Strawberry (fraise) liqueur made by macerating strawberries in spirit. BN Cartron, Dolfi, Monin, Pagès.

Strega a yellow Italian liqueur made from herbs and flowers.

Suze (BN) a gentian-flavoured liqueur (16°).

Syrup a mixture made from sugar and water or sugar and fruit extracts or juice. In cocktails the most commonly used are sugar syrup, grenadine and orgeat. Gomme Sirop made of sugar, water and gum arabic gives smoothness to cocktails without making them oversweet; it can be bought commercially.

T

Tequila a spirit made from the fermented sap of the agave plant; the special variety used grows in an area round and neighbouring the town of Tequila.

Tía Maria (BN) a strongly-flavoured coffee liqueur based on rum and made in Jamaica. Kahlúa and other coffee liqueurs can be used as substitutes.

Triple-sec orange liqueur based on orange peel and spirit; one of the best of the curaçaos (see Curaçao). Made by a number of producers but best known under the brand names Cointreau and Grand Marnier.

V

Van den Hum (BN) a South African liqueur made from local oranges and herbs.

Poster by Dudovich for Carpano Vermouth.

Vermouth a wine flavoured with herbal extracts (15°–18°). All vermouths are based on white wine and the dark ones are coloured with caramel:
Dry (often called French), very dry and pale with not more than 40 g (1½ oz) sugar per litre (1¾ pints).
Sweet white, much sweeter, more scented and with more colour than the dry (called bianco by the Italians).
Red, coloured, sweetened and scented—150 g (5 oz) sugar to a litre (1¾ pints)
BN Carpano, Cinzano, Dolin (Chambéry), Gancia, Martini, Noilly Prat, Riccadonna etc.

Verschnitt a German word for a mixture of neutral alcohol and brandy.

Verbena (verveine) liqueur (BN) a herb liqueur made in southwest France; the yellow variety is sweeter and smoother than the green.
BN Verveine du Vellay.

Vieille Cure (BN) a liqueur from the Gironde made of brandy and aromatic herbs.

Violette, crème de a liqueur made from violet petals.

Vodka a spirit with very little flavour, originating in Poland (40°). Vodka is distilled from fermented cereals and from other raw materials, and is rectified with herbs to produce a discreetly flavoured alcohol. BN Finlandia, Smirnoff, Stolichnaya, Wiborowa, Zubrowka.

W

Whiskey/Whisky see Bourbon, Canadian whisky, Irish whiskey, Rye, Scotch.

Williamine a sweetened blend based on pear brandy.

Y

Yvette, crème de a liqueur made from violet petals.

Index 1

Recipes

Abbey, 56
Abbey Cocktail, 56
Absinthe Cocktail, 101
Absinthe Drip, 101
Absinthe Special, 101
Acacia, 56
Acapulco (rum-based), 39
Acapulco (tequila-based), 95
Acapulco Gold, 39
Addington, 102
Adios Amigos, 39
Admiral, 102
Adonis, 102
Adry, 80
Affinity Cocktail, 88
After Dinner, 112
After Dinner Cocktail, 112
Afternoon Cocktail, 25
After One, 56
A.J., 35
A1, 56
Alaska, 56
Albemarle Fizz, 57
Alcudia, 57
Ale Flip, 130
Alexander, 25
Alexander Baby, 39
Alexander's Sister, 25
Alexis Heck, 25
Alfonso, 57
Algonquin, 80
Allen, 58
Almond Eye, 112,
Amabile Beone, 112
Ambassador, 95
Amber Dream, 58
Ambrosia, 35
American Beauty, 25
American Beauty Special, 25
American Fizz, 58
American Flyer, 39
American Grog, 137
American Legion Margarita, 95
Americano, 102–3
American Rose, 25
Amer Picon Cocktail, 103
Amer Picon Cooler, 103
Amer Picon Highball, 103
Amontillado Cocktail, 103
Amour Cocktail, 130
Ampainen, 72
Amsterdam, 58
Angel Face, 35
Angelo, 72
Angel's Delight (pousse-café), 113
Angel's Dream (pousse-café), 113
Angel's Kiss (pousse-café), 113
Angel Special, 142
Angel's Smile, 72
Angel's Tip (pousse-café), 113
Angel's Tit (pousse-café), 113
Angel's Wing (pousse-café), 113
Angostura Fizz, 104

Anticipation, 113
Antilles, 39
Antoine, 104
Ants in the Pants, 58
A1 Pick Me Up, 123
Apéritifs, cocktails based on, 100–111
Aphrodisiac, 137
Appendicitis, 58
Apple Blossom, 35
Apple Brandy Cocktail, 36
Apple Brandy Highball, 36
Apple Cocktail, 36
Applejack Cocktail, 36
Apple Today, 137
Après Ski, 72
Apricot Brandy Coller, 114
Apricot Daiquiri, 39
Apricot Lady, 114
Apricot Nog, 39
Aquavit Fizz, 104
Arago, 25
Arak Cooler, 104
Archbishop Punch, 130
Argentine Julep, 130
Around the World, 40
Arrow Head Cocktail, 80
Artillery, 59
Artillery Punch, 123
Astronaut, 40
Atholl Brose Cocktail, 114
Atlantic Cognac, 26
Attila, 105
Auld Man's Milk, 126
Aurore, 40
Aurum, 105
Aviation, 105
Azteca, 95
Aztec Punch, 124

Bacardi, 40
Bahamas, 40
Bahamian Delight, 105
Bahia, 40
Balalaika, 73
Baltimore Eggnog, 126
Bamboo Cocktail, 130
Banana Bliss, 26
Banana Cow (milk-based), 126
Banana Cow (rum-based), 41
Banana Daiquiri, 41
Banana Royal, 41
B and B (Benedictine and Brandy), 26
Banshee, 114
Barbara Cocktail, 73
Barbarella, 142
Barbary Coast Cocktail, 88
Barbican, 88
Barbotage, 130
Barracuda, 41

Barrier Reef, 59
Bartender, 59
Bayou, 114
Beer, cocktails based on, 128–35
Bee's Knees, 59
Belladonna, 73
Bellini, 130
Benedict Cocktail, 88
Benedictine Cocktail, 114
Benedictine Frappé, 114
Benedictine Scaffa, 114
Bermuda Rose Cocktail, 59
Bermudian Cocktail, 59
Bernice, 73
Between The Sheets, 26
Big Bamboo, 41
Bilberry Grog, 137
Billy Hamilton, 26
Bishop (hot drink), 137
Bishop (wine-based), 130
Bitter Highball, 105
Black and Tan, 130
Black Cloud see Black Russian
Black Hawk, 80
Black Pearl, 130
Black Russian, 73
Blackthorn, 114
Black Velvet, 130
Black Watch, 89
Black Widow, 41
Block and Fall, 115
Blood and Sand, 89
Bloody Bull, 95
Bloody Bullshot see Bullshot
Bloody Mary, 74
Blue Blazer, 137
Blue Bottle, 59
Blue Hawaiian, 41
Blue Jacket, 59
Blue Lady, 115
Blue Lagoon, 74
Blue Sea, 41
Bois Rose, 105
Bombay, 27
Bordeaux Cooler, 130–1
Bosom Caresser, 26
Boston Eggnog, 126
Boston Flip, 80
Bourbon, cocktails based on, 79–87
Bourbon and Soda, 80
Bourbon Collins, 80
Bourbon Cooler, 80–1
Bourbonella, 81
Bourbon Highball, 81
Bourbon Mist, 81
Bourbon Sour, 81
Brandy, cocktails based on, 23–34
Brandy Alexander Milk Punch, 126–7
Brandy Blazer, 27
Brandy Champerelle, 27
Brandy Cocktail 1, 27
Brandy Cocktail 2, 27

Brandy Collins, 27
Brandy Daisy, 27
Brandy Eggnog, 127
Brandy Fizz, 27
Brandy Flip, 27
Brandy Gump, 27
Brandy Punch, 124
Brandy Sour, 27
Brandy Toddy, 27
Brandy Vermouth Cocktail, 28
Breakfast Nog, 28
Broken Spur Cocktail, 131
Bronx, 59
Bronx Dry, 59
Bronx Golden, 60
Bronx Silver, 60
Brooklyn, 81
Brunette, 115
Buccaneer, 124
Buck's Fizz, 131
Bullshot, 74
Burgundy Cocktail, 131
Burgundy Punch, 131
Byrrh-Cassis, 105
Byrrh Cocktail, 107
Byrrh Special, 60

Cacatoes, 28
Café Curaçao, 115
Café de Paris, 60
California Lemonade, 81
Calimero, 28
Câlin Cocktail, 115
Calvados, cocktails based on, 35–7
Calvados Cocktail, 36
Calvados Cooler, 36
Calvados Rickey, 36
Calvados Sour, 36
Camilla Cocktail, 60
Camomile and White Wine, 137
Camomile and Wine, 124
Campari Orange, 107
Campari Shakerato, 107
Campay, 107
Canadian Whisky, cocktails based on, 79–87
Canebiére, 107
Cape Codder, 74
Cape Cod Jack, 36
Capri, 107
Captain Collins, 81
Caramba, 60
Cardinal, 61
Carin, 61
Carioca, 115
Carnival, 28
Carrol Cocktail, 28
Caruso, 61
Casablanca, 42
Casino, 61
Cassis Cocktail, 81
Castle Dip, 36

Catherine Blossom, 142
Cavalieri (rum-based), 42
Cavalieri (vodka-based), 74
Cecema Punch, 124
Chablis Cup, 131
Champagne Cocktail, 131
Champagne Julep, 132
Champagne Verbena, 132
Champerelle (pousse-café), 115
Champs-Elysées, 28
Chancellor, 89
Chapala, 95–6
Chartreuse Tonic, 116
Cherry Blossom, 115
Chi-chi, 74
Chi-chi (Frozen), 74
Chinese Itch, 42
Chocolate Punch, 137
Chocolate Soldier, 28
Chocolate with Two Flavours,
    142
Churchill, 89
Cider brandies, cocktails based on,
    35–7
Cider Grog, 137
Cinderella, 142
Claret Punch, 132
Claridge Cocktail, 61
Classic Cocktail, 28
Close Encounters, 28
Cloud Burst, 61
Cloud Buster, 132
Clover Club, 61
Club Martini, 61
C 9 J Punch, 42
Cocktail Apéritifs, 100–111
Cocktail Digestives, 112–22
Coco Loco, 42
Coconut Tequila, 96
Coconut Tumble, 42
Coco-oco, 142

Coffee Amaretto, 137
Coffee and Bitter Orange Punch,
    124
Coffee Calypso, 138
Coffee Diablo, 138
Coffee Nog, 29
Cognac Cocktail, 29
Cognac-Mint Frappé, 29
Cognac Orange, 29
Cognac Perino, 29
Commodore, 81
Conca d'Ora, 61
Conchita, 96
Conclave, 142
Cool Banana, 116
Cool Caribbean, 116
Coquito, 116
Corpse Reviver 1, 29
Corpse Reviver 2, 61
Corpse Reviver 3, 29
Corpse Reviver 4, 116

Corsican Bounty, 116
Covadonga, 107
Covino, 107
Cowboy, 82
Crème de Menthe Frappé, 116
Crillon, 107
Cross Bow, 61
Cuba Libre, 42
Cuba Libre Supreme, 116
Cuban, 30
Cuban Cocktail, 43
Cup Crillon, 43

Daily Mail, 82
Daiquiri, 43
Deep Valley, 62
Dempsey Cocktail, 62
Dérobade, 75
Digestives, cocktails based on, 112–
    122
D.O.M. Cocktail, 62
Don Pablo, 43
Double 007, 43
Dou Dou Fizz, 142
Dragon Lady, 44
Drakkar, 62
Drambuie Eggnog, 127
Drambuie Swizzle, 117
Drunken Apricot Punch, 132–3
Dry Americano, 107
Du Barry Cocktail, 62
Dubonnet Cocktail, 62
Dubonnet Fizz, 107
Duke, 117
Dummy Daisy, 142
Dunhill '71', 30
Durango, 96
Dynamite, 133

Eaglet, 133
Earthquake, 96
East India 1, 30
East India 2, 107
El Conquistador, 44
El Diablo, 96
El Jardinero, 44
Ellisse, 30
El Metraya, 117
El Pepino, 44
El Presidente, 44
El Zorzal, 45
Embassy Royal, 82
Esprit Cartésien, 82
Estoril 81, 45
Evans, 82
Evergreen, 96

Fallen Angel, 63
Fantasia, 75
Farmer's Joy, 142

Favourite, 30
Felicitation, 142
Fernet, 30
Fernet-Branca Cocktail, 63
Festrus, 75
Fiesta, 45
Fiesta Cocktail, 45
Flambé, 108
Flamboyan, 45
Flamingo, 75
Flying Scotsman, 90
Fond de Culotte, 108
Frostbite, 96
Frosty Amour, 75
Frosty Dawn, 117
Frosty Lime, 143
Frozen Daiquiri, 45
Frozen Mint Daiquiri, 45
Frozen Pineapple Daiquiri, 45
Frozen Scotch, 90
Frozen Southern Comfort, 117
Frozen Steps, 75
Frozen Strawberry, 97
Fruit Cup, 143
Fruit Punch (non-alcoholic), 143
Fruit Punch (with rum), 124

Gato, 63
Geronimo Punch, 46
Gibson, 63
Gimlet, 63
Gin, cocktails based on, 55–71
Gin Alexander, 117
Gin and Bitters, 63
Gin and It, 63
Gin and Tonic, 63
Gin Fizz, 63
Gin Sling, 63
Gin Tropical, 64
Gipsy, 75
Glad Eye, 108
Gloom Chaser, 117
Gold Coconut, 117
Golden Cadillac, 117
Golden Dawn, 64
Golden Dream, 117
Golden Fizz, 64
Golden Fling, 46
Golden Gate, 46
Golden Gleam, 30
Golden Medallion, 30
Golden Rum Punch 1, 124
Golden Rum Punch 2, 125
Golden Screw, 64
Golden Slipper (based on
    digestives), 118
Golden Slipper (gin-based), 64
Golden Tea, 138
Goldie, 46
Gold Time, 46
Granata Cocktail, 64
Grand Nord, 118

Grand Prix, 75
Grasshopper, 118
Green Dragon, 118
Green Lady, 64
Green Room, 30
Grenadine Shake, 144
Grog, 138

Hair of the Dog, 90
Harry Lauder, 90
Harvard Cocktail, 30
Harvard Cooler, 36–7
Harvey Wallbanger, 75
Havana Beach Cocktail, 46
Hawaiian, 64
Hawaiian Brandy Cocktail, 37
Hawaiian Coffee, 46
Hepmaïstos, 46
Herculys, 30
Highland Cooler, 90
Highland Milk Punch, 127
Honeymoon (based on Calvados),
    37
Honeymoon (non-alcoholic), 144
Honey Suckle, 46
Honolulu, 64
Horse's Neck, 30
Hot Brandy Flip, 31
Hot Bullshot, 138
Hot Buttered Rum, 139
Hot Drinks, 136–40
Hot Jamaican Cow, 139
Hunter, 82

Ice-Breaker, 97
Incorruptible Champagne, 144
Indian Summer, 46
Irish Cheer, 90
Irish Coffee, 139
Irish Whiskey, cocktails based on,
    88–94
Island Cream Grog, 139

Jack Rabbit, 37
Jack Rose, 37
Jack's Special, 144
Jaffa, 118
Jamaica Joe, 118
Jamaican Cow, 127
John Collins, 64
Juliana Blue, 64–5

Kahlúa Alexander, 118
Kangaroo Jump, 65
Kava Bowl, 125
Kentucky Colonel Cocktail, 82
Kentucky Sunset, 82
Kentumi, 144
King Alfonse, 118

King George V, 90
Kingston, 46
Kir 8, 133
Kir Royal, 133
Kiss in the Dark, 65
Kiss Me Quick, 108
Klabauter Man, 139
Kriss, 31

Ladies' Cocktail, 82
Lady's Dream, 82
La Florida Daiquiri, 47
Lait de Poule 1, 31
Lait de Poule 2, 127
Lait de Poule with Lime, 144
Last Order, 31
Lemon Mint, 144
Leningrad, 118
Liaison, 31
Lime and Blackcurrant Tea, 144
Lime Martinique, 144
Linstead, 90
Loch Lomond Cocktail, 90
London Cocktail, 65
Long Green, 118
Los Angeles (based on Bourbon),
  82
Los Angeles (based on Scotch
  whisky), 90
Lucky Dip, 76

Macca, 108
Mahui Fizz, 47
Mai Tai, 47
Mai Tai Mix, 144
Mamie Taylor, 90
Manhattan, 82–3
Manhattan Dry, 83
Manhattan Perfect, 83
Manilla Sunset, 47
Maple Leaf Cocktail, 83
Margarita, 97
Maria Bonita, 47
Maria Theresa, 98
Martini 1 (original recipe), 65
Martini 2 (Dry Martini), 65
Martini 3 (Extra Dry Martini), 66
Martini 4 (Medium Dry Martini)
  66
Martini 5 (Special Dry Martini),
  66
Martini 6 (Sweet Martini), 66
Martino Tea, 139
Matador, 98
Matouba, 125
Mauresque, 108
Maya, 47
Mazel Tov, 119
Merry Widow 1, 108
Merry Widow 2, 108
Merry Widow 3, 119

Merry Widower, 109
Mexican Grandma, 144
Mexico y Espana, 109
Miami Beach, 90
Michel, 109
Milk, cocktails based on 126–7
Milk Punch, 127
Millionaire, 31
Million Dollar, 66
Milvea, 66
Mint Julep, 83
Mint Tomato, 144
Mockingbird, 98
Mojito, 48
Mona Lisa, 119
Monon 1, 133
Montana, 31
Moomba, 48
Moonlight Cooler, 37
Moon River, 67
Morning Dew, 119
Morning Glory 1, 31
Morning Glory 2 (based on
  bourbon or Rye Whiskey), 84
Morning Glory 3 (based on
  Scotch Whisky), 91
Morning Glory Daisies, 109
Morning Glory Fizz, 91
Moscow Mule, 76
Moulin Rouge, 32
Mount Fuji, 109
Mucaro, 48

Negroni, 67
Nevins, 84
New Fashioned, 32
New York, 84
Night Cap, 139
Night Shade, 84
Nonalc Mai Tai, 145
Non-alcoholic cocktails and drinks,
  141–9
Not Too Bad, 48

Old Fashioned, 85
Old Nick, 85
Old Pal, 85
Olympic, 32
Omnia, 76
One Ireland, 91
Opal, 67
Opening, 85
Orange Bloom, 109
Orange Blossom, 67
Orange Daiquiri, 48
Orange Fizz, 109
Orange-Peppermint Shake, 145
Orange Punch, 125
Oriental, 85
Orleanian, 85

Paddy Cocktail, 91
Pall Mall, 67
Palmer Cocktail, 91
Panache, 76
Pan American, 85
Pancho Villa, 98
Papaya Royal, 48
Paradise, 119
Parrot, 109
Parson's Special, 145
Patricia, 76
Peach Daiquiri, 48
Pendennis Cocktail, 68
Penguin, 32
Peppermint Pick Me Up, 139
Perfect Affinity, 91
Perfect Martini, 68
Perfect Rob Roy, 91
Pernod Bitter Lemon, 110
Pernod Riviera, 110
Petit Futé, 48
Phoenix Gin Sling, 68
Picador Cocktail, 98
Pick Me Up, 32
Pimm's No. 1, 110
Piña Colada, 48
Piña Colata, 145
Pineapple Cobbler, 145
Pineapple Cooler, 145
Pineapple Fizz, 48
Pink Explosion, 110
Pink Gin, 68
Pink Lady, 68
Pink Melon Delight, 145
Pink Panther Flip, 145
Pink Pussy, 110
Pink Squirrel, 119
Pippi Long Drink, 32–3
Pisco Punch, 119
Planter's Punch 1, 48–9
Planter's Punch 2, 49
Platinum Blonde, 119
Playa Delight, 68
Playmate, 33
Plum Shake, 145
Pompier Daisy, 134
Po-Pomme, 37
Port and Starboard (pousse-café),
  119
Port Flip, 134
Port Light, 85
Pousse L'Amour (pousse-café),
  119
Pousse-Rapière, 134
Prelude, 110
Prince Charles, 33
Princess Mary, 68
Princess Pride Cocktail, 37
Princeton, 68
Punches, 123–5
Pussy Cat, 145
Pussy Foot 1 (rum-based), 49
Pussy Foot 2 (non-alcoholic), 146

Quarter Deck, 49
Quebec Cocktail, 85
Rainbow 1 (pousse-café), 119
Rainbow 2, 120
Ramos Fizz, 127
Rattlesnake, 85
Red Hackle, 33
Red Light, 146
Red Lion, 68
Red Lips Cocktail, 76
Red Sombrero Cocktail, 146
Regate, 68
Richelieu, 85
Ricoliano, 49
Riviera, 147
Road Runner, 76
Roadster, 69
Roberta, 76
Robert Burns, 92
Rob Roy, 92
Rolls Royce, 33
Roman Sling, 69
Rose, 69
Rose 2, 110
Rose of Warsaw, 76
Royal Clover Club, 69
Royal Coco Punch, 49
Royal Fizz, 69
Royal Romance, 69
Royal Russian, 76
Royal Smile, 69
Rubis, 86
Rum, cocktails based on, 38–54
Rum Alexander, 120
Rum Collins, 50
Rum Fizz, 50
Rum Float, 50
Rum Gimlet, 50
Rum Orange, 50
Rum Orange Grog, 139
Rum Orange Punch, 125
Rum Sour, 50
Rum Tonic, 50
Rusty Nail, 92
Rye and Dry, 86
Rye Cocktail, 86
Rye Collins, 86
Rye Highball, 86
Rye Lane, 86
Rye Sour, 86
Rye Whiskey, cocktails based on, 79–
  87
Rye Whiskey Cocktail, 86

Saint Germain, 120
Salome, 69
Salty Dog, 76–7
San Cristobal, 50
Sangria, 134
Sans Souci, 125
Savoy 90, 120
Sazerac, 86

Scanex, 77
Scarlet Cocktail with Orange, 147
Scarlet O'Hara, 120
Scorpion, 51
Scotch Collins, 92
Scotch Frappé, 92
Scotch Frog, 77
Scotch Mist, 93
Scotch Old Fashioned, 93
Scotch Sour, 93
Scotch Whisky, cocktails based on,
    88–94
Screwdriver, 76
Shamrock, 93
Shannon Shandy, 120
Shark's Tooth 1, 51
Shark's Tooth 2, 51
Sherry Cobbler, 110
Sherry Cocktail, 110
Sherry Eggnog, 127
Sherry Flip, 134
Side Car, 33
Silent Third, 93
Silk Stockings, 98
Silver Fizz, 69
Silver Jubilee, 69
Silver Streak, 69
Singapore Sling (based on
    apéritif), 110
Singapore Sling (gin-based), 70
Sir Walter, 51
Ski Bunny, 140
Ski Wasser, 147
Slim and Trim, 51
Sloe Gin Cocktail, 120
Smash, 77
Smiling, 134
Snake in the Grass, 120
Snowball, 120
Snow Flake, 77

Soly Sombra, 51
Sorbet and Tea Punch, 147
Southern Belle, 86
Southern Ginger, 86
Spicy Ginger Tantalizer, 147
Spring Time, 78
Spritzer, 135
Stinger, 34
Strawberry Daiquiri, 51
Suissesse, 110
Summer Cooler, 147
Summer Fun, 34
Summer Mint, 120
Summertime, 51
Sunny Dream, 120
Sunset, 52
Sunset Tea, 140
Surfing, 52
Sweet Eden, 34
SWI, 78
Swinger, 147
Sylvia, 52

Talisman, 52
Tampico, 110–1
Tea with Mint, 147
Temptation, 86–7
Tempter, 120
Tenderfoot Mint, 147
Tequila, cocktails based on, 95–9
Tequila Cocktail, 98
Tequila Daisy, 98
Tequila Orange, 98
Tequila Straight, 98–9
Tequila Sunrise, 98
Tequila Sunset, 98
Tequini, 99
Three Miller, 34
Three-Three-Three (333), 37

Tia Eggnog, 127
Tidal Wave, 122
Tip Lady Daiquiri, 52
Tipsy Guava, 147
T.N.T. (brandy-based), 34
TNT (Tequila and Tonic), 99
Tobago Punch, 125
Tom and Jerry, 140
Tomato, 111
Tomato Cucumber Cooler, 147
Tomato Mint Cocktail, 148
Tom Collins, 70
Tops Smile, 34
Trapiche Cocktail, 52
Trapiche Syrup, 148
Trinity, 111
Troika, 78
Tropical Kiss, 52
Tropical Mimosa, 53
Tropical Storm, 78
Tropic of Capricorn, 53
Tsarine, 78
Tutti Frutti Verbena Cocktail,
    148–9

Up-To-Date, 87

Valencia, 122
Vallée d'Auge, 140
Vanderbilt, 34
Velvet Hammer, 122
Verbena Creole, 140
Virgin Mary, 149
Vodka, cocktails based on, 72–8
Vodka Collins, 78
Vodka Gibson, 78
Vodka Gimlet, 78
Vodka Imperial, 78
Vodkatini, 78

Waikiki, 87
Waratam, 53
Ward Eight, 87
Waterloo, 53
Wax, 70
Wembley, 93
Western Electric, 135
Western Rose, 70
Westminster, 87
Whip, 34
Whisky Cobbler, 94
Whisky Cocktail, 94
Whisky-Lime Grog, 140
Whisky-Mint Cocktail, 94
Whisky Sangaree, 94
Whisky Toddy, 87
Whist, 37
White Heather, 70
White Lady, 70
White Lily, 71
White Rose, 71
White Russian, 122
White Satin, 122
White Witch, 53
Whizz Bang, 94
Wine, cocktails based on, 128–35
Winter Warmer, 140

Xères Cocktail, 135
Xochimilco, 122

Yankee Doodle, 34
Yellow Daisy, 71
Yellow Dwarf, 149
Yellow Parrot, 122

Za-Za (Zara), 71
Zombie, 53

Index 2

Terms, Ingredients and Accessories

Absinthe, 100, 150
Advocaat, 150
Aguardiente, 150
Allasch, 150
Amaretto, 150
Ambassadeur, 150
American Whiskey, 79
Amer Picon, 150
Anesone, 150
Angostura bitters, 150
Aniseed, 13, 150

Anisette, 13, 150
Aperol, 150
Apéritifs, 100–1, 150
Applejack, 35, 150
Apricot/apricot liqueurs, 12, 112
Apricot brandy, 12, 150
Aquavit, 150
Arak, 150
Armagnac, 12, 13, 14, 23, 24, 112,
    150
Aurum, 150

Bacardi rum, 38, 150
Baileys Irish Cream, 150
Banane, crème de, 12, 24, 150
Banyuls, 150
Bars
accessories for, 16
basic ingredients for, 16
bottles for, 12–13
equipment for, 16
fresh produce for, 16
keeping insects away from, 13

private (at home), 12–13
public, 11
storing spirits and liqueurs, 13
Beer, 9, 13, 128
Benedictine, 13, 150
Bilberry liqueur or crème, 151
Bitters, 151 see also Angostura
    bitters
Blackberry liqueur, 151
Blackcurrant liqueur see Cassis,
    crème de

Blend, 151
Borovicka, 151
Bottles
  choice of, 12–13
  storage of, 13
Boukha, 151
Bourbon, 12, 79, 151
Brandy, 13, 14, 23–4, 100, 112, 123, 151
Buck, 19
Byrrh, 151

Cacao, crème de, 12, 151
Calvados, 12, 13, 14, 23, 35, 151
Camomile, 123, 151
Campari, 12, 100, 151
Canadian whiskey, 79, 151
Cassis, crème de, 12, 151
Chambéry, 151
Champagne, 13, 18, 128, 151
Chartreuse, 12, 151
Cherry Brandy, 151
Chill, how to, 22
Chocolate, 23, 151 see also cacao, crème de
Cider, 35
Cider brandies, 35
Cinzano, 12, 151
Cobbler, 9, 19
Cocktail apéritifs, 100–1
Cocktail digestives, 112
Cocktails
  art of mixing, 14–16
  history of, 9–10
  recipes, 22
  serving, 18
Cocktail snacks, 18
Coconut, 38
Coffee liqueur, 12, 151
Cognac, 12, 13, 14, 23, 24, 112, 151
Cointreau, 12, 23, 151
Cola, 13
Collins, 19
Cooler, 9, 19
Cordial, 151
Corn whiskey, 151
Cream, 23, 112
Crusta, 9, 19
Cuarante y Tres, 151
Cup, 9, 19
Curaçao, 12, 23, 38, 151
Cynar, 151

Daiquiri, 10, 19, 38
Daisy, 9, 19
Danziger Goldwasser, 152
Decoctions, 136
Digestives, 112
Drambuie, 13, 152

Dubonnet, 152

Eggnog, 19
Eggs, 126
Electric mixer, 16
Equipment bar, 16

Falernum, 152
Fernet-Branca, 24, 152
Fix, 9, 19
Fizz, 19
Flip, 9, 20
Floater, 20
Floc, 152
Frappé, 20
French, 152
Frost, how to, 22
Frozen, 20
Fruit juice, 22 see also name of fruit

Galliano, 13, 152
Genever, 55, 152
Gentiane, 100, 152
Gin, 9, 12, 14, 23, 55, 152
Ginger/ginger ale, 13, 24
Glasses
  different types of, 16–17
  mixing, 15
  right temperature for, 18
  sizes for short and long drinks, 19
Glayva, 152
Grain spirits, mixing, 14, 24
Grand Marnier, 12, 23, 152
Grape spirits, mixing, 14, 24
Grappa, 152
Grenadine syrup, 23, 38, 152
Grog, 20, 136

Herb-based liqueurs, 12–13
Highland Malt, 152
Holland see Genever

Ice, 15, 16, 22
Infusions, 136, 141
Irish Mist, 152
Irish Velvet, 152
Irish Whiskey, 12, 79, 88, 152
Izarram 13, 152

Jack Daniel's, 152
Julep, 9, 20

Kabänes, 153
Kahlúa, 12, 153

Kirsch, 153
Korn, 153
Kummel, 153

Lemon, 23, 35, 38, 55, 79, 95, 123
Lillet, 153
Lime, 38
Long drinks, 19
Lowland malt, 153

Madeira, 9, 153
Malibu, 153
Malt Whisky, 153
Manderine, 153
Manderin liqueur, 12, 153
Maraschino, 153
Marc, 153
Marie Brizard, 153
Marsala, 153
Martini & Rossi, 153
Measures, 22
Menthe, crème de, 12, 153
Mezcal, 153
Midori, 153
Milk, 126
Mint, 24, 112 see also Menthe, crème de
Mirabelle, 153
Mistelle, 153
Mixer stick, 15
Mixtures, 13, 14, 24
Monin, 153
Mulled Wine, 20

Noilly Prat, 12, 153
Noyaux liqueur, 12, 153

Old fashioned, 20
Orange/orange juice, 13, 35, 39, 55, 112
Orange flower, 123
Orange liqueur, 12, 23, 55, 95, 153
Orgeat syrup, 153

Parfait Amour, 154
Pastis, 12, 100, 154
Peach liqueur, 154
Pear brandy, 154
Peppermint liqueur, 23
Pernod, 12, 100, 154
Pimm's No. 1, 101, 154
Pineapple juice, 38
Pineau of Charentes, 100, 154
Pisco, 154
Plum brandy, 154
Port, 9, 154
Pousse-café, 21
Prunelle brandy, 154

Pulque, 154
Punch, 9, 21, 123
Punt e Mes, 154
Quinquina, 154
Raspberry liqueur, 12, 154
Ratafia, 154
Ricard, 154
Rickey, 9, 21
Rock and Rye, 154
Rum, 12, 14, 23, 38, 123, 154
Rye whiskey, 12, 79, 154

Sabra, 154
Saint Raphael, 154
Sambuca, 154
Sangaree, 9, 21
Schnapps, 154
Scotch whisky, 12, 79, 88, 154
Shakers, 15, 16, 22
Sherry, 9, 101, 154
Short drinks, 19
Shrub, 21
Sling, 9, 21
Sloe gin, 154
Smash, 9, 21
Soda, 23, 100, 141
Sour, 21
Southern Comfort, 13, 154
Steinhager, 154
Strainer, 22
Strawberry liqueur, 12, 155
Strega, 13, 155
Suze, 155
Syrups, 22, 141, 155

Tea, 123
Tequila, 12, 95, 101, 155
Tia Maria, 12, 155
Toddy, 21
Tonic, 13
Triple-sec, 12, 23, 155

Van den Hum, 155
Verbena, 123
Verbena liqueur, 155
Vermouth, 12, 35, 55, 79, 88, 100, 101, 155
Verschnitt, 155
Vielle Cure, 155
Violette, crème de, 155
Vodka, 12, 14, 72, 155

Whisky/whiskey, 12, 14, 79, 88, 155 see also type of whisky
Williamine, 155
Wine, 13, 14, 20, 128

Yvette, crème de, 155